Praise for Reimagining Death

"We cannot heal our relationships with the natural world, others, and ourselves until we heal our relationship with death and grief. With *Reimagining Death*, Lucinda Herring charts a course for this essential healing—a course that is both practical and spiritual, personal and universal."

—BRIAN FLOWERS, funeral director, founder of the Meadow Natural Burial Ground, and past president of the Green Burial Council

"This is the book we have all been waiting for! As a sacred partner in this complex journey of living and dying, Herring's wisdom and poetic renderings resonate completely with what is in my heart. Her stories remind us that nature is our constant companion, offering solace, mystery, possibility, and at times absolute proof that there is much more to life and death than what most people believe. This book can help us transcend our fears of death and find the authenticity and beauty in life that is always there."

—JERRIGRACE LYONS, founder and director of the nonprofit Final Passages, the Institute of Conscious Dying, Home Funeral, and Green Burial Education

"Lucinda Herring embodies the emerging ethic of natural, meaningful, and conscious threshold and after-death care. Her book empowers us all to trust our intuition and find ways to say goodbye that are both practical and transformative. She has captured the generous spirits of the home funeral and natural burial movements perfectly."

—LEE WEBSTER, former president of the National Home Funeral Alliance, education chair of the Green Burial Council, and founding member of the Conservation Burial Alliance

"With her innate wisdom, depth of understanding, and compassionate approach, Lucinda Herring embodies the sacred and offers us the possibility of an honoring, transformative, and loving experience of death. This book offers 'peace of the green' and is a profound gift to us all."

—CLAIRE TURNHAM, UK-based founder of
Only with Love and chair of the Home Funeral
Network

"As an active, long-time member of the National Home Funeral Alliance and the founding director of Heart Land Prairie Cemetery, a prairie restoration burial ground in central Kansas, I have longed for a book that I could give to people interested in what lies at the very heart of this work. *Reimagining Death* is that book. I am so grateful for Lucinda Herring for sharing her stories and practical instruction and for reminding us all of a deep abiding wisdom we share as human beings. Caring for our own dead in tender, environmentally friendly ways has the power to help heal our souls, our relationships to each other, and to reinstate our place in the cycle of life."

—SARAH CREWS, president of the National
Home Funeral Alliance and director of Heart
Land Prairie Cemetery

Reimagining DEATH

STORIES *and* PRACTICAL WISDOM *for* HOME FUNERALS *and* GREEN BURIALS

LUCINDA HERRING

FOREWORD BY DAVID SPANGLER

North Atlantic Books
Berkeley, California

Published by
North Atlantic Books
Berkeley, California

Cover design by Jasmine Hromjak
Cover photo courtesy of Lindsay Soyer
Book design by Happenstance Type-O-Rama

"Hospital to Home Funeral Blueprint" appears in this book courtesy of Lee Webster; "The Long Conversation" courtesy of Laurie Riepe; "Undertaking" courtesy of Donna James; "And We'll Adorn His Body" courtesy of Judith Adams; and "Bringing Eric Home" courtesy of Shelley Sherriff

Printed in the United States of America

Reimagining Death: Stories and Practical Wisdom for Home Funerals and Green Burials is sponsored and published by the Society for the Study of Native Arts and Sciences (dba North Atlantic Books), an educational nonprofit based in Berkeley, California, that collaborates with partners to develop cross-cultural perspectives, nurture holistic views of art, science, the humanities, and healing, and seed personal and global transformation by publishing work on the relationship of body, spirit, and nature.

North Atlantic Books' publications are available through most bookstores. For further information, visit our website at www.northatlanticbooks.com or call 800-733-3000.

DISCLAIMER: The following information is intended for general information purposes only. We encourage individuals to consult natural after-death care providers, as well as their health care providers or faith communities before administering any suggestions made in this book. Any application of the material set forth in the following pages is at the reader's discretion and is his or her sole responsibility.

Library of Congress Cataloging-in-Publication Data
Names: Herring, Lucinda, author.
Title: Reimagining death : stories and practical wisdom for home funerals and green burials / Lucinda Herring ; foreword by David Spangler.
Description: Berkeley : North Atlantic Books, 2019.
Identifiers: LCCN 2018031617 (print) | LCCN 2018040542 (ebook) | ISBN 9781623172930 (E-book) | ISBN 9781623172923 (paperback)
Subjects: LCSH: Burial—Environmental aspects—United States. | Funeral rites and ceremonies—Environmental aspects—United States. | Environmental responsibility—United States. | BISAC: SELF-HELP / Death, Grief, Bereavement. | FAMILY & RELATIONSHIPS / Death, Grief, Bereavement.
Classification: LCC GT3203 (ebook) | LCC GT3203 .H47 2019 (print) | DDC 393/.9—dc23
LC record available at https://lccn.loc.gov/2018031617

1 2 3 4 5 6 7 8 9 KPC 24 23 22 21 20 19

Printed on recycled paper

North Atlantic Books is committed to the protection of our environment.
We partner with FSC-certified printers using soy-based inks
and print on recycled paper whenever possible.

This book is dedicated
to my mother
Irobel Foshee Herring (1927-2001)
and to my father
Harold Francis Herring (1924-2010).
May the legacy
of their love
and stewardship of family, land, and place
bless this book and bless its readers.

With the drawing of this Love and the voice of this Calling

We shall not cease from exploration
And the end of all our exploring
Will be to arrive where we started
And know the place for the first time.
Through the unknown, remembered gate
When the last of earth left to discover
Is that which was the beginning;
At the source of the longest river
The voice of the hidden waterfall
And the children in the apple-tree

Not known, because not looked for
But heard, half-heard, in the stillness
Between two waves of the sea.
Quick now, here, now, always—
A condition of complete simplicity
(Costing not less than everything)
And all shall be well
And all manner of thing shall be well . . .

—T. S. ELIOT, from "Little Gidding" in *Four Quartets*

CONTENTS

ILLUSTRATIONS

These illustrations are in the color photo section.

PAGE ONE: Jake Seniuk's Last Art Installation
> *"Jake Lying in State at Home"*
> *Courtesy of Tristan Seniuk and family*
> *"Undertaking"*
> *Courtesy of Tristan Seniuk and Donna James*

PAGE TWO: Preparing Jake for Natural Burial
> *"Jake and His Mushroom Shroud"*
> *Courtesy of Tristan Seniuk and family*
> *"Sons and Friends Lowering Jake into Green Grave, The Meadow,*
> *Ferndale, Washington"*
> *Courtesy of Tristan Seniuk and family*

PAGE THREE: Painting Caskets during Home Vigils
> *"Painting the Casket at Home"*
> *Courtesy of Olivia Bareham / Sacred Crossings, www.sacredcrossings.com*
> *"Boys Decorating Vahe's Casket"*
> *Courtesy of Olivia Bareham / Sacred Crossings, www.sacredcrossings.com*

PAGE FOUR: Eric Ivan Field's Home Vigil
> *"Eric Home from the Hospital Hours after His Death"*
> *Courtesy of Eric Field's family*
> *"A Friend Built the Pine Casket and Then Word Went Out to the*
> *Community for Anyone to Come and Decorate It."*
> *Courtesy of Eric Field's family*

PAGE FIVE
> *"Eric and His Son Loren"*
> *Courtesy of Eric Field's family*
> *"Eric's Sacred Space near the Window"*
> *Courtesy of Eric Field's family*
> *"Eric Was Dressed in Garments He Had Worn in Ceremony in Africa*
>   *and Placed in His Casket with Messages, Sacred Items, and a Wreath*
>   *His Wife Wore at Their Wedding."*
> *Courtesy of Eric Field's family*

PAGE SIX: Animals and Home Funerals
> *"Fanny and Keisha at Keisha's Home Vigil"*
> *Courtesy of Fanny Porter and Keisha*
> *"Lisa and Her Beloved Dog Clover at Her Home Vigil"*
> *Courtesy of Olivia Bareham and Lisa Schiavello*

PAGE SEVEN: Jeanne and Dorothy
> *"Jeanne Caring for Her Mother Dorothy at Home"*
> *Courtesy of the Lepisto family*
> *"Dorothy's Handmade Casket and Green Burial"*
> *Courtesy of the Lepisto family*
> *"Jeanne at Her Mother's Graveside Service"*
> *Courtesy of Deborah Koff-Chapin, artist/photographer*

PAGE EIGHT: Leonard Daniel Hamby's Natural Burial
> *"Leonard Daniel Hamby's Daughter Elizabeth at His Natural Burial,*
>   *Ramsey Creek Preserve"*
> *Courtesy of Dara Ashworth and family*
> *"Leonard Daniel Hamby's Shroud Burial, Ramsey Creek Preserve"*
> *Courtesy of Dara Ashworth and family*
> *"Hannah, the Family Dog, Died the Morning after Leonard 'Treat Man*
>   *Dan' Was Buried. Kimberly Campbell of Ramsey Creek Kindly*
>   *Buried Hannah next to L. Daniel Hamby So They Could Be Together*
>   *in Death, as in Life."*
> *Courtesy of Dara Ashworth and family*

PAGE NINE: Ramsey Creek Preserve

"*Entrance to Ramsey Creek Preserve, First Conservation Burial Preserve in North America, Established by Dr. Billy and Kimberley Campbell in 1996*"

Photo by John Christian Phifer/Courtesy of JCP and Ramsey Creek Preserve, Westminster, South Carolina, www.memorialecosystems.com

"*Ramsey Creek Natural Burial Headstone*"

Photo by John Christian Phifer/Courtesy of JCP and Ramsey Creek Preserve, Westminster, South Carolina, www.memorialecosystems.com

PAGE TEN: Prairie Creek Conservation Cemetery/
Heartwood Preserve

"*A Shroud Burial at Prairie Creek Conservation Cemetery, Gainesville, Florida*"

Photo by Melissa K. Hill, Courtesy of Prairie Creek Conservation Cemetery, www.prairiecreekconservationcemetery.org

"*Metal Disc Used to Mark Plots in Grid System at Heartwood Preserve, Trinity, Florida*"

Photo by Andrea Ragan/Courtesy of AR and Laura Starkey of Heartwood Preserve, www.heartwoodpreserve.com

PAGE ELEVEN: Larkspur Conservation/Kokosing Nature Preserve

"*Sapling Casket, Larkspur Conservation, Taylor Hollow, Tennessee*"

Courtesy of John Christian Phifer, executive director of Larkspur Conservation, www.larkspurconservation.org

"*Flower Pathway at Kokosing Nature Preserve Burial Ground, Gambier, Ohio*"

Courtesy of Heidi Hannapel and Jeff Masten of Landmatters, a multidisciplinary consulting firm committed to healthy communities and sustainable landscapes, www.thelandmatters.com. "Kokosing Nature Preserve," www.kenyon.edu/directories/offices-services/philander-chase-conservancy/kokosing-nature-preserve

PAGE TWELVE: Esther Sutin's Burial/Eloise Woods
Natural Burial Park

"*Ellen Macdonald Reads Love Notes at Her Mother Esther Sutin's Service.*"
Courtesy of Ellen Macdonald, owner of Eloise Woods Natural Burial
Park, www.eloisewoods.com
"*Love Notes around Esther Sutin*"
Courtesy of Ellen Macdonald, owner of Eloise Woods Natural Burial
Park, www.eloisewoods.com
"*Grave Marker for Esther Sutin's Natural Burial*"
Courtesy of Ellen Macdonald, owner of Eloise Woods Natural Burial
Park, www.eloisewoods.com

PAGE THIRTEEN: White Eagle Memorial Preserve

"*Shroud Burial in Winter, White Eagle Memorial Preserve, Goldendale,*
Washington"
Courtesy of Jodie Buller and the Fink family, White Eagle Memorial
Preserve, www.naturalburialground.org
"*White Eagle Shroud Burial*"
Courtesy of Jodie Buller and the Fink family, White Eagle Memorial
Preserve, www.naturalburialground.org
"*Director Jodie Buller Making a Grave Beautiful before Natural Burial*"
Courtesy of Jodie Buller, White Eagle Memorial Preserve, www
.naturalburialground.org

PAGE FOURTEEN: The Meadow Natural Burial Ground

"*A Procession with Shrouded Body on Caisson*"
Courtesy of Brian Flowers, The Meadow Natural Burial Ground at
Greenacres Memorial Park, www.molesfarewelltributes.com
"*An Early Green Burial at The Meadow Natural Burial Ground*"
Courtesy of Brian Flowers, The Meadow Natural Burial Ground
at Greenacres Memorial Park, Ferndale, Washington, www
.molesfarewelltributes.com

PAGE FIFTEEN: Biodegradable Casket and Shrouds

"*Biodegradable Wicker Casket/Hand-Dug Grave at Steelmantown Cemetery, South Jersey*"

Courtesy of Edward Bixby, proprietor

"*Theresa's Shroud Burial*" (cover of the book)

Courtesy of Lindsay Soyer, photographer

"*Beautiful Shroud Burial at Eloise Woods Natural Burial Park*"

Courtesy of Ellen Macdonald, owner of Eloise Woods Natural Burial Park, www.eloisewoods.com

PAGE SIXTEEN: Judy's Home Vigil

"*Mother and Daughter, Judy's Home Vigil*"

Courtesy of Lynn Hays, artist/photographer

"*Judy's Goodbye*"

Courtesy of Lynn Hays, artist/photographer

"*1,000 Paper Cranes from Judy's Elementary School Students*"

Courtesy of Lynn Hays, artist/photographer

"*Painting Judy's Casket at Home*"

Courtesy of Shanti Lousteneau, artist/photographer

FOREWORD

*I*n 1963, my father and I had the only argument we ever had about a book I was reading. The book in question was Jessica Mitford's *The American Way of Death*, which had just been published. I was home for a visit from college. Dad came into the living room one evening and saw me reading it. He had an immediate reaction, telling me that I was too young (I was eighteen) to be reading about death and that I must be getting morbid to read an "awful book" like that. Surprisingly, given that our family home was filled with books of all kinds, he asked me not to have it in the house. This was an unprecedented request from my liberal, loving, gentle father, which is why it has stuck in my memory all these years.

It was the first time I realized the depths to which my father refused to confront in any way the topic of death. It was an attitude that hardened as he got older. Any time the subject of death or dying would come up, he would leave the room. He refused all attempts, on the part of my mother or me, to discuss what arrangements he would like when his death came. He left it to my mother to make her own arrangements, which she did by willing her body to the local medical university to be used by medical students learning to do autopsies, after which her remains were cremated and mailed in a box to Dad. He never opened that box.

After Mom's death, Dad lived alone in their house in Ohio, putting off efforts my wife and I made to have him move out to Washington State to be with us. He died one night in bed of a sudden heart attack. A friend found his body two days later and called me.

By the time we got to Dayton, where he and Mom had lived, he was already in a funeral home and ready for burial.

The funeral director, a young, friendly woman, asked me what my dad's wishes had been for his funeral. I was at a loss to answer her. Fortunately, I remembered two comments he had made. One, made years earlier, was that he wished to be buried next to his father in a plot that had been in the Spangler family for a couple of generations. The second was something he'd said to me when the box with Mom's ashes had been delivered. He'd said he'd like the box buried with him.

With this to go on, the funeral director said she would handle everything, and she did. The main problem was that the graveyard where Granddad was buried was a small one in rural Ohio some distance from where Dad had been living. There was no problem taking the body there, but its distance meant that only one of our family friends could attend. Consequently, the graveyard service, which I, as an ordained minister, was able to conduct, consisted of me and my wife, our family friend, the funeral director, and a couple of men associated with the graveyard. It hardly seemed fitting for a man who had loved life so much and had been loved by so many in return. Yet, it seemed the best I could do at the time, especially given the rapidity with which events unfolded and having so little knowledge of any desires my father might have had.

In this wonderful book, Lucinda Herring writes, "Turning toward death is not easy. Most of us actively avoid thinking about it. We are quite content to push the inevitable down deep, promising ourselves we will get to 'all that' another day." This was certainly true of my father, though not of my mother, who was quite easy and candid about discussing her death and what she wished to do with her body. But the "turning" toward death that Lucinda writes about is not merely toward the *event* of death and care for the body and for those who mourn; it is not just about acceptance or knowing what to do when "the time comes." Behind her stories and her practical suggestions for home vigils and natural burials lies a deeper, powerful message grounded in her holistic vision of life. It's a message about how we can be more whole human beings and, in the process, contribute to the emergence of healthier, more harmonious life for ourselves and for the world.

I have had the pleasure and privilege of knowing Lucinda for many years. I have always admired her passion and compassion, her joy in life, and her commitment to finding and enlarging the connections between our increasingly technological society and the natural world that surrounds us. She has a talent for creating rituals and celebrations that bring people together with each other and with the beauty and gifts of nature. This talent illumines her work as a home funeral guide, working at the boundary between life and death, grief and joy, pain and release.

This is a practical book about what to do when someone dies and you wish to not only care for the body in ecological and natural ways, but also care for yourself and others who grieve the loss of a loved one. It helps you navigate the legalities of society and the expectations of the commercial funeral industry. It helps you find a calm center in the midst of the storm and equally importantly, it gives important insight into how to care for the passage of the one who has died. Depending on your belief, there may be an afterlife waiting for the one who has passed on, but even if you do not believe this, it is certain the dead live on in us in our memories and imagination. In either case, how we treat and honor the transition of this person from physical life will have an effect in either destination.

Beneath the practicalities, though, and resonating through the many stories, there is an undercurrent to this book, like the bass line supporting the melody. This is the idea that life, death, and the world are inextricably and interdependently linked in a wholeness. How we deal with one affects how we deal with the others. Appreciating, honoring, and attending to this wholeness is something our ancestors instinctively appreciated. Many of their customs around both life and death reflected this. It's an awareness and a worldview our culture, faced with the challenges and dangers of ignoring this interconnectedness, is struggling to reclaim.

One of the ways we may do so is in bringing the naturalness of death back in from the cold and reimagining how we treat our dead or, as Lucinda felicitously puts it, in the "greening of death." We may not all opt for a home funeral, but we can all participate in new and powerfully healing ways in blending death with life in the celebration of a soul's passage into a new form of existence.

I didn't tell all the story of my dad's death and passing over, so let me do so now. All my life, I've been aware of the subtle, nonphysical dimensions of the earth. From my perspective, these constitute an ecology of life every bit as diverse as anything we find here on earth. Because of this, I have always viewed death not as an ending of anything but as another kind of birth, a portal into this vast, subtle ecosystem. It is a view that Lucinda shares as well and, although she in no manner insists on it in this book, leaving each reader to have his or her own conclusions about the nature of reality, it is there as another vibrant undercurrent in her stories and her perspective.

When Dad died I had no knowledge of what he might wish to help him with this passage. I could only hold his soul in my love. But as the hour of the funeral approached, I suddenly knew with certainty what I needed to do and say. Did this information come from Dad's soul in touch with my own? I don't know, and it doesn't matter. The important thing was that it arose from a wellspring of love and honor both for him and for the momentousness and joy of this moment of transition. And though it was undoubtedly odd for the funeral director and her assistants as I conducted a short, simple, and entirely improvisational ritual on Dad's behalf, I knew without question it was empowering for him and came from a place of mutual attunement. I must have done something right, for when I finished, I clearly saw both my mother and father standing by their joint grave, holding hands, smiling at me, and looking radiantly happy in their new life together.

Whether imagination or true vision, it doesn't really matter. What counts is that in that moment I felt deeply connected to my father—to both my parents, really—and to all he had given me in my life. I felt that an important circle of life had been lovingly completed, giving me a foundation for moving on.

It's exactly this kind of deep completion and the empowered moving on of all concerned that is at the heart of Lucinda's book. With eloquence and love, she has given us here more than a book about death. It is a testament to life and its inexhaustible possibilities.

David Spangler

May 2018

PROLOGUE:
The Calling

With the drawing of this Love and the voice of this Calling
We shall not cease from exploration
And the end of all our exploring
Will be to arrive where we started
And know the place for the first time . . .
And all shall be well
And all manner of thing shall be well . . .

—T. S. ELIOT, from "Little Gidding" in *Four Quartets*

I am sitting at my father's elegant inlaid desk, by an open window looking out on the Alabama land I love. It is late afternoon and countless birds flock to the bowls of water I have put out for them in the forest clearing. Chipmunks scamper beneath the great drifts of fallen leaves, and the place, with one of us home, seems happy and alive again, glowing in warm russet light. Everything is welcoming me back. Early this morning I rose and took a walk across the ravines to our spring, dry and dusty from extreme drought, but a flowing fountain still in the depths of the limestone caverns beneath me. I offered prayers and songs to the spirits of our land, greeting them once more as beloved friends, asking for their support and guidance. I know they hear me.

I have returned to my family land to begin work on the book you now hold in your hands—a book about caring for our own dead again, as we used to do long ago; about the gifts of home funeral vigils or wakes; simple green burial; and other natural, creative, and innovative ways to care for our bodies after death. It is fitting that I begin my writing here, within log cabin walls that have surely, in their two hundred years, borne witness to many families caring for their own dead. Here, in the beauty of a room overlooking the forest, where both my mother and father died: Irobel Herring in 2001, and Harold Herring nine years later in 2010.

My family cared for the bodies and souls of our parents after death, rather than entrusting that sacred task to strangers in the local funeral home. "Local" in our area means forty miles away, which is why it made perfect sense, at least to me, for us to do the honors. We—four daughters, one son, spouses, and grandchildren—all "set up" (as Southerners would say) with Mama and Papa for a time. We bathed, anointed, and dressed them, read poetry, and sang hymns. We kept watch, holding them close within the heart of things—our hearts, our hands—until we were ready to let them go.

The spirits of Papa and Mama draw in close to me as I write— my ancestors now, still stewards of this place. I have built an altar for them both, to honor Samhain/Halloween/Day of the Dead. It is especially meaningful, for I am here on their land, rather than back home in the Pacific Northwest, where I have lived for the last thirty years. Photos of Mama and Papa rest on the windowsill, near the very spot where each of them took their last breaths, and where they entered the green realms of death on their own terms. The photos are surrounded by autumn leaves, faded and dry now, which rustle occasionally in a silent breeze. A candle flickers, spilling light onto the jiggers of Jack Daniel's whiskey I have placed nearby to sustain and delight them. I am filled with a quiet and abiding sense of peace and intention. I know that all shall be well.

Mama and Papa invoked the words "All shall be well" often in their lives. The saying was a favorite of theirs, attributed to Julian of Norwich, a Christian mystic and theologian from the fourteenth century. "All shall be well, and all manner of thing shall be well": T. S. Eliot weaves the words into his poem "Little Gidding" from *Four Quartets;* I weave them in here, for the words have become an invocation and prayer for me in my work now as an alternative funeral director, minister, and home funeral and green burial guide. For me, it is an invocation for healing and wholeness in our relationship to death itself—a chance to transform our fears and heavy thought forms and "return home," by reclaiming after-death care practices that are more natural, instinctive, nourishing, and ecologically sustainable for all.

I offer this saying to you as we turn together toward a contemplation of death—our own, and the loss of those we love. Turning toward death is not easy. Most of us actively avoid thinking about it. We are quite content to push the inevitable down deep, promising ourselves we will get to "all that" another day. But if you are reading these words, something in you is already willing to turn and begin opening the doorway. Perhaps you have experienced the transformative gifts of a home funeral vigil and are eager to learn as much as you can. Perhaps you have heard of the huge environmental impact associated with conventional burial and even cremation, and wish to make different choices when you die. Perhaps working with a funeral home when your mother or father died left you longing for something more.

It is my hope and intention that you, as reader, will be inspired and empowered to reimagine the way your body, or that of your loved one, will be cared for after death—and to get those wishes and plans in place long before they are needed. Such conscious intention about our own mortality can help create a greater sense of ease about dying—a knowing that, indeed, all shall be well, no matter what the end of our lives may bring. Being prepared for our deaths enables us to actually turn around and live our lives more fully.

As a home funeral and green burial guide, I help others understand that there is a relatively unexamined aspect of end-of-life
planning that is nevertheless important to think about and include.
I refer specifically to the "gap" time between the moment one dies
and the time when the body is taken away to its place of final disposition. In my experience, most people have never factored this
important part of death's threshold into their final wishes. When I
ask people if they have thought about their funeral plans, many will
assure me that everything is already in place, perfectly handled. "Oh,
I'm going to be cremated. Nothing fancy." Or "Yes, I've bought a
burial plot and my family knows my wishes."

But then I ask: "Have you thought about the moment of your
death, how you want that to transpire? What about the time immediately afterward, and the hours before you are taken away for your
cremation or burial? What will they be like? What if you die suddenly in a car accident and find yourself in a coroner's morgue?
What if you die in a hospital rather than at home? Have you imagined these scenarios and thought about how you wish your body and
your soul to be treated?"

In many traditions, the hours and days right after a death are
vitally important and sacred. They are viewed as a precious opportunity, a holy interval, when our souls and spirits have enough time and
support to fully leave our physical bodies behind. Those who love
us are also supported to have real closure and a chance to say goodbye. Here is the third stage of death's threshold—the time of active
dying being the first, and the moment of death being the second.
(See Appendix A for a more detailed discussion of these three
stages.) In our fear and dread of "being dead," we have forgotten the
gifts and potential of slowing everything down and being present
to all that might emerge in the third stage—that sacred "time out
of time." It does not matter whether this interval is simply an extra
hour before the funeral service arrives, a few hours spent adorning
our mother with flowers and saying prayers at the funeral home,

or a full three-day vigil. The decision is up to us and, of course, dependent on the circumstances of the death. But it's important to know that it is legally possible to ask for the time we need, and that we have an innate right to make such choices for ourselves and for our loved ones.

When I talk about this, people often look at me with a dazed expression. I can tell such inquiry has never entered their minds. We are so conditioned now as a culture to accept without question that the body is taken away immediately when someone dies. In the midst of our grief, we believe we must stop everything and call a chosen funeral service, so that strangers can whisk our loved one away to places unknown, to rooms behind closed doors—out of sight; out of mind, please; and the sooner the better, really, for everyone concerned.

If the time is right, that's when I might share ways we can begin reimagining the way we "do death" in our society. (When I say "our," I am addressing primarily we of the modern Western world.) Many of us have had hard, if not traumatic, experiences with today's funeral industry. The growing impersonal corporatization of funeral homes in this country makes the cost of asking strangers to care for our dead increasingly high—financially, emotionally, and spiritually. Yet we don't know any other way to handle matters when a loved one dies. We have not been educated and informed of all our options (conveniently so for the industry).

So we listen to the funeral director and give away our power and right to participate in Aunt Betty's care. We agree to embalm our father, though the thought of filling his dear body with chemicals is surreal and disturbing. Our beloved mother is sealed away forever in an airtight steel-gasketed casket and then placed in a concrete vault in the ground—both of which obscure the dark, fertile earth waiting to welcome her home. We leave the graveside early and we go back to work and try to get on with our lives. And we wonder why we cannot concentrate on our jobs or focus on our children's needs, and why we feel so numb and disoriented in our days.

We are dying (and living) in profoundly disconnected ways. The circles of real intimacy in our lives are broken, and we have little understanding of how to change. Such separation begins with our relationship to death, which has been banished from the cycle of life, relegated to overfull morgues in hospitals, embalming rooms and coolers in funeral homes. I am convinced that our fear and denial of death underlies much of our inability to live whole and connected lives.

The pace of our days is frenetic and stressed; we live only in our heads and conditioned minds and forget to take care of our bodies, our relations, and the earth from whence we come. Nor do we turn to the body and earth for wisdom—something indigenous cultures have never forgotten to do. We are oblivious to our interdependence with all other sentient beings on this planet, and the possibility of communion and co-creation with that great web of life. Cut off from the reality of our own mortality, we are cut off from nature itself and from what it really means to be human. In denying death, we deny the very substance from which we are made—matter, *mater*, the Mother. This denial is woven with a collective negation of the Feminine in our psyches as well. Such fragmentation makes it very difficult to live balanced lives, and to know the sacred wholeness of who we really are.

As I write these words, I feel the danger of spinning out into abstractions of the mind and leaving the body behind. Perhaps you feel the same, reading these paragraphs. It's a lot to think about, much less try to integrate. And it's about death—the dreaded enemy who will someday come knocking at our door. Maybe it's best to go get a warm cup of tea and find comfort for a while. Go outside and feel your feet firmly planted on the ground. It's earth wherever you are. But come back to these pages, for I have stories to tell, and inspirations that I hope might ease your angst for a time. If we can open to death again, we can learn what it means to co-create with that mystery, with our bodies, our earth, our true natures. In doing so, we can begin to reimagine what is possible at the end of life, and learn how to bring beauty, creativity, life, hope, and healing back in caring for our dead.

The good news is that more and more people are opening to these "new," actually old ways of being present at death's threshold. T. S. Eliot's poem is appropriate here:

With the drawing of this Love and the voice of this Calling

We shall not cease from exploration
And the end of all our exploring
Will be to arrive where we started
And know the place for the first time.

As I read these words, I think of all the families who naturally and instinctively are "arriving where we started" long ago—and reclaiming the right to care for the bodies of parents, children, and friends after death, in shared and creative communion once again. I celebrate all the remarkable transformative and healing moments I have witnessed—when people, "knowing the place for the first time," shed their fears of being with the dead, and realize how normal and real and beautiful it can be to show up and participate in a dear one's care. Touching our mother's body with love and reverence as we bathe and dress her for cremation. Picking up shovels and pickaxes to dig our friend's grave ourselves, lining his final resting place with moss and ferns, and singing and crying together as we fill in the dirt and return his shrouded body to the earth. All this within the intimacy of one's own circles of love, in conscious relationship to land and place, and with awareness and consideration for the greater circles and web of life on this planet.

"We shall not cease from exploration." How true this is for those of us who are saying "yes" to this reclamation and pioneering work together. Many of us are women, which makes sense, as we were the original caretakers of the dead before funeral care became an industry. Many of us are baby boomers, accustomed to doing things our own way, and rebelling against the status quo. Just as we helped create the natural home birth movement in the 1970s, we are now working at the other end of life, demanding that home funeral vigils and natural after-death care be reestablished once again. There is also a younger generation joining us now—calling themselves the "Death Positives" and reimagining even how we have been working, thus keeping our movement alive and generative and relevant for those coming after us. This is to be celebrated.

Individuals, families, whole communities are joining together to create a vital network and growing cultural and political movement for innovation and change. The National Home Funeral Alliance and the Green Burial Council are organizations that have formed from these shared endeavors, along with the Funeral Consumers Alliance, which helps protect families' rights within the funeral industry. New, innovative alliances in the conservation burial ground movement are currently on the horizon, which will generate stronger collaboration between the home funeral movement and those committed to burial practices that restore and preserve land and ecosystems for the future. To me, these are ever-widening circles of wholeness and healing. Though the focus of these organizations and alliances differs, there is a shared vision to educate people about their innate legal rights to choose more natural and sustainable ways to care for the dead; and to ensure that home funeral vigils, green and conservation burials, and other ecological forms of disposition are readily available death care options for the future.

I have been blessed to be part of this paradigm shift since its beginnings in the 1990s, and to have experienced the exciting ways individuals and groups are manifesting their passions and shared visions. The level of commitment and willingness to think outside the box and to bring all our gifts, talents, and resources to the table inspires me. Though the work is hard and demanding, and often done without fanfare or recognition from others (as is the case with most pioneering efforts), people in the movement deeply support one another. This makes our efforts more resilient and sustainable for the long run. Probably most of us would agree that Love "drew us," to rephrase T. S. Eliot's words—love for a dying family member or friend who asked for more natural care of his or her body; love for land and cherished places in need of conservation; love for planet Earth as a living, conscious being in need of our care.

I know that Love "drew me" to this Calling—love for Earth as Gaia/Great Mother, and love for my own mother, who introduced me to the wonders and magic of the natural world, and whose remarkable death was a pivotal point in my own journey. When I returned home to our mountain land to help my mother die, my personal relationship to death deepened in ways I am still exploring today. The transformative initiatory experiences I had with my mother and family on the mountain—especially with nature and spirit and the land itself—left an insistent question in my heart and soul: *What does it mean to co-create or partner with nature, our bodies, and the earth at the threshold of death?*

My explorations and efforts to answer this question have shaped everything I do today. I must admit I had no idea what I was getting into. Never in my wildest dreams did I think I would become a licensed funeral director (albeit a "green," alternative one) in my sixties, at a time of life when most of my friends are retiring. Never did I think I would be waking in the middle of the night to help a family bathe the dead body of their loved one, or stand with a gravedigger, teaching him how to pile biomass on a shrouded body before filling in the grave. Such work is not for the faint of heart or body. Nor is it my idea of a calm and peaceful way to head toward retirement—or the lack thereof, since it turns out this pioneering work rarely pays the bills and is certainly not a lucrative "career" choice for anyone (though I have spent years of magical thinking trying to make it so). Yet something within my heart keeps saying "yes" to this inquiry, even when my rational mind daily protests the very real levels of stress and uncertainty such an affirmation brings.

The stories and practical wisdom shared in this book come directly out of my personal journey and commitment to reimagine death, and to work with others to find their own unique and special imaginations of what it means to die, and to care for our own dead again as a sacred act of love. I am only one voice in the remarkable collective response to this Calling, and I will be sharing some of the many creative ways others are joining this great movement for healing and change. In essence, this Call springs from Earth itself, an invitation to remember and "return home"—and from our own hearts and shared longing to recover the full dimensions of what it means to be human, and to live and die naturally, with awareness and with wisdom once again.

Please note: There is a Resources section at the back of the book. Please refer to that section for further information, websites, and book references mentioned in the Prologue and in each subsequent chapter.

Practical Wisdom: Home Funerals Lost and Found

Up until the mid-nineteenth century, American families cared for their own dead at home. Often teams of women in communities would come in to bathe, dress, and lay out for viewing a deceased person; and everyone would gather round the corpse in the best room or parlor of the house. People understood that the body needed to be kept cool, but artificial interference with the body, such as embalming, was rarely, if ever, a part of after-death care in family life.

During the U.S. Civil War, when thousands of soldiers died on battlefields in the South, families, particularly wealthy Northern ones, paid field surgeons to develop embalming techniques to preserve a loved one's body until it could reach home. Thomas Holmes, considered one of the founding fathers of the modern funeral industry, perfected embalming methods during this time, and became a leading influence on his fellow undertakers. The funeral industry formed around the growing practice of embalming bodies for viewing and services.

When Abraham Lincoln's body was embalmed in order to travel by train across the country from Washington, DC, to Springfield, Illinois, and to be viewed publicly by thousands of people, the whole concept of preserving bodies with chemicals rapidly gained popularity, helping pave the way for modern-day after-death care practices. People (almost always men) became specialized "funeral directors," offering embalmed viewings and increasingly elaborate caskets and services in funeral "parlors" as a burgeoning business. Thus began the great migration of the dead away from the home, and from a family's natural and loving care, into the hands of "professionals"—whose services inevitably included business strategies and the bottom line. These professionals either consciously or unconsciously dismissed the fact that their businesses were based on the unnatural use of toxic chemicals, heavy industrial manufacturing of metal and endangered-species woods for caskets, and widespread environmental abuse of land and resources.

There are good people in the modern funeral industry profession whose hearts are dedicated to helping families in their time of loss and grief, and who do a magnificent job of caring for others. But the model upon which today's funeral services are based is outdated, deeply flawed, and unsustainable for anyone's future, including those who are entering the profession today. The industry is in trouble, particularly the mom-and-pop independent local funeral homes in rural areas. The rise of funeral service corporations means that families receive increasingly impersonal and commodity-based care that is both financially and emotionally costly, and often empty of real meaning and closure. The idea of the "full-service funeral"— where the body is taken away and embalmed, viewing and services happen on site at the funeral home, and families are encouraged to pay thousands of dollars to purchase the most elaborate and "protected from the elements" caskets to best honor their loved one—is no longer viable or even desired by much of the public. Cremation is fast becoming the disposition of choice around the country, based on financial, environmental, and convenience concerns. And more and more people are choosing "greener," more ecological after-death options.

The growing interest in home funeral vigils and green burials is a natural and instinctive response to the ways we have been caring for our dead in the last 150 years in this country. Now we are learning how to care for loved ones in ways we used to do—in comfortable, familiar places where we can be ourselves, and where the dead can be held and supported in a field of love rather than being whisked away too rapidly to stark, cold morgues and the impersonal care of strangers. And where they can be laid to rest in natural and life-giving ways. In reclaiming the sacred act of caring for our own dead, we are "returning home"—to ourselves, to our bodies, and to the earth.

A Story of the NHFA's Beginnings

In my mind and heart, the National Home Funeral Alliance began on a frigid January night in 2010, though the organization had been in the works for a couple of years. Beth Knox, founder of Crossings in Maryland, gathered with others in 2008 to honor Crossings' tenth anniversary, and its work to educate people about their sacred right to care for their own dead. That celebration was the first networking event and shared acknowledgment that home funeral advocates needed ways to come together and support each other in the work. Char Barrett hosted a gathering in the summer of 2009 as part of the Funeral Consumers Alliance biennial conference in Seattle, with Jerrigrace Lyons of Final Passages and some of her students. (Jerrigrace had also been training home funeral guides, like Beth Knox, for ten years.) Karen van Vuuren started Natural Transitions in Boulder, Colorado, soon after, and hosted a conference for home funeral advocates in October 2009, as well as a follow-up organizational meeting the next day, from which came the first leadership team of thirteen who would initiate the next steps in creating an official alliance.

Char Barrett, a licensed funeral director who started her own funeral service in 2007, A Sacred Moment, Inc.—offering home funerals and green burials—was head of that leadership team. Char and I had completed Jerrigrace's home funeral training together five years before, and when Char chose to expand her funeral service to Everett, Washington, she asked me to join her. I was grateful for the opportunity to do so, as it meant I could get my funeral director's license and still remain true to the home funeral/green burial movement. On the night when the NHFA officially started for me, Char and I were on our first case together. This case happened the day before A Sacred Moment's Everett doors were even open for business, initiating us from the very beginning of Char's newest endeavor into the power of what we were choosing to do.

We were sitting in the front seat of Char's car, in the parking lot of a city church, taking a small respite from holding a funeral that had already been going on for hours inside. Before the altar lay a young man, tragically murdered. We had managed to bring his body to the church, unembalmed and natural, dressed in his Bob Marley T-shirt and baseball cap, so that all his schoolmates and the community could gather round him and mourn. We had decorated his cardboard casket with beautiful silks and had overnighted sheepskin coverings to hold him close in a cozy biodegradable bed. He would be laid to rest in a green burial the next day. These tasks were a strong awakening for all our staff, because of the raw emotions and brutality of what we were handling. I remember a steady freezing rain beating down on the windshield while Char and I groped for snacks and water to sustain us before heading back inside. The bright red and blue lights of police cars surrounding the church flashed eerily in the gathering darkness, leaving no doubt of the public nature of our efforts, and our unwavering commitment to give this family the services they wanted and needed anyway.

Right in the midst of this drama, Char's cell phone rang, and on the other end there was a chorus of voices—Jerrigrace, Beth, Karen, Marian Spadone—letting us know that Oregon had just passed legislation that would make it far more difficult for families to care for their own dead, and especially for home funeral guides to educate and support them (thanks to the funeral industry lobbyists there). We needed a more public presence, and to form a legal and political entity right away, one that could protect families' innate right to care for their own dead, and also represent those who were becoming home funeral educators and guides. The National Home Funeral Alliance came into greater manifestation that night.

I see now that this was a seminal moment in the home funeral movement. I watched Char, in the semidarkness of the cold car, take a deep breath and agree to be the first president of a newly forming board of directors. And I remember taking a deep breath myself, feeling the implications of that decision for Char's barely budding new endeavor, and for me, Jan, and Chris, who made up the rest of her staff. We were in the midst of helping a family grieve in different ways, and bury their boy in a natural grave, and we were at the same time helping form a national alliance of all those who were answering this Call. I remember feeling the weight and also the excitement of that sacred moment. I was grateful, and am to this day, to be a part of the efforts of these pioneering women who were bound and determined to make natural after-death care a viable and sustainable possibility for families once again. And to reimagine a great paradigm shift in this country and, with dedicated service, make that transformation a reality.

As I write these words, the NHFA is in its eighth year of service and is going strong with almost 1,500 members from forty-seven states, five provinces, and seven countries. Char did an epic job as president for the first few years, and Beth Knox offered her skills, grace, and wisdom as second president afterward. Then came Lee Webster from New Hampshire—a force of nature who, from the beginning of her involvement and through her time as president, raised the bar of what was possible, and brought everyone else along with her in those herculean efforts. I quote these words from the NHFA website: "It needs to be stated that most of what we have accomplished in each year, Lee has done ¾ of it singlehandedly. She has been a tremendous gift to our movement." Thanks to Lee—and her fearless board members, including Sarah Hawley Crews, who is now the fourth NHFA president—the NHFA is today a strong and remarkable resource for families and communities who wish to care for their own dead. It serves also as the foundational support for all those wishing to take up this work as home funeral and green burial educators and guides.

1

RETURN TO THE MOTHER

And for all this, nature is never spent;
There lives the dearest freshness deep down things;
And though the last lights off the black West went
Oh, morning, at the brown brink eastward, springs—
Because the Holy Ghost over the bent
World broods with warm breast and with ah! bright wings.

—GERARD MANLEY HOPKINS,
from his poem "God's Grandeur"

*L*et us return now to the place where we started; to my family's mountain land in Alabama. This time to a balmy, full-moon night in May 2001, when I arrived home to be present for my mother's departure from this world. I chose Mama's story as the first one for this book, as my desire to have a home funeral vigil, and my experiences at Mama's final threshold, form the foundation of all that I am doing now as a green funeral director and natural after-death care minister and guide.

Mama was always a good storyteller, and in her death, she created one of her finest tales. Naturally, this rendition is my version of what happened. If you asked my sisters or brother what transpired, you would hear very different experiences. My story of my mother's death is actually an entire book that I have worked on for years. I have focused on the parts of Mama's story that are most relevant to our inquiry here—what it meant to me to return to my mother in her dying, and find a new relationship to death; the dramas and adventures that ensued when I came home to a family that was unprepared for my certainties and enthusiasm for having a home funeral and caring for Mama's body ourselves; and how nature and the spirits of land and place were integral players and support for all that unfolded at Mama's threshold.

I felt the urgency of the hospice nurse's words on the phone: "If you want to be present for your mother's death, please return to Alabama as soon as you can." As hard as it was, my teenage daughter Eliza, burdened by exams and the end of sophomore year in high school, chose to remain behind on our island with friends. The flight from Seattle was long and Papa was late picking me up in the truck, so it was almost midnight when we reached the last winding curve into our mountain cove.

A huge, luminous orb of a moon hung low over the mountains, beckoning like a portal in the night sky. I wondered if the pull of the full moon was helping Mama finally let go. At least its light could be her radiant escort—dancing in the creek waters and spilling over red clay furrows, newly planted with corn. Its brightness turned the gates at the entrance to our land silver, and lit up the steep, rocky drive as the truck bumped and jostled its way up the hill and came to a silent halt in the clearing.

No loud honk of the horn, as Papa usually did to herald arrivals home, no matter what the hour. Not like the good old days when Mama stayed up waiting, vegetable soup bubbling on the stove, keeping the top half of the door ajar so light from the kitchen could pour out a welcome. I so wanted to see my mother, hurrying down the stone flagged steps, wiping her hands, damp from late night dishes, on her denim skirt. Holding out her arms to me halfway down the walk; mouth pensive but eyes bright; seizing me in a tight, quick little hug, as was her way. Filling empty spaces with buoyant words: "You're home, Lu, on the mountain again. Look at the maidenhair fern. Hasn't it grown? I've put clean sheets on the Papa Bear bed. Hope that suits you. Isn't it *good* to be here?" I would smile and nod, drinking in my mother's textures and smells—old cotton garden sweater, onions, garlic, bourbon—and something else—something I depended upon completely—the "dearest freshness deep down things."

I turned to Papa, who was resting his head on the steering wheel, as if reluctant to face the stark truth waiting inside. "You don't look so good, Papa," I ventured, hesitant to break his reverie. Usually pretty spry, Papa had defied his male family's penchant for keeling over early from heart attacks and managed to look younger than his seventy-seven years. His life as a trial lawyer, civic leader, husband, and father had been good to him, and his days on the mountain now, cutting firewood, driving the tractor, and tending to the gardens, kept him vital and resilient most of the time. Now, in the glare of the truck light, I could see Papa wasn't taking care of himself. Sadness hung on him like a weight, drawing the corners of his mouth down, rounding his shoulders.

"Well, I don't feel so good, either," Papa finally answered, forcing a little smile just for me, before climbing wearily out of the truck and groping for my bags in the back. "I'm glad you're here, Lulie," he called over his shoulder, his voice soft and tired. I watched my father move unsteadily toward the screen door, as if he found the worn, familiar walkway suddenly strange and uncertain territory to manage. I felt shaken too, reluctant to come face to face with the stark reality waiting within. So I stood on the stone flagged walk, seeing with eyes sharpened by grief the richness of all that my family had created on our land—all that Mama had to let go of now in her dying.

Mama and Papa had found our hundred-year-old log cabins in forgotten places up in Tennessee and transported them here to our mountainside in Alabama. Two yellow poplars and a cherry tree looked as if they were holding up the back screen porch, where ancient plows, iron tools, and baskets hung on the log walls, and deer antlers guarded the doorway. This porch was a whole other room in the summertime, with a bent willow couch and chairs, a table for eating meals outside, and overhead fans that spun lazily in the light. Beyond, in the corner of the clearing, another log cabin towered to the treetops; this one, an old tavern, with timbers two feet wide, heavy poplar beams, and skylights open to the stars. This was Papa's law office, with wall-to-wall books, Oriental rugs, and space upstairs where children and family slept on visits home.

I could not imagine life on the mountain without Mama. She was the warp and weft of our family's weaving. It felt as if some cold, relentless hand of fate was pulling all the threads off the loom, leaving the rest of us to unravel. Ever since the hospice nurse's call, I had felt more frayed and porous, more on the edges of things. Now, home in Alabama, the veils between worlds seemed so very thin. Maybe it was the full moon talking to me through the dense woods and thickets. But it felt like more—some heavy, observant presence, vast, cold, and impersonal, and yet as close and familiar to me as my beating heart.

"Are you Death?" I said aloud. "Are you waiting and watching in our woods? Are you coming now for our mother?" Only silence answered. Then, suddenly, from across the gully, a barred owl's garbled call came. Its mate responded, right over my head—a high, plunging wail, so close to my feelings, it was as if she uttered her cry on my behalf. I wondered, hearing the haunting sounds pierce the darkness, if the owls might be Death's chosen voice, answering one of his own: me, there in the moonlight.

I tried to turn my attention to all things alive—the smell of moist new leaves and freshly turned soil; moths flickering around the screen porch light. "Please help us," I whispered to all the vibrant life of the mountain. "You who live and die with some semblance of ease, and do not suffer death as we do. Be with Mama now. Give her all the support she needs to fly away. Comfort us, we who are so sad and left behind."

A quiet breeze swayed the branches of the poplar trees. Again, a strong presence came, but this time the energy was warm and loving, embracing me like a mother. The whole of the mountain with all its intricate life seemed to draw near, as if to witness the passing of one of its own. Red oak, hickory, beech, and sweet gum trees bowing to the woman who greeted them daily on her walks down to get the mail. Native plants Mama painstakingly transplanted to avoid their destruction elsewhere—bloodroot, trout lilies, trillium, ginseng, Solomon's seal. Perhaps these were all listening and paying tribute, giving their benefactress thanks; every tiny woodmouse, spider, tick, and tree frog watching, waiting for our mother to let go.

Feeling such companionship from the life of the forest, I managed to open the screen door and step inside. Our dog, Happy New Year, waiting by the kitchen door, sniffed my hand in welcome. Despite the late hour, Mama's kitchen was warm and welcoming. A fire crackled in the big open stone fireplace, with its iron hook and cooking pot next to the flames. There were my sisters, Margaret and Shay, worn out and wondering what had taken me so long, patiently waiting up for me all the same. They were drinking coffee in their nightgowns at the old oak table and came over to hug me, not asking me why I had lingered outside. We were all operating from a place of shock and numbness. I remember we didn't talk of much. Knowing that I would want to see Mama, my sisters both walked up the back stairs with me to the bedroom, with tall windows open to the night air, and a fire almost spent, its embers only a red glow in the shadows.

A hushed sorrow filled the room. I had not seen my mother for several months, since Christmas, and I was shocked to see her body so frail and thin. I instinctively curled up on the bed and lay down beside her, longing to take away the ravages of disease I saw before me. Mama's skin was papery thin and pale. She looked gaunt and hollowed out, her body a rickety frame about to splinter. Yet, there was a haunting beauty in her countenance, too—her true self, rising from within, and shining. She was sleeping, her eyes closed and her breath faint on my cheek. As I lay next to her, listening to her labored breathing, I realized that the mother I had always known would not be there when she opened her eyes. I had not grasped that bitter reality, had pushed it away in denial. Now I could no longer do so.

Mama had been increasingly ill for nine months, suffering terribly when the breast cancer she had battled before returned to her bones. The disease ate her vertebrae, breaking her back and making her bedridden. Such cancer is truly cruel, because the pain is unbearable when the tumors reach the skeleton and nerves. Papa and my sisters had been dealing with this agony for months. Blessedly, the metastases eventually reached Mama's brain, and to everyone's relief, her greatest pain disappeared. But this progression also took our mother away, far into herself. She could no longer read or write, nor could she speak. At least we could talk to her, although she needed hearing aids for even this to happen. When she was sleeping, as she was now, she was already gone, inhabiting a different world.

Saying goodnight to my sisters, I turned off the bedside lamp and lay in the darkness next to my sleeping mother, a wave of unrest settling in my chest. The fact that Mama and I would never talk again reminded me of all the times we had been unable to communicate; the years when we fought and said hurtful things to each other; the chilly silences that lived between us. The grief of our misunderstandings, and an inability to right them now, weighed heavily on my heart. When I was eight, I wrote Mama a poem thanking her for the gift of words. How sad that words would become the source of our greatest confusion with one another. At least we continued to write each other over the years. I treasure my mother's letters, for they show her ever-present love and support of me, from afar, even when she could not handle me in person. Now, no more letters. No more words. I would never hear her voice again.

I tried to breathe, tried to stay open, close to my body and feelings. Lying on the quilt, I began to grow calm, with Happy New Year thumping his tail against the floorboards, and Papa downstairs, calling one of our cats, Biddie, to come in away from the coyotes. In, out, in, out; Mama and I breathed together, and as this synchronous pattern continued, I reached for memories that could help me feel less distant from my mother.

Mama and I had always shared an inner landscape of inspiration, a place of bright beauty that lived at the very root and heart of who we were. This was a quiet and hidden source, rarely spoken of aloud. We did speak of it together once, sitting on the front porch swing, drinking iced tea and enjoying the soft light of an Alabama afternoon, basking in shared understanding. I wrote the following words after that day: "Ours is a green glad melody of mossy footpaths and bubbling wellsprings; ivy clad stone walls hiding secret gardens, the laughter of children in apple trees. Ancient voices call out in chorus one hallowed and life-filled song: Christ, King of the Elements; Lord of the Dance; Christ of the sunlight, the treetops, the dripping rain...."

Though Mama and I shared this communion with Christ, I went on in life to explore many other paths, cherishing most the sacred authenticity of each individual human being's own understanding of what it means to be alive. I have always needed freedom to explore without the bonds of any religious path restricting my way, wanting to understand the nature of consciousness itself, and how that is expressed in the complexity and sacredness of all life. This took me far from my Southern Episcopalian roots, far from my mother in many ways. But I never let go of the vision of a "green and growing" Christ, a force of Love and Renewal interwoven with the natural world, and emerging wherever "two or more" are gathered—whatever or whoever that "two or more" might be. This is what I shared with my mother, and what I instinctively knew would help me most in reconnecting with her before she died.

That night, lying next to Mama, I drew upon that long-ago afternoon when we had laughed with delight, and spoken of all that lived within us as possibility and promise. The full moon shone down through the skylight over the bed and bathed us in its beauty, and I felt the radiant presence of angels, those ones Mama had always believed in and loved. Were they drawing near around us, hovering close at the borderlands, waiting and watching, reporting for duty now?

The next morning at breakfast, Margaret said she had felt faeries on the front porch. Mama was the one who taught us such things, who kept angel books by her bed, and who woke us when we were little to ask if we had danced with the wee folk in the night. I was the child who took Mama literally, studying everything I could get my hands on to understand parallel levels of existence, green realms that intersected ours in life and now, it seemed, in death as well.

I imagined a troupe of faeries stationed on the porch, told to keep watch in case Mama decided to leave in the wee hours of the morn. They were a motley bunch, those faery escorts for my mother. Tough and wizened, their bark-brown faces melded easily with the surrounding trees. Clad in tattered leaves from the forest floor, smelling of leaf mold and limestone caverns, they perched on the stone steps or the wooden rails, chattering and singing to themselves, their voices as clear as the underground springs of water flowing down off our mountainside. Theirs would be a sacred task, one of immense importance and joy—to accompany dear, darling Irobel on her final journey home.

Mama disappointed that troupe of faeries and angels, though. In the afternoon, Cindy, the hospice nurse, shook her head in surprise and said her patient was much stronger, not ready to depart. As I walked down to the garden to pick salad greens for lunch, I saw that this threshold would have its own wisdom and timing, and that I had to be part of Mama's passage, no matter what it asked of me. Little did I know that Mama's soul was asking the family to all come home, to spend a crucible of time together—from one full moon to the next full moon—before she could fly away free.

For an entire month, all four sisters and our brother were home again, living together, cooking meals, helping Papa in the garden, and caring for our mother night and day. Most of us simply moved in to the cabins for the duration. We were fortunate to be able to do this. I was a self-employed teacher and minister. My brother Hal was an environmental journalist in Montana. Shay had already taken time off from her painting and teaching art in Virginia. Margaret lived nearby and had flexible hours as a nurse. My youngest sister, Nancy, had small children, and so she and her family drove six hours back and forth from North Carolina almost every weekend. Eliza, my daughter, also came once during those weeks to tell her grandmother goodbye.

My siblings and I had not been together in one place for any length of time for more than twenty-five years. Cloistered away together up on the mountain, normal life stopped; time seemed to spin backward or disappear entirely from our days. There we were—sleeping and waking, day after day, as we did when we were children, amongst a menagerie of dogs and cats, some resident, some visiting weekly. All our old, habitual patterns of relating resurfaced in strange and bemusing ways, making it easy to believe the years we had spent becoming adults were fruitless efforts of a fleeting dream. But our common shared purpose of caring for Mama and Papa, and showing up for whatever was asked of us in the moment, chiseled away at surface disputes; made room—albeit at times uneasy—for our differences; and affirmed our bedrock connection with one another. This was something Mama must have needed before she could tell us goodbye. And when the time came for our mother, Irobel, to leave, nature and spirit got together to create one of the wildest exits any human soul might ask for, in honor and celebration of her days.

―――――――――――

"I'd like to speak to the 'Wild Sister from the West.'" It was Melanie, the hospice social worker, on the phone, trying to mask concern with humor.

"That would be me," I said, trying to match her bantering tone. "I'm Lucinda, the second daughter. I've just gotten here from Washington State, and yes, I'm the one interested in having a home funeral for Mama. It would be great to talk with you, Melanie. When do you think you'll be coming?"

The previous day, I had asked Cindy in private about the normal procedures once a patient dies. I had shared that we would love to care for Mama's body ourselves and have her with us at home, maybe for as long as three days, as people used to do when they laid their loved ones out in the front parlor. We would fill the room with ferns and wild hydrangea from the garden, light lots of candles, sing "Lord of the Dance," and read the 139th Psalm. Such care would help us grieve and come to terms with Mama leaving us. I had told Cindy that my island community had begun taking care of loved ones when they died, and how doing so had transformed our lives, and our way of seeing death. (I omitted the parts about transporting friends to the crematorium in a VW bus with Tibetan prayer flags flapping in the wind, deciding it might not help my plea in the long run.)

Cindy had listened well, said it would be up to Papa to decide, and seemed fine with my asking. Now it looked as if she might be more worried about my ideas than she let on, since the entire hospice staff knew all about me, and it was only Monday morning. I should have known. My wishes were not exactly common practice anymore in Alabama—or in any other state, for that matter. Now most of us allow complete strangers to care for our dead, and we never even question what it costs us to give that gift and privilege away.

The social worker's voice on the phone interrupted my thoughts. "I can come see y'all about three o'clock," she said. "I'd like to talk to your father too—see how he's holding up." *You mean, you want to see how my father feels about my ideas,* I thought. I realized that I should never have spoken to the hospice team first before talking to Papa and my family. Now I was going to have to move fast. We were a wild and woolly bunch who loved each other fiercely and were deeply loyal to the bonds of blood and kin, but communication could be decidedly ornery at times, especially in situations of stress and difficulty like the one we were facing now losing Mama.

Though I wanted a home funeral badly, there were already "a whole lot of hitches," as my Aunt Mimi used to say. Mama could die at any minute, and I sure couldn't keep her body without everyone else agreeing. Saddest of all, I couldn't ask Mama how she wanted to be cared for now. It was too late. What if she didn't want such an affair? And how would I procure a little pine casket for her, something I was determined to do, and make that happen in time? I knew taking over tasks the funeral home normally handles does require some work beforehand, to keep things legal and in line with the system that hospices and funeral directors usually follow. I could handle that part. It was broaching my ideas with the family I dreaded.

Escaping the kitchen before anyone could ask me what Melanie wanted, I made my way up to the old logging road and let the hush of the forest and the limestone ridges soothe my frazzled nerves. I leaned up against my favorite boulder, letting its ancient strength sustain me, and turned to examine my own behavior. It was hard to admit, but truly, the biggest hitch lay within me. I was exhibiting attachment to this idea big time—a behavior most unbecoming to my years of Buddhist practice. Okay, I told myself, watching the blue jays dart among the branches, and wishing at that moment I could be one, instead of the errant "Wild Sister from the West." *I'll try to be more detached, more mindful, strike a lighter tone of being. Right. Since when had I ever managed to do that with my family?*

It is, at times, a hard row to hoe, trying to be the person I am, in a clan who dislikes anything too intentional or self-conscious, and who has a natural distrust of ritual and ceremony, especially if it comes from me. My family has grown to appreciate my holiday offerings—sitting in the dark together for Winter Solstice, walking through candlelit woods to an outdoor manger on Christmas Eve, or building huge bonfires in the meadow for Midsummer's Day. But resistance is a natural component of those times. Actually, I understand. After all, we each strive for spiritual freedom in my family, and my inordinate love of festivals and rituals borders on religious coercion. Or so my family members say.

I should have known my wishes for bringing a "meaningful experience" to Mama's death would be viewed in the same light, but somehow I had convinced myself that, this time, surely, in the face of death, things would be different. I was, of course, quite wrong.

When I got back to the cabin, everyone was eating lunch and doing the dishes. Shay asked me why the social worker had called. So I told everyone what was on my mind. Papa listened and was immediately open, loving the idea of caring for Mama ourselves. But Shay and Margaret were doubtful and didn't want to have to think beyond what was right in front of them to do.

I knew that a home funeral would be more work, on top of everything else we were doing, and acknowledged this to my sisters. It was easy for *me* to propose such a laborious extra endeavor. I had not been caring for Mama night and day for months as they had been. Both were beyond weary, and overwhelmed. So I assured them I would take on all the tasks, since it was so important to me. But I could see the idea still made them uncomfortable, and that was disheartening.

Papa wanted to be there when the social worker came, but it turned out he had an appointment in town, and Shay and Margaret went with him. After they left, I called Nancy, who had lived out in Oregon for years before returning home to the South, and so better understood my West Coast ways.

"Mama would never even go out of the house without putting lipstick on," Nancy reminded me. "She sure wouldn't want to go out in her nightgown in a body bag, like a piece of dry cleaning. And I think she would want us to care for her ourselves. It's a good idea, and I'll definitely help you out, Lu."

So I felt optimistic when the social worker arrived. Melanie and I had a good conversation over tea, though of course she had hoped to speak with all of us. I laughed when she asked me if I was one of those "pagan" types she had heard of. I told her if "pagan" meant following our own natural instincts, then yes, I supposed I was. She went out to the car and brought me a CD she had carried around for months because no one seemed to be interested in it. It was called *Graceful Passages,* a beautiful guide for the dying, from all traditions, with music and comforting words. I didn't tell her I knew the artist who had created it, that he had lived near me on Whidbey Island for a time. I felt like a person from another country receiving a gift package from home. Still, hospice seemed open and supportive, as long as Papa was on board, and I heartily agreed our father should have the final say.

A conversation with my brother Hal in the kitchen a few nights later left me less hopeful. I learned everyone had been talking about my home funeral request, without talking to me, and that most were resistant to the idea. Hal was a bit intrigued, liking the idea of taking a door down and laying Mama out on it in the dining room, as folks used to do. But only in theory. As he reminded me, we were not on Whidbey Island. This was Alabama, and it was hot and humid, and there were lots of flies. And what was the point anyway, since Mama would be simply dead and gone?

Where Mama's consciousness would go after dying was the source of several discussions after supper in those weeks we were home, heated and wonderful really, but hard, as I always ended up feeling so alone. Papa was with me in feeling that Mama might need our companionship, and he certainly believed she would be winging her way to heaven afterward, but whether that meant we should keep her body after death for a time, he couldn't say. All my siblings are strong environmentalists, and some share what Hal said so eloquently one night—that yes, he thought each person's consciousness is unique, like a snowflake, but after death, we probably just merge back into the fabric of things, back into nature, becoming an "elemental kind of joy" again. So if that was the case, some argued, was there really a need to care for Mama's soul and body after death?

I knew there was a need—my own, and probably everyone else's as well—to have enough time and opportunity to do things our own way when Mama died. Unless one has experienced the difference between that kind of spaciousness and calling the funeral home right away to pick up the body, it's hard to even understand how it can be so helpful. I tried to reassure everyone that I just wanted more time, to light a few candles and read to Mama, and prepare her for departure. Yet everyone's habitual reaction to my "fiestas" as Hal called them, and West Coast ways, and an inability to understand why I would even want to handle Mama's body after death, meant they were uncomfortable with my request. So I left it all up to Papa, as I had promised. But our father, torn between the conflicting feelings of his five children, and unable to truly face Mama's death himself, left the matter hanging, unresolved. At some point, I realized I had to let go of my dream of having a home funeral with my family.

However, I never let go of wanting a little pine casket for my mother. I hated feeling Mama would have to lie on a cold marble slab in the morgue and not be held and contained in any way. Better to have a cozy little wooden box to sleep in, wrapped up warm with quilts and blankets, and flowers and herbs to keep her company, than to be so utterly exposed. No, Mama needed a boat to take her across the seas of change. My Celtic soul could not imagine anything less.

Whenever I brought the subject up of Mama having a pine casket, I was met with sighs of frustration and resentment, so I eventually stopped talking about it. But I held the idea in my heart still. I spent a lot of time online looking for anyone nearby who could make me a pine box, one I could go fetch and bring home. One day I found an Amish man in Tennessee who built pine caskets, but of course, the Amish have no telephones. So I called the Chamber of Commerce in Monteagle, Tennessee, and asked how to get in touch with the craftsman. The lady at the desk was so kind.

"Honey, I'm bored to tears in this office, and a ride out in the country will do me a heap of good. I'll go look that man up for ya, and ring you back later on." I was overcome with the woman's generosity and hung up the phone, feeling optimistic for the first time. But she called back a few hours later to regretfully inform me the Amish man had moved away, and there wasn't a soul anywhere nearby who could make my Mama a box. I thanked her profusely and got off the phone, knowing I was going to have to give up that idea as well.

Through dreams and intuitions I began to feel that Mama wanted me to accompany her somehow on a soul level—to listen and watch for the deeper patterns of her journey, which were unfolding beneath the surface of our days. Her illness was so full of pain and dissolution. If I could remind her of those inner landscapes we shared, it might be helpful. I also sensed she wanted me to hold a different vision of her death, not the bleak, heavy, constricted one of fear and aversion we were all carrying, but a "greener," more light-filled and buoyant way of seeing. If I could find a way to inhabit that place myself, and rest at times in a field of peace and acceptance, perhaps it would be a reminder for her to do so as well.

It was not easy to hold this vision of green gladness through endless days of changing bedsheets and diapers, and watching Papa's shoulders slump with grief and despair. And listening to my daughter Eliza sob on the phone late at night on the other side of the country. Or, most painful of all, watching Mama in her debilitated state agitatedly fold cloth napkins over and over in her lap, an act that broke our hearts to witness. Having to depend only on raised eyebrows, hand squeezes, and cries of pain to know what a mother might need for her final journey was excruciating for everyone, and there were constant misunderstandings in navigating those relentless days together.

It was inevitable that the fault lines of our family would surface in the threshold of Mama's death. Unfinished business in families almost always emerges when one member dies, especially if it is a parent. Our clan was no exception. The liminal nature of death seems to flush out everyone's strengths and weaknesses, longings and fears, so that they are all present at the same time in the same place. Makes for a tangled mess most of the time.

There were days when I was overcome with grief about my decision to raise Eliza out West, far away from my Southern family, and anxious that the way I was helping Mama on a soul level might simply be wishful thinking on my part. Maybe I was making up this way of connecting with my mother because I was not as close to her as my other siblings were. Though I longed to be a part of things in my family, I often felt separate and alone.

When I began trying to cultivate a different relationship with Death, something I felt Mama wanted me to do, I got in touch with some of the reasons I was so fervent about having a home funeral, and about creating a meaningful experience with my family. Wanting to care for Mama myself was my way of taking back some semblance of control in a situation where I actually felt powerless. It was my own effort to defy Death and to ease my primal fear of that merciless presence, coming soon for the mother we loved. That fear was present in everything I was doing, but I had not admitted it to myself. I truly needed to feel close to my family again, in the face of this uncertainty and fear, and I especially wanted to feel a part of things during the empty and lonely time after Mama was gone. Since I had grown accustomed to feeling connected to others through "meaningful experiences," I had put a lot of hope in having a home funeral vigil that might soothe and comfort us all.

Realizing all this was freeing, and helped me understand that everything we were experiencing could hold meaning—our yearnings, our efforts to connect, even all our struggles and pain. Each of

us had a gift to give—Margaret's competent nurse hands smooth-
ing Mama's sheets and turning her gently with so much care; Shay
coming up the stairs with vegetable soup and wildflowers on a silver
tray to nourish Mama's body and soul; Hal bounding up the stairs
with his coffee to sit on the windowsill next to Mama, their mutual
respect and love rising in the room like a prayer; the days Nancy
braved reentry into our shut-away time—bringing her husband Stu
and children Will and Lila to brighten our days; Papa rarely sleeping, wheeling Mama's hospital bed over to the bottom of his bed,
so he could lie sideways and hold Mama's hand through the night.
Witnessing these acts of care connected me naturally to everyone,
and helped me know we were all being held in a great field of love
and sacredness, even when we could not feel it or had lost our way.

I began to seek out moments of ease and beauty, even joy, in our
days, and I kept them close, sharing them with my mother, heart to
heart. Reminding her daily that "all shall be well, and all manner
of thing shall be well." The hummingbird, with his sparkling green
back and his tiny wings, would whirr a welcome each day as I sat
on the upstairs balcony outside—near enough to watch Mama, but
outside in the glories of the May morning. And the wood thrush,
Mama's favorite bird, sent his lovely, consoling notes out into the
trees so they would land on the pillow, next to Mama's ear, and
bring her peace. She could see the many forest birds landing on
Papa's feeders, and our cat, Harvey, stalking them in the bushes. A
sudden movement, a door slamming, a child running up; and all
the birds would rise like one being, swiftly into the sky. Gone. I
watched this happen over and over, and I knew nature was teaching
Mama how to die.

Retreating to the natural world was always my way back to the
"dearest freshness deep down things," to a clear and indisputable
connection with my mother, and to my own core strength and knowing. I would walk over to our spring most days and sit next to the
little pool of water that emerges from the limestone crevices after
rain. A gentle wind often came, making the treetops sway and the

leaves rustle companionably around me. Dragonflies hovered over the water, squirrels and chipmunks would scamper along branches and chitter back and forth, and the limestone itself seemed to wake up from an ancient sleep and offer strength and solace for my heart and bones.

I felt called to cultivate a living, ongoing dialogue with the land itself to fulfill my promise to Mama to hold a different perspective and understanding of her death. In the times when I could relax and stay grounded in my body, and rest in the earth itself, and in the greater fields of intelligence and sentient life around me, I felt closer to my mother, as if she too were resting there. As if she (and I with her) were learning to rest and to trust in the very nature of Death itself.

———————

Monday morning, June 4, 2001, dawned still and blue. I lay in bed, wondering if we all felt as clearly as I did that Mama was going to die that day on the full moon. There was a heightened sense of possibility and mystery, as if the gateways were already standing open.

Late the night before, the phone had rung, and I had rushed to get it so it wouldn't wake the others.

"Is that Lucinda?" a man's voice asked. "Yes," I said, wondering who in the world would call at such an hour. "This is Don Jenkins from Franklin, Tennessee. I hear your mama needs a box."

What a strange sensation—to hear an unknown voice reminding me of my heart's desire. I could barely respond.

"Uh, yes, yes. That's right. I did need one … but, well …" It was then I knew. Mama was going to die the next day on the full moon. Even though a stranger was answering my long-sought-after prayer, it was all too late.

"You see, Don," I spoke breathlessly into the phone. "Mama is going to die tomorrow, so I can't come get a box now. I need to be here with my family. I really appreciate your offer, but I had to let go of the idea a few weeks back." My voice trailed away, and there was a moment of silence on the phone. Don seemed to be pondering something.

Finally, he offered gently: "Well, I'm still willing to make your mama a box, and I'll bring it to you to boot." I could not believe what I was hearing. I had given up entirely, let go of my wish to have a pine box for Mama, and now the universe was offering one up via the goodness of a mountain man's heart. Or the emptiness of his pocketbook, Hal said later, cynical but intrigued. I was too caught up in the way spirit came through for me at the last minute, to even question the man's intentions.

"If Mama goes tomorrow, we'll need it then," I said, thinking there was no way this warm stranger could accommodate those plans. "Well, I better get busy" was all he had to say. So I ran to Papa, sitting in the armchair next to Mama, moonlight shining down on her covers like a blessing, and I told him the strange news. "Surely we can't say no, Papa. Doesn't it seem like God or Mama has a hand in this somehow?" Papa seemed filled with the same mystery I felt, and said yes immediately. I went to bed that night elated. Tomorrow, Mama would receive her lovely pine box, just as I had dreamed, just in time for her departure.

I walked up on the logging road after breakfast the next morning, knowing that it was Mama's last day on earth. When I leaned against the limestone rocks, I felt the same sweet, embracing presence that gathered me up the evening I had arrived home—the mountain energy that held me like a mother. With a kind of shock, I realized that this energy had all along included Death as well—that they were one and the same.

Hearing the grandchildren's voices throughout the day, so full of life as death descended, added an incredible sense of wholeness and made me so grateful for home deaths. On one level we were merely experiencing all one day could bring us—and this included a mother dying upstairs. Maybe it was because we had been living with it all so long: when the time actually came, it felt so calm and ordinary.

One by one, we gathered around Mama's bed, by the windows opening to the forest she loved. We stood there silently, Papa with one hand cradling Mama's head, the other stroking her arm. I was

struck with our father's presence, like a guardian keeping watch at
the gate while his Irobel did what she needed to do to leave us.
We watched and listened to Mama's rhythmic, labored breathing.
Outside, the everyday sounds continued—the carpenter bees buzz-
ing in the ceiling of the balcony, a dog barking down in the cove.
Yet even these sounds seemed hushed, expectant, waiting. Mama's
loud breathing dominated the room. Just the way she breathed while
giving birth to all of us, I thought. Only now, she is giving birth
to herself. Long moments of no breathing happened. I felt us all
hold our breath, too, wondering if this time would be the last. Then
Mama would start again. There was an incredible heaviness in the
room, almost stifling, and I felt as if I were being pressed into the
floor.

Suddenly, outside the window, a wood thrush called—his clear,
plaintive notes piercing the room's heaviness with light. "Irobel,
come," he seemed to sing. As if in answer, Mama stopped breathing
for the last time and softly, with a tiny rush of energy I felt flut-
tering through my own chest, our mother seemed to slip away. For
one fleeting moment, I saw light burning beyond, or within, her
tiny form, like sunrays pouring into a darkened room. My body felt
excited, elated, and filled with the freshness one finds standing under
a waterfall, or walking in the dew of a new day.

The bedroom suddenly felt immense, as if the strength of
Mama's leaving had stretched the boundaries of the walls. None
of us could move. It could only have been a few minutes, but it felt
like forever, as if we were frozen in a painting for all time. Then
suddenly, without warning, the spell shattered. I tell people now that
when Mama crossed over, all heaven broke loose on the mountain.
Because it did.

One minute, the woods were silent and still. The next moment,
seemingly from out of nowhere, waves of wind came rushing through
the tops of the trees, like a thousand whispering voices. The skies,
so clear before, darkened, and a bolt of lightning flashed, ripping
through the woods close by. Its light illuminated the clearing, and

everything glowed with unearthly hues. A huge clap of thunder, like a bomb exploding on the mountain, extinguished all the electricity at once. Wind lashed the branches to and fro, and tore at the open window frames where Mama lay. I felt the wind's wetness on my face, heralding torrential rain, which came moments later in sheets, like a great waterfall pouring from the skies all at once, pounding down around us, drumming incessantly on the tin roof, and making such a racket, we had to shout to be heard.

So much for the peaceful after-death vigil I had hoped for. No sitting quietly by Mama's side, reading the 139th Psalm, or lighting candles around her bed. Dogs were barking madly and cowering under Mama's bed. Everyone was rushing madly around, shutting windows and comforting screaming children.

Only Papa and I were left standing by Mama. I didn't move from my place by the window, held by the wonder of the storm, but also imagining our mother might feel abandoned by everyone suddenly. I didn't want her to feel alone. A comforting peace seeped into the room, gathering us up in its embrace. Rain drummed on the roof so loudly that it muffled all other noise, creating a shut-away place, a holy place, made sacred by sound. I hated to break that feeling, and I could not muster the energy to speak anyway. It was way too full in the room for talking. Finally, after what seemed ages, Papa looked at me and said in a funny voice, "This happened when Jesus died." He patted Mama's arm, obviously awed that nature found Irobel's death worthy of a great storm as well. I nodded, looking at the tiny form of my mother and marveling that such an enormous force of elemental power had come to take her home. It surely seemed as if all the commotion had shown up just for her, since it had happened within minutes of her leaving.

"Who *are* you?" I whispered, shaking my head. All at once, I was seeing my proper Southern mother in a new light, and feeling how very big she really was. I had always prided myself on being different from Mama, more untamed and wild. She had stayed within the boundaries of being a wife and mother and had never needed to be

anything else. Yet, her love of wild things was always there, informing her life and her death now. Such a connection all poured out
when the gateway opened, and she transcended the limitations of
her human self. A laugh escaped me, suddenly, at the absurdity of it
all, and I wondered: Was it proper to feel almost exhilarated, when
Mama was there before me, growing so cold and still?

I looked out the window and saw Nancy standing in the rain, her
head raised to the sky, letting sheets of water cascade down her face
and neck. "I'll be back soon, Papa," I said, kissing his head. The wet,
slippery limestone rocks of the pathway felt good to my bare feet as
I navigated my way to the drive, running with rivulets of water and
gravel. I stopped where I could see open sky, lifting my face to the
pouring rain.

Hard drops of water beat down on my head and ran down my
neck under my shirt, making me shiver. I breathed deep, drinking in
the energy. Everything gleamed and shimmered with wet light. The
rush of the wind in the trees sounded like hundreds of voices again,
whispering Mama's name. I felt the doorway of Death flapping back
and forth, tossed hither and yon by mighty elemental forces and
beings of nature who seemed truly gleeful, celebrating the return of
one of their own. Our spring was chanting a welcome-home song,
overflowing its banks and tumbling down the mountainside with
abandon.

Here was the festival I had longed for, to honor Mama. I need
not have done anything. It was already arranged, and it was so much
greater than anything I could have imagined. Was Mama dancing
somewhere, looking down on us all? Could she feel how much we
loved and celebrated her that day?

―――――――――――

It is said that if we can let go of our attachments, they may well
return to us, in ways we never dreamed possible. The day Mama
died, I learned this so intimately. I had let go of everything, all
expectations of caring for Mama's body ourselves and having a

home funeral—all except the hours it would take for Don Jenkins to get there with Mama's pine casket.

Don! In the wild aftermath of the death, I had totally forgotten him. I came in out of the rain to hear that he had called, at exactly the hour Mama died, to say the box was finished. I called him back and told him I didn't think it was safe to travel in such a storm. But Don just laughed and said it would be an adventure, and he was coming anyway, because, after all, hadn't my mama died, and didn't I still need a box? There was no stopping the man.

But would he get there in time? Papa had called Cindy, because she was supposed to come out, declare her patient dead, and fill out the paperwork. If she got there first, and Don took a long time in coming (it was a two-hour drive), I would have to plead all over again to keep Mama's body awhile. Well, I needn't have worried. A whole other drama was unfolding on Mama's dying day, a baffling twist and turn of events we are still pondering to this day.

I went downstairs to tell our housekeeper Ava goodbye. She had been with us all day and hated to leave, but she was anxious about getting home in the driving rain. She honked as she drove by the kitchen window, her headlights shining eerily in the half-light. It was only suppertime, but so dark we couldn't see anything outside the windows.

Fifteen minutes later, the phone rang. Kim, Shay's husband, answered; it was Ava. She was distraught, talking a mile a minute into the phone. How she had driven down the hill and made it to the end of the lane that met the main road out of the cove. How she had to stop because the road was completely covered in water. How, to her horror, she had found Cindy's red sports car, almost on its side in the ditch, with flash flood waters swirling all around it and no Cindy inside. Ava had searched everywhere for the nurse, but the steady rain and the gathering darkness made it impossible to continue.

"Surely she got out of there," Ava cried, her voice weak with fear. "Y'all have got to get down there as quick as you can."

A shock ricocheted through the house with that phone call. Papa, Kim, Shay, and Margaret pulled heavy raincoats on and drove down in the truck to search for Cindy. They said later that they just stood in front of the ruined car and cried.

Nancy and the children were in the back cabin, and Hal had rushed off to the airport to get his wife and baby, so I was left alone in the house. I climbed the stairs and went to sit by Mama. The electricity was still out, but a faint glow of natural light from outside the window revealed her quiet, unmoving form. For a moment, it was easy to believe my mother was just sleeping peacefully, through all the din and commotion. But when I touched her forehead, she was icy cold and her skin shone translucently pale in the twilight.

I spent a few moments lighting all the candles I had placed on the window seat that afternoon, when we knew Mama was dying. It was a calming thing to do since my mind was so agitated about Cindy's accident. When I had twelve candles lit, I stood and surveyed my work, grateful for the few moments of tranquility found in the midst of chaos, and for the aura of sacredness I felt hovering all around Mama's final resting place.

Mama seemed very close by still, as if she were looking down on me, smiling a little at my stubborn refusal to let storms and possible tragedy prevent me from lighting those candles I had fought so long and hard over. Thinking she might hear me, I asked Mama if she could see anything from her viewpoint. Surely there would not be two deaths in that one wild portal, and surely the nurse, who had cared so deeply for us all, would not be going with my mother now.

Some time later, the phone rang, loud in the quiet room. I ran over and picked up the receiver. There was static on the line, but on the other end, Cindy's voice, calling from a house way up in the cove. A family had picked her up in their four-wheel drive truck, but the phones had been down at their home, and it had taken her all this time to get through. I could hardly speak, I was so relieved. I told her to hold on, and we would come pick her up as soon as we could. As I hung up the phone, the electricity came back on. The lights turning on all over the house felt like beacons, heralding the grand news that Cindy was alive and well.

When Cindy walked in our door, she was a mess—worn out, drenched, her hair wet and bedraggled, but laughing and so glad to be with us all. She was inundated with hugs from everyone, all equally sodden and cold from their escapades and search for her. When I told her how grateful I was that she was alive, she looked at me with a knowing grin.

"Well, Lucinda, you got your wish. Your mama's death papers were in my car, and by now, they must be almost to the highway. The roads are under a foot of water and impassable, I'd say. No funeral man's gonna get here tonight, that's for sure. I won't even try and call them. See, I told you things have a way of working out." Indeed. What powers were afoot that holy evening? I felt strangely elated—not because I had gotten my way, but because, in the face of all we had been through, it didn't seem to matter anymore.

It had been six o'clock in the evening when Don and his friend Bob set out with Mama's casket. Now it was after ten, and there was no sign of them. I knew it was a two-hour drive and would likely be longer with the storm and flooding. But I was getting worried. We had a late supper and sat around, waiting for Mama's miracle casket to arrive.

The truck finally lumbered up the hill at midnight, the headlights barely penetrating the pelting rain. Papa and I both went outside to greet the men and let them know they were in the right place. Don was getting out of the driver's seat and slapping a baseball cap on his head to keep off the water, and his friend was coming round from the other side with a flashlight. I stuck out my hand to shake Don's, but suddenly that didn't seem to be enough for the monumental task he had just accomplished for us, so I threw my arms around his neck instead and gave him a big hug, stranger that he was.

"Don, I'm Lucinda. You made it! And this is my father, Harold Herring."

Papa embraced Don too and called him an angel to bring a coffin for Mama through such a terrible storm. Bob chuckled and said it had taken them six hours to do what normally takes two, because whole roads were washed out, and some fields looked like lakes instead of land. They joked they would have done better with a boat instead of a four-wheel drive pickup truck.

I could tell Don was eager for me to see his handiwork, so we opened the back of the truck and peered inside. It was dark and shadowy, but not enough to hide the fact that the box I was seeing was so big, it filled the entire bed of the truck. It was not anywhere near the size of the measurements I had sent him. I just stood there in the rain, slowly grasping the fact that my beautiful pine box, small and perfectly made for a tiny mother, was in fact a huge plywood monstrosity that barely fit through the kitchen door and would have to be left on the screen porch with the dogs. It even had little legs.

I could not let these wonderful souls see my disappointment, so I swallowed my feelings and told them it was beautiful (even though it seemed Don had not followed any of my instructions). What had gone amiss with my perfect plans? Maybe the measurements I'd given him were way off, which is probable, given my state of mind when I sent him the fax. To this day I'll never know.

We asked the men in for coffee and gingerbread. Once the subject of the storm was mined, we talked of sundry things, as if we had all the time in the world. It was the wee hours of the morning then, so, as true Southerners, we offered them a place to stay for the night, even though there was not a free bed on the premises and our mother was lying upstairs, only a few hours dead. The men would hear none of it, saying they were looking forward to their next adventure, hoping the full moon would make an appearance to guide their way home. Papa paid them a generous sum (they asked for only $100!), and the men bade us goodbye, shook everyone's hands, and drove off into the darkness and wind and rain. Mama's angels, just reporting for duty.

I walked out on the porch with my nephew Bass, and just could not believe my eyes. The box was enormous. "Lucinda," Bass said, "Michael Jordan isn't dead yet. Maybe we should save this for him and use it as a wood box in the meantime." By that time, I was hysterical. All I could think about was the funeral men's reaction to our chosen casket for Mama. Papa said it was the most beautiful box he had ever encountered, with a twinkle in his eyes, though, in many ways, he really meant it. It was charged with Love.

I stumbled up the stairs, so tired I could not see straight, and went to sit beside Mama for awhile. Papa was going to sleep next to her one last time, and I realized, through my fog of weariness, that he could do that because the universe had granted my wish after all. But it was all a cosmic joke. All of it. I turned to protest to Mama that I had had enough, and lo and behold, she was smiling. Truly. She had died with her mouth open slightly, and we had not touched her or moved her in any way. Now, as I looked, I saw that her mouth had closed into that funny little smile she always reserved for us when she was deeply amused. There were laugh crinkles around her eyes. Mama was laughing. I shouted for everyone to come, and people from various parts of the house congregated around Mama's bed to see the wonder of her change. Maybe Mama's laugh lines were her final goodbye, an acknowledgment of my efforts to be of service, but most of all a reminder to stop taking myself so seriously.

―――――――――

The next day could have been any other early summer morning on the mountain. The door was open onto the balcony, and fresh air drifted in, cool and inviting. Outside the windows a cardinal landed on the birdfeeder, its feathers a splash of scarlet against lush green foliage. There was a trail of baby powder from the bathroom all across the wooden floorboards where Papa had showered and gotten dressed. I wondered how he felt doing that normal task with Mama lying on the bed, cold and dead. Had he avoided looking over at her, or had he talked to her the whole time as if she were only resting?

From where I stood in the open doorway it was easy to believe, for a minute, that Mama was still with us. But when I got over to the bed and saw her pale features frozen on the pillow, I could hardly breathe. Death's starkness filled the room, like sharp and cutting steel slicing the soft morning air into jagged pieces.

Eliza had just arrived after an overnight flight. I was worried that she would be too tired to help care for Mama, but she said it was important to her, that it would be her goodbye. She and Nancy and I made a circle around Mama, standing there for a moment in silence. None of us had ever bathed a dead body before, but somehow the task before us felt old and familiar, a sacred task I knew as well as I knew myself.

Looking around the room, I realized with a sigh that all my good intentions to have everything ready for Mama's after-death care were buried under the chaos of the previous day. I had wanted to follow the instructions indicated by Rudolf Steiner and outlined in Beth Knox's *Resource Guide,* from her organization Crossings: Caring for Our Own at Death. *Remove all clutter from the room.* Well, we had a room piled up with dirty bedclothes and Papa's shoes scattered all across the floor. *Have special cloths neatly laid out, candles and fresh flowers, and warm water ready in a ceremonial bowl.* Well, the candles had burned out during the power outage, and most of the towels and suitable cloths were in the laundry basket. *Use rose oil "to soothe the environment and lessen fears in the dying."* Too late. *Use lavender oil to anoint the deceased.* Ah, that we could manage. We had lavender, thanks to Margaret, and I could use one of Mama's antique bowls for the ceremonial washing.

"Thank you for helping me," I said, squeezing Nancy's and Eliza's hands. "Thank you also, Mama, for still being here with us. I'm grateful."

We had to somehow get Mama's nightgown off, which was no easy task since she had become stiff and rigid overnight. Lifting her arm, I felt as if it could easily snap off in my hands if I wasn't careful. "Let's just cut the nightgown off with scissors," Eliza suggested.

What a practical idea. I could always count on Eliza to solve a mechanical dilemma.

It was stark taking Mama's nightgown off and seeing her skin, pale gray and mottled, her bones shining through. Dark blood had pooled at her back and behind her knees. Her face had changed in the night again. The tiny smile was gone, and her mouth hung slack and crooked. She was so cold it felt like holding burning ice to touch her arms and legs.

"Breathe," I reminded us all. "We can do this together."

I found myself grateful it was just the three of us. "The Trinity, Mama. The Three Graces, at your service," I whispered. A quiet peace fell over us as we worked, slowly bathing Mama's face and neck, her chest and belly, washing under her arms, making sure she was clean between her legs. I put a drop of lavender oil on her forehead and on her joints, and caressed her palms and feet with oil, as Beth Knox suggests in her book. I traced a Celtic cross on Mama's heart with the lavender oil as a final blessing of love.

Downstairs, the men were talking loudly in the kitchen, and Bass was tossing Hal's baby son New Harold up in the air, making him squeal with laughter. But Nancy and Eliza and I were tucked away upstairs, in a temple of our own making. I thought of Papa, standing next to Mama in the dawn light that morning, stroking her legs and talking to her softly in a final goodbye. Such a gift. And now, it was fit and right that the women were here for Mama—the daughters and granddaughter, born of her flesh and blood, performing this last rite and sacrament for the woman whose body gave us bodies, and whose life made our lives possible.

Nancy insisted Mama would want her makeup on—her face powder, with the tattered puff and smeared mirror I loved to play with when I was little, her cream rouge for giving herself "a bit of color," her bright red lipstick. Mama's mouth was always tiny, and her lips thin. Now it was even harder to trace the lines of her mouth. I thought it was going to make Mama look garish and awful, but

Nancy was right. It helped to have color in her face, to match her jacket's bright yellow hues.

When we were almost finished, Shay and Margaret and Papa came upstairs. Papa was so grateful to us, saying Mama looked beautiful. Margaret and I picked out the quilt we would use to line the casket, and some little pillows off the bed covered in starched white embroidered cotton. I went downstairs with those things and asked the men to bring the big box from the screen porch to the dogtrot, which was big enough to accommodate it.

We were going to have to carry Mama down the stairs. That was a bit tricky, but I knew it could be done simply by pulling the edges of the sheet up around her and making a kind of swing hammock—with someone on each end carrying a knot and someone holding her body in the middle. It would be awkward navigating the steep, narrow stairs, but not impossible. Papa and Kim and Hal took up this task readily, so I waited down below for them. I felt a pit in my stomach when they actually appeared up on the landing with the twisted bundle in their arms, but it all happened so fast Mama was in her big cozy box in no time.

Shay came up from the garden with a wonderful bouquet of wildflowers and ferns and placed them on Mama's hands, near her heart. Margaret put the little Peace pillow she had given Mama next to her cheek, and straightened the quilt that covered Mama's body—her last gesture of goodbye. Nancy tucked poems and pictures from her children Will and Lila next to Mama and placed her own hands on Mama's one last time. Eliza tucked a letter in the pocket of Mama's jacket. Bass came in and placed a poem in the bottom of the box, his face a study in concentration. Holly, Hal's wife, leaned their baby over the box so he could get one last glimpse of the grandmother he had known only a short while, while Hal stood in the doorway watching, his eyes glittering with unshed tears.

Standing in the hallway staring down at our mother, I found that my legs were shaking so hard that I had to kneel beside the coffin and steady myself by taking a deep breath and focusing on Mama's face. I was struck suddenly with the finality of Mama leaving us. We called Papa and together the men lifted the top and put it in place, sealing the sight of our mother away from us forever. I said my own little honorings quietly to myself, holding Eliza's hand tightly while Hal nailed the top down, the sound of the hammer echoing loudly in the still morning air.

Around noon we heard the funeral men coming up the hill. I dreaded the sound but had to smile when I saw the four-wheel drive Suburban hearse. It was fitting to our lives up on the mountain to have a four-wheel drive take our mama into town. It was the next best thing to taking her ourselves in the van. I felt sorry for the two men who got out of the hearse. They were dressed in tight black coats and pressed pants that must have been sweltering in the heat. In fact, one of them broke out in a sweat when we led them up the steps to the porch and he saw how big the box was they were going to have to carry. I think they were expecting to take Mama out on a gurney, not pick up some enormous, heavy box and carry it to the hearse. Papa took one look at the situation and sized it up fast.

"Hal, Kim, Bass—can you help me do the honors here? I want to carry Irobel ourselves." They gathered round the box and, moving in sync like one being, lifted Mama up on their shoulders. From the looks of it, the burden was heavy, but the men who loved the woman within walked as if they were carrying light. They were there for Mama one last time, helping her leave, bearing her away from the home and the land she had created and loved so long. As Mama's box moved slowly and steadily down the stone flagged path, the wood thrush sang his clear, liquid notes from the cedar tree, bidding the Lady of the Land a fine farewell.

I returned to my mother as she lay dying, and reached across years of misunderstanding and distance to reconnect and to support her passage from this world. Though laced with struggle and loss, I managed to find comfort, communion, even delight with Mama in the end—filled with the "freshness deep down things" and a renewed imagination of all that is possible when we die.

I use the phrase "Return to the Mother" metaphorically here to capture the complexities of what it means to connect with nature and land as sacred partners; to trust the wisdom of our bodies and senses and direct experience; to heal the repression and abuse of the Feminine, which is so linked to the domination and destruction of the earth and the environment; and to embrace death once again as a natural and sacred part of life. All of these elements are inextricably linked together in my heart and mind. To address one is to address the others; to heal one is to heal the others. Such an understanding is both personal and collective for me, and has helped define my life, and all that I bring to others in my educational work and ministry.

Trust is one of the primary gifts of this reclamation and healing for me. I am learning to trust "what is," to trust all that life brings, no matter how hard, and to trust in Death itself, as my teacher and ally. It is not easy to trust, in the midst of difficult and painful times. Yet the more I manage to do this, the stronger and more resilient I feel, and the more capable I am of handling whatever life brings my way. To be able to face the challenging demands of death (and life) with greater ease and acceptance can be a transformative gift. I know, because I experienced this with my mother. Though her death was heartbreaking, it also held uplifting energies of healing, celebration, and joy. Like the apple blossomed promise of a May morning—in the midst of mourning.

Practical Wisdom: Discerning if a Home Funeral Vigil Is Right for You

My mother's story conveys the complexities and challenges that can arise within families who are contemplating having a home funeral vigil. The other stories in this book focus more on the gifts and beauty of caring naturally for our own after death. Such blessings are certainly present in Mama's story as well, but the struggles and uncertainties I had with my family are good lessons and well worth highlighting here.

Make sure your family are all on board with the idea of a home vigil, or are at least okay with some family members taking on the task of caring for a loved one after death. As you saw in Mama's story, Papa, Shay, and Margaret had been doing the heaviest caregiving for our mother for months beforehand. Hal and I were out West, and Nancy had tiny children. The thought of continuing to care for Mama's body after death was simply too much for my sisters, understandably so. In the end things worked out well, as those of us who had the energy and desire to take care of Mama's body could. But we were able to care for Mama only because the storm happened, and carved out enough time and spaciousness for us to do so. I don't know what would have happened if the storm and flooding had not cloistered us all away up on the mountain naturally. We had never decided together to keep Mama's body—something vitally important to do as a family if you wish to have a peaceful and harmonious home vigil experience.

Know that there will probably always be family members who simply are not drawn to care for the dead. There will also be those who are actively resistant, even to someone else in the family handling the care. If these people are key players, this stance must be taken into consideration in discerning whether a vigil is right for the family. I have been involved with families where the dying person was the only one who actually wanted a home funeral to happen. Once that person was dead, the vigil fell to family members who ended up feeling resentful and unhappy about the whole state of affairs. This is not a good scenario for a successful home funeral.

Know upfront that bringing the idea of home funeral vigils to families who have never considered such care can be a delicate task, especially if those family members are your own! In hindsight, I wish I had broached the subject of caring for Mama after death long before I arrived home to help her die. We would have had more time to imagine it together, air all our concerns and resistances in less stressful circumstances, and work out a plan that suited all. I recommend being this proactive if you can. I also know that hardly anyone will be, so if you find yourself in my position, it's far more successful to talk with the family before setting things in motion with hospice and other outside people!

Sometimes home funerals are seen as the domain of the "culture creative" or "New Ager." I was dubbed the "Wild Sister from the West" (meaning West Coast new spirituality ways) by Alabama's hospice staff. My family was worried that I might do something that did not suit us all—especially Mama—when in fact, I just wanted enough time to light candles, say a few prayers, and bathe and dress our mother as a final act of love. Home funerals are not new; they are the traditional way we used to care for our dead. We are simply reclaiming our innate right to be more actively and creatively engaged when someone we love dies. Home vigils are not for everyone, nor are they possible in every situation. Yet, when the circumstances are right, caring for our own dead can be a healing and transformative experience of love.

2

GREENING THE GATEWAY OF DEATH

Washing with rose otto and water,
anointing with frankincense oil,
I caress the skin of his cold corpse,
talking as though he could hear.
Cloaking his body in pure white cotton

I let loose my hold.

I arrange this discarded outer garment
on a table of bed-sheet and ice,
drape the remnant of him
in shiny white silk,
bedeck it with evergreen boughs.

—DONNA JAMES

When my mother died in 2001, I had not yet solidified a path of working intentionally and professionally at the thresh-old of death. In fact, I was very much immersed in celebrating the thresholds of life and newness with young families and children in my island community. In those years, I created The Festival Guild, an organization dedicated to building community through seasonal festival-making and fun. My courses and circles for parents and children offered ways to connect with one another, the natural world, and the soul of the earth through the seasons with art, ritual, and celebration. Together we learned to "green the gateways" in the cycle of the year.

We felt apprenticed to the land itself in this adventure—to the meadows and evergreen forests, to the Salish Sea and the sandy shores of our island home. It was as if by honoring and celebrating the earth's seasonal wheel in relationship to a beloved place, a whole body of understanding and lost wisdom was made available to us again. Our ancestors knew such awareness, and indigenous people still do. Yet, for the most part, being in dialogue with land and place is a way of life forgotten by modern-day human beings, especially we of the Western world.

Such wisdom taught us how to open the doors of our perception once again. We learned to take time out of our busy, hectic lives to relax and breathe, and be in our bodies, hearts, and senses; to inhabit our imaginations rather than our cut-off conceptual minds; to sing and dance and laugh and play; and to rediscover our living connection to nature's seen and unseen realms of life. We relished the chance to grow young again, and to join our little ones, who lived still in an open place of wonder and surprise, and saw everything—stones, ferns, blackberries, beetles, hedgehogs, wind, and rain—as friends and companions, sacred "others" to listen to, play with, and love.

I became an interfaith minister in those early years because I saw how hungry people were, especially parents, for new rituals and meaningful ceremony, for spiritual nourishment not tied to any one church or organized religion. We longed to be true to our own spiritual pursuits—but to do so in the company of others. We shared creativity, stories, and good food, and we tried to align our daily lives with more natural rhythms and ways of being. We strove to build real and sustainable community where we could feel more fully alive, more connected to the earth and the larger circles of life, and be there for each other through all of life's transitions, joys, and sorrows. These longings led us to explore the nature of thresholds themselves and what I call "threshold awareness." This is the capacity to recognize and work with times of transition and change in more conscious, intentional, and sacred ways. It is also the ability to support one another in easing the challenges and difficulties that often arise when we are asked to transform and grow.

No other threshold brings us to our knees like death does; it is still the hardest passage to accept and navigate, no matter how conscious or prepared we think we are. The liminal experience of death thrusts us into the great unknown. All that we thought we knew is called into question. This can be a hidden gift, an invitation for us to know the larger dimensions of ourselves—our wholeness and true natures. And yet the transformation itself requires so much of us. And the pain of losing those we love is an unbearable journey. Yet, bear it we must, somehow.

While I was helping my mother die, I felt an invitation from Death itself to draw nearer, to become more intimately acquainted with what it means to be human, to live in a body, to be incarnated, and to die—what it means to cross that final threshold. So when I returned home to my island, I began to focus more on the end of life, and to apply all that I had been learning with others in community, all my explorations and adventures as minister and "festival maker" and guardian of gateways, to helping others navigate the passage of death with greater ease and resiliency and well-being.

My parents' favorite phrase, "All shall be well, and all manner of thing shall be well," became a kind of mantra for me at that time. What if we could find some semblance of knowing that, beneath all loss and heartache, there is still a place where all is well, all is whole? An impossible task, but one I still longed to explore. What kind of comfort and reassurance can we give those facing death, and how can we help soothe the trauma and suffering of families who lose someone they love? Can we discover ways to help transform the fear of death itself, and lighten the heavy thought forms we all carry about dying?

On the Nature of Thresholds

My exploration of threshold experience was an important part of trying to answer the questions above. Understanding what often happens to us when we are at a crossroads or important passage in life can help us imagine the best ways of handling such transition and change. Thresholds are always an opportunity for us to grow and expand our awareness; to become more alive, more connected to something greater than ourselves. They are doorways into the Sacred and are a way to reconnect with our deepest capacities of wholeness.

Yet, when we find ourselves on shores of change, and when the foundation and moorings we thought were steady and secure fray and unravel around us, we often tend to batten down the hatches and simply endure the ordeal until it's over—especially if we have just lost a loved one to death, or learn we are terminally ill. When we are going through shock and loss and pain, we cannot remain open; we contract and shut down in many ways instead. It is difficult not to do so, because our brains and bodies are wired to retreat in the face of real or perceived threat or danger, in the face of raw grief and dismantlement. Sadly, however, such a response means we can end up inhabiting a much more limited and diminished state of being, sometimes permanently.

If we can learn how to "resource" ourselves—which is a neuro-biological term for calming ourselves down, resting, finding ways to inhabit the parasympathetic part of our brains, rather than the "fight, flight, or freeze" response from the sympathetic nervous system—then our threshold experience can often be less traumatic, more resilient and generative in the end. We can breathe, and find ways to relax, ways to be more spacious and steady in the face of change. Hopefully, we can inhabit a more open, curious stance, rather than retreat; try to go with what is happening, rather than resist and fight the inevitable, and sink into depression or despair. This can make all the difference in whether our minds and hearts become more wounded and defended, or whether we can eventually transform and find new, more healing, expansive ways to be.

Yet what can we actually do to resource ourselves at the threshold of death? I knew instinctively that everything I had learned working with families and children, and building community with each other and with the natural world, could be beautifully applied to finding our way in the midst of the chaos and confusion of death. I also knew that home funeral vigils, and caring for our own dead, are natural containers to support not only the deceased, but all those around him, to experience death in more resourced and supportive ways, both practically and soulfully.

So I trained with Jerrigrace Lyons of Final Passages to become a home funeral guide, and I became part of those early years of the home funeral movement, as an advocate and practitioner on my island and in the greater Seattle area. With every family I helped, I saw how home funerals can help soften trauma and suffering at the end of life and can bring people back into a more intimate and living relationship with death itself.

Taking more time and space after someone dies offers us a greater chance to be ourselves, to have a more direct experience, and to follow our natural instincts and knowing. We can create whatever we need, and find effective and supportive ways to cope with the shock and loss we are experiencing. We can go even further, and actually bring life-giving energies of art, beauty, and gifts from the natural world to lighten death's stark reality. It is vital that we have enough time and opportunity for these kinds of responses to happen. Home funeral vigils offer us this sacred container, this chance to "green the threshold of death" with new imaginations of closure and healing.

The Gifts of Home Funeral Vigils

I was blessed to work with Glen and Celeen in the early days of my work as a home funeral guide. When Glen died of a brain tumor, Celeen and their children David and Alyssa and their community created a vigil that remains in my heart and mind as a beautiful example of how we can "green the gateway of death" by caring for our own at home, and by bringing art and nature and shared ritual to an otherwise heart-wrenching and difficult time. This family's journey taught me so much about the possibilities of experiencing death differently, from a place of open trust and shared community involvement.

Glen and Celeen had deep roots in Christianity and were also part of our island Waldorf school community. They were part of an international organization called Shematrix as well, whose work seeds sacred circles of ceremony and healing for men and women around the world. The kind of home funeral vigil that we created for Glen was shaped by Celeen and Glen's immersion in these spiritual paths—rightfully so, for home vigils should capture the uniqueness and essence of the person who has died, and reflect the natural expression of the family and friends left behind.

As reader, you may feel that Glen's home vigil is something your family would never do. I understand, having experienced within my own family resistance to my "Whidbey Island ways" of caring for Mama's body after death. I encourage you to read Glen's story and take from it what you will, and to translate my choice of words and language to fit your own way of doing things. For example, the idea of "sacred space" could become "special or comfortable space." "Holy listening" could become "paying attention to patterns that emerge" or simply being observant and knowing what would be helpful at any given time. You will know how to translate.

After my experience with Glen and Celeen, I went on to become a licensed funeral director with Char Barrett at A Sacred Moment, Inc. I experienced many different kinds of home funerals in the years

I worked there, and these helped me know that the kinds of vigils we can create are as unique and different and fascinating as we are. Thank goodness.

I remember driving up into the Cascades to a run-down trailer, with wrecked cars in the yard, and dogs barking madly behind chain-link fences. A home vigil was going on for a man who had died outside on the porch in a metal swing. His body was lying there still, covered with a faded quilt, his eyes staring out at the great mountain that rose up behind his house, a dark and brooding guardian. The neighbors were all there, sitting on the porch drinking beer, or standing out in the yard smoking cigarettes. There was a matter-of-fact air, a casual acceptance that the big man lying on the porch was biding his time, and they were there to bide it with him. A radio was blaring out from the open doorway, and a Willie Nelson song came on that seemed to celebrate every aspect of that vigil scene. It was a wild and wonderful affair, and I was gifted to be there.

Please pick and choose from the following story as you will. I have chosen to tell Glen and Celeen's story as a teaching tale. This way, the gifts home vigils can offer us are highlighted in the sharing. It is my hope you will find some elements to inspire your own imagination so you can create, when the time comes, a home vigil that is exactly right for you.

The Gift of Holy Listening, or Kything

Part of "threshold awareness" and keeping watch as a gatekeeper at the end of someone's life involves what I call "holy listening." I spoke of this in my mother's story—how I tried to pay attention to all the levels of what was transpiring in her death, and to listen especially to what seemed to come from Mama's soul, from her own understanding of what was happening to her. This required a kind of intuitive attunement, since we could no longer communicate through words.

I like the word "kything," first used by the author Madeleine L'Engle in her well-loved children's book *A Wind in the Door*, and explored further in the book *Kything: The Art of Spiritual Presence* by Louis M. Savary and Patricia H. Berne. Essentially, kything means the art of communion between souls, a spiritual skill we can all develop. It is my experience that the art of kything, or holy listening, can be very helpful in all three stages of death's threshold, including planning a home funeral vigil if the person dying has not or cannot articulate those plans himself. This was certainly true in Glen's case.

When Celeen and I met to plan Glen's home funeral vigil, their family was in that "bardo of dying" time, when things change from moment to moment, and nothing feels clear. There is a sense of urgency as well, because it is obvious there is little time left. And Glen was already past the point of being able to communicate coherently. I remember sharing with Celeen how a person's soul seems to bypass the personality and ego structure more and more as death approaches, allowing another kind of consciousness to emerge. I shared with her about practicing a kind of holy listening with my mother's soul as she lay dying—how we had an entire communication, with her nodding and smiling—even though she was very deaf, and I had forgotten to put in her hearing aids that morning, so she could not have possibly heard me in the physical dimension. I suggested we try to commune with Glen in a similar way.

When we both "tuned in" to Glen, we received a surprisingly clear message. We were to arrange for Glen's friends from the Waldorf school to build his pine casket in the next week, and no later than the Saturday when the men from Glen's Shematrix circle were going to gather. Those men would take the casket into their ceremony, to bless it for Glen's passage. In addition, that day was January 31, Imbolc/Candlemas Eve. Celeen and I had celebrated many festivals together, and she and Glen and their children loved Candlemas. It felt special that Glen's casket would be blessed in the festival doorway of renewal between the last of winter and the beginning of early spring.

Glen's men circle arrived Friday night, January 30, some from as far away as Chicago and Kansas City. They gathered around Glen's bed the next morning and gave him their blessings—smudging him with sage, drumming, playing flutes, speaking what was in their hearts to say to this man, their brother—he who was preparing to die. After a moving morning, the men carried Glen's casket away with them into their day of ceremony. The pine box would reside in the middle of their sacred circle and be consecrated there, before being returned to the house that evening.

The men shared later that at 1 p.m., after lunch, a ray of sunlight poured into their circle, and this sunray fell upon the casket resting in the middle of the room. It was at this moment that Glen took his last breath. Perhaps Glen was that warm sunlight, coming to tell his brothers goodbye, and to have his own hand in blessing the casket made for him. Everyone felt Glen's presence strongly in the room, though they had no idea until later that this was the time he actually began leaving his body.

None of us thought Glen was ready to go, though in looking back, it was obviously beautiful timing on his part. Four months before, Glen had experienced his first brain seizure within a men's sacred circle, and some of the same men who were present for Glen's death took care of him those many months before. This was a shocking and demanding task at the time, one that affected each man deeply; and, for some who had come from far away, a reason to be back with Glen on January 31.

The divine order of Glen's portal was palpable in the room for all of us. It brought us consolation and strength. I could sense Glen's pleasure in seeing us gathered together around his body. Despite the energies of death, a tiny smile graced his countenance. We had listened and kythed well with Glen's soul, it seemed, in a joint community effort that felt like a seamlessly choreographed dance—Glen's own finely orchestrated departure—one that gifted us all.

The Gift of Sacred Space and Time

Celeen, in her holy listening, felt that we should plan for a full, three-day Anthroposophical vigil, since Rudolf Steiner's teachings and their children's Waldorf experience were so meaningful to their family, and the school community was their strongest local support of love. This meant setting up a twenty-four-hour watch for Glen, which felt right, as it seemed to both Celeen and me that Glen did not want his body left alone, even at night.

So one of Celeen's friends organized a list so that people could sign up for two-hour slots around the clock. All three days filled up in no time, and we began having to double-book the slots. I realized then that such a vigil truly addresses the emotional needs of people in community who want to be able to give in a real and meaningful way. One friend shared with me recently that she sang for Glen during her middle-of-the-night slot, and that this experience, her first with a dead body, inspired her to later sing to her mother and to a man in her church after they died.

This round-the-clock vigil would give Glen comfort and companionship, if he needed such care, for his next steps away from incarnate life. We soon realized, however, that it didn't feel right for people outside the family to spend the first night with Glen. He was still lying in the hospital bed in the living room upstairs and, though there were many people coming and going in the house, they would be leaving at some point, and Celeen and her children could then be with Glen on their own. So we decided to create Glen's "sacred space" in a room downstairs, and move him there the second day, so that all those coming to visit him could do so without infringing on the family's privacy. This was a good solution, one I have utilized many times since in other home funeral vigils. The family often needs alone time to grieve, without having to relate to others all the time, as helpful and caring as those visitors might be.

Creating a vigil—however that might look and feel to you—goes a long way in helping everyone feel more comfortable, more open to everything death brings. People working together to create a place of rest and beauty for the one who has died often feel held in a collective field of intimacy—one that can sustain them afterward, when the adrenaline of the first days disappears. I have seen how helpful it can be to invite others to respond and bring something of who they are to the shared effort—something no one else might think of to contribute. This invitation to be creative—to bring art, imagination, nature, and beauty to a time of loss and sorrow—can be so nurturing and healing. It can empower us to be more present, less defended and afraid. We are not alone; we are facing this death together.

I saw this so vividly with Glen's vigil. Two fathers in the Waldorf community had already built Glen's pine box with care, and their creation was simple, elegant, and full of love. We set up the lid of the casket on a table in the kitchen, with paints and markers and ribbons, so all the children who came to the vigil could paint pictures and write messages to Glen on the top. Alyssa, Glen and Celeen's daughter, wrote on the lid the many ways he had taught her how to live, and painted a huge red flower of life in the middle of her words, which became the main focus of all the art the children contributed. The Waldorf teachers spent hours creating tissue-paper stained-glass windows of a sun rising over a mountain behind Glen's casket—shapes of new life and promise. When sunlight poured through the windows, the warm, vibrant splashes of color brought life and nourishment to the room.

There is something instinctive about bringing life forces from the natural world to balance and ease our experience of death. Fragrant evergreen boughs lining the casket; daffodils perched jauntily behind Glen's ears; sap from his favorite tree placed lovingly by Alyssa on his throat; special pebbles from the beach; a single carnation, startlingly pink, between his pale and bloodless fingers. Each gesture was the response of someone's soul—their heart wish to soothe and enliven the wan, lifeless hues and waxy textures of the dead. I saw that such offerings also helped people feel more needed and useful, more connected to the beauty unfolding there.

The Gift of Creating Beauty

When the room was ready on the second day, and people began to arrive, I spent time observing the body language of those entering the vigil space. I saw that the power of what we, as a community, had created for Glen helped people be less afraid and resistant. I think many who came had never been in the presence of a dead body. I watched them open the side door and enter slowly, hesitantly, breath held in, features contracted. Then the sheer beauty and soul of the space would embrace them. I heard gasps, sighs, as people breathed out spontaneously and visibly relaxed, able to move forward in a freer way. Not everyone: Some stayed back the whole time, near the door, as if by doing so, they could make their escape as soon as possible. Others kept their eyes closed, sitting quietly and then leaving. Some stayed distracted, tracking children and not allowing themselves to drop into deeper places. Many, however, seemed quite awed and ready to experience the gifts present there.

I am reminded of the poet John O'Donohue, who wrote so eloquently of the power of Beauty: "The wonder of the Beautiful is its ability to surprise us. With swift, sheer grace, it is like a divine breath that blows the heart open."[1] And this: When we encounter something beautiful, "there is a sense of homecoming ... we awaken and surrender in the same act ... we can slip into the Beautiful with the same ease as we slip into the seamless embrace of water; something ancient within us already trusts that this embrace will hold us."[2] I cannot think of a more perfect way to express how the beauty of a home vigil can help us rest in death itself once again.

---

[1] *Beauty: The Invisible Embrace* by John O'Donohue, 7.

---

[2] Ibid., 2.

The Gift of Home Vigils for Children

One of my most vivid memories of Glen's death happened on the first night. I was walking into the living room to bring the dry ice we would be placing beneath his body later on. Alyssa was standing next to the bed, crying softly. Her friend Charlotte was standing next to her, one arm around Alyssa's waist in such a protective, loving way. With her other hand, Charlotte was stroking Glen's arm, speaking quietly to Alyssa as she did so. This natural capacity to touch and be with death without fear, as a compassionate gesture for her friend— the daughter who was suffering so much—was remarkable. Both girls were twelve years old.

Many children who came to Glen's vigil were naturally curious and accepting. Even though a few seemed fearful, wonder and inter- est won out over hesitancy for most. I cried several times witnessing the wise sheltering instincts of parents for their little ones. A child would go up to Glen, and soon a mother would be there, drawing close and putting her hand on her son's head, or stroking his back, letting him know he was not alone in the face of death. One father grabbed his daughter's hand and went forward, urging his girl to lean into his big, firm body while they stood silently gazing down on Glen's still form. There was something so strong, and yet so vul- nerable, about these scenes. So achingly human.

The Gift of Blessing and Spontaneous Ritual

Late the first night of Glen's vigil, after everyone else had gone, Celeen and I, and the children, each with a chosen friend, blessed Glen's body with lavender water, giving thanks for each part of this special man. His mind, enjoying thinking and reading; his heart, caring and loving in such a generous way; his hands, playing the guitar and building bookshelves. We were tired and giddy, and so grew silly and full of giggles. Celeen felt Glen approved of us "lightening up," and so we did. Alyssa blessed his nose and all the funny smells he used to talk about. When David blessed his ears and hearing, coyotes yelped right outside the windows. David helped his mother and me lift his father into his casket. That night, Celeen and Alyssa slept on the sofa right next to Glen, grateful for the chance to be so close with him still.

We created a special service spontaneously the next morning. All the Shematrix women and men returned to help transport Glen from the living room to the downstairs vigil space. Glen had nudged someone the night before, saying he would love for his body to go outside in nature one last time. So we created a procession, with the men carrying Glen in his casket all around the garden. A friend played the flute, and I drummed a heartbeat sound on Glen's drum, as we walked slowly and reverently through an arbor and around the house.

At one point, I felt an urge to stop, and the thought came that Glen wanted his body right on the earth. So I turned and said we should pause and put the casket down. One man helping carry the casket gasped when I said those words, because he had felt the same thing in his body, and the casket and Glen had suddenly become unbearably heavy. This was a very physical experience, one that helped me sense how embedded we are in the earth and in each other. Reflecting back on this, I feel I was using a somatic felt sense that was open to Glen's continuing spirit presence there with us in the garden. I saw that such a sense was an integral part of listening in the portal of death, staying grounded and rooted in the land, and being open to messages from the unseen dimensions of consciousness around us.

What a moving sight to see Glen lying there in his pine box, a smile still gracing his features, despite the onset of rigor mortis and change. There on the wet, mossy grass, on the land he loved, with the crows cawing from the roof of the garage, the sun offering a layer of warmth to soothe his dissolution, and the morning air so fresh and new. We stood in a circle holding hands around Glen, and sang "Dona Nobis Pacem" in four-part round, our voices creating a sound field of resonance and love. This was the family's special blessing song. David, so strong for his sixteen years, led the men in their part, and this brought many of us to tears. As the men lifted Glen up and we made our way back inside, they reported that the casket seemed lighter, their burden lifted. As if in affirmation, the crows rose up in a great cloud of black wings, calling out to Glen to follow them into the vast blueness of space and sky.

The Gift of Departure Rituals

Often, the greatest need for some kind of acknowledgment and ritual happens at the end of a vigil, when the deceased person must depart from the house for the very last time. Family are either ready and relieved to see this moment come, or they are even more reluctant to release a loved one, having had such intimate time and connection. Either way, it is often helpful to do something meaningful and comforting when the transition to the crematorium or cemetery arrives.

Family and friends can carry the person themselves to the waiting vehicle in a solemn or lively procession. There can be music and singing if that feels right, prayers and blessings, or jokes and hilarity. Having something like rose petals on hand can be beautiful, so that everyone can scatter them in front of the departing body. These are simple and nurturing things to do. The chance to imagine special ways to say farewell is part of the gifts home funeral vigils bring.

Glen's departure was a welcome release of all intentional ritual, having done much of that in the days before. Celeen put on Glen's favorite rock and roll music and invited everyone to dance around the room wildly as a way of saying goodbye. I'll never forget my removal man Sean's face when he came to the door, which had been flung open with abandon so that people could spill out into the garden. There we all were, gyrating and spinning around Glen's casket, and singing along with the music.

Sean told me later he had never encountered a family saying goodbye in such a way, in all his years of transporting the dead. Our enthusiasm must have been infectious, because he took my suggestion that he should see a bit of Whidbey Island before he headed back to the mainland, and that Glen might appreciate one last visit to the beach. We all loved thinking of Glen and the removal man hanging out with the wind and waves on the shores of Puget Sound, a fitting and perfect metaphor for the next stage of Glen's crossing.

The Gift of Normalizing Death

Having three days with Glen's body helped us be with death in the midst of life. Though the vigil was certainly a time-out-of-time experience, the fabric of daily existence remained and was deeply comforting. The container of holding we created together made room for everything, so that we could be ourselves in the midst of momentous change. We were grounded in the physical—good food, back rubs, firing up the hot tub, cleaning the bathrooms, encouraging each other to nap or go outside for fresh air. Feelings were welcome and held—grief, despair, anger and confusion, happiness, laughter and joy—all were part of the tapestry of those days. In Celeen's words, "This is very, very painful, but I am not suffering. I am remarkably relaxed, held by the Love that is everywhere."

I am remembering the first night, with Glen still lying in the living room in his hospital bed, growing pale and cold. The warmth of laughter and music playing all around him; the clink of dishes in the kitchen; the aroma of soup simmering on the stove; a voice singing quietly in a corner; someone sobbing. Children coming shyly up to touch Glen's face and hands—feeling safe and comfortable, held by a tangible field of normality and deep acceptance. This is death, and it is a natural part of life—our lives right now, in this house, at this time. I think the very ordinariness of Glen's death became, in the end, the most sacred and valuable gift of all.

———

I have one more home vigil story to tell—this one dear to my heart because it represents how natural and instinctive home vigils and green burials can be, even if one has just heard of those possibilities and has never experienced such care before. The day I met with Jake and Donna and his sons Tristan and Markus and their friends, a luminous double rainbow formed over the house as I got in the car to go home. It seemed like a gift for Jake and his family, and for me—a sign of the great potential and blessings of caring for our own in ways that care for the earth as well.

Fierce Beauty: The Gift of Planning Your Own Home Vigil/Green Burial

Jake Seniuk and his wife, Donna James, contacted me for a green burial consultation. Jake was dying of cancer, and he really fancied being buried in the mushroom suit he had seen in a TEDx Talk by Jae Rhim Lee, the founder of Coeio. (See the Resources section for chapter 9.) Regrettably, I had to tell him those suits were not available for humans yet, but that a natural burial was, and I would be honored to help him with that choice. After hearing that families can care for their own dead at home in Washington State, and can drive a loved one from the house to the burial ground themselves, Jake and Donna were eager to learn more.

I was grateful for the chance to work with Jake while he still had the energy and desire to make his own plans. It is not often that I can meet with the person who is actually dying, and help him imagine what he most wants. Usually a family calls me, and I work with them instead to craft a vigil—hopefully based on the dying person's wishes, but often just arising out of the present moment and what the family can handle by then. Being able to work directly with Jake before he died was a privilege, one that strengthened my resolve to help people plan ahead, imagine what they really want, and share those wishes in person with family and friends. It is my experience that picking a team, and facing one's death together with the ones you love, can be one of the most powerful gifts you can give yourself and others before you die.

We gathered in the cozy living room, friends and family making a circle of togetherness around Jake, who was so weak he had to lie on a chaise lounge in his silk bathrobe and only occasionally sit up to add his voice to our conversation. There was no question about who was in charge though. Jake was dying, and he was orchestrating all details of his departure, like the artist and wise sage he was.

"Let's look upon this after-death care as my last art installation," Jake said, his voice carrying a lightness of being nobody else in the room was feeling. "You can even mount me on the wall if you like," he joked, making his sons laugh, and Donna smile through her tears. As the home funeral vigil and green burial guide, I was there to help Jake's loving team learn how to care for his body after death, wrap him in the linen shroud he had chosen to be buried in, and transport him themselves in a van to a natural burial ground—where Jake's beloved earth could receive him back in simple and life-giving ways.

We went around the circle, and people spoke first of their hopes and fears, so that the truth and reality of why we were there could live and breathe in the room, informing us. I asked if anyone had any concerns about Jake being at home after death. Jake's son Tristan admitted he was worried about his father's body smelling. Wouldn't that be a problem? I assured him that there would be no smell to speak of if Jake were bathed and dressed, and they used dry ice to cool the body down. I thanked Tristan for being so forthright with his question. It helped drop us to a level of sharing that was more intimate and real right away.

One of Jake's friends had the courage to express his anger and aversion to the whole idea of Jake dying, much less having a home vigil. Jake's response was so moving. He acknowledged his friend's feelings and didn't try to change them in any way. At the same time, Jake spoke of his own growing interest in the great adventure he was facing, and how he hoped his death, and caring for his body afterward, could be a teaching and help heal the way we think about dying. I witnessed Jake's friend shift his resistance and become one of the key contributors in our training that day. He went on to participate in Jake's home vigil and even drove the van that carried Jake's body to his final resting place.

I watched Jake drink in this honest sharing from those he loved, and find nourishment and support to turn more consciously toward his pending death. He seemed to settle into a greater understanding of what lay before him, willingly taking part in practical planning, but holding always the deeper vision and spirit of what was transpiring for us all. Jake's strength of soul and his grace helped everyone else in the room come to a greater acceptance and peace that day.

Though Jake was not expected to die right away, he was gone within a week of our gathering, as if the support generated by that circle lent him courage and resolve for his journey. His home vigil—with sons Tristan and Markus doing the paperwork and handling the dry ice, Donna's attentive care, and others there to aid and comfort—was, in Donna's words, "transformative." After shrouding Jake's body, and placing mushrooms in the folds, in honor of his original wish to have an Infinity Burial Suit, Jake's team drove his body themselves up the highway to The Meadow, a green burial ground in Ferndale, Washington. This caring for Jake at home, and laying him to rest in a natural grave, helped weave his creative life and death together as one. It was Jake's final gift of art, in collaboration with his willing family and friends—a gift of fierce beauty and wholeness.

Donna's poetry about her journey with Jake is part of that fierce beauty, her own gift from the threshold:

Undertaking

I

In search for meanings of his lifetime's labors,
he and I mine the underworld

of dreams, memoir, Bavaria,
hallucinations of ayahuasca.

With bills, assets, letters to answer;
manuscripts to ready for an editor's desk;
works of art to place in museums,
I assume authority for his outer life.

Sculptures, wire cutters, cameras,
Dr. Grinspoon bud, a pension,
two young men and one young woman—
heirlooms I prepare to inherit.

II

As this ark, our home, lurches in the storm,
I spoon-feed him morphine and rice pudding,
shoulder my lover on his ten-minute
wobbly odysseys toward the toilet,
secure a bucket for a purge of vomit.

His intimate body slows, slackens,
thins, groans, stops filtering poisons.
I witness. I watch him:
He surrenders himself to the reaper.
He is gone. Carted off somewhere.

III

Washing with rose otto and water,
anointing with frankincensed oil,
I caress the skin of his cold corpse,
talking as though he could hear.
Cloaking his body in pure white cotton

I let loose my hold.

I arrange this discarded outer garment
on a table of bed-sheet and ice,
drape the remnant of him
in shiny white silk,
bedeck it with evergreen boughs.

IV
For three days, this body and I
sit together with our friends.
Some handle paperwork,
one procures ice,
most sleep through the night.

Some cook, all eat, one weeps, two joke.
We telephone, photograph, replay legends,
meditate on the difference
between a body and a life;
feel the vanishment.

V
We fold linen flaps over feet and face.
Wrap and tie four ribbons into thick white knots—
not too tight around the neck—
transmuting visage to memory.

We transport a package stowed
in the cargo compartment of a van.
Five cars caravan
up the freeway toward a meadow.

We walk the remains to a grave,
consign matter to earth,
a mortal's final estate,
where it is taken under.

Scepter

At your bone feet, we settle a stone
first anniversary. Liver, heart, brain
one-fifth decomposed already.

Stone scrubbed smooth in Elwha's waters.
Stone the color of your hair that grows yet
with your nails as microbes eat soft tissue.
Stone to outlast your fleeting cells, to endure
with your spirit—lithe forest sylph, laden,
as soil after a violent half-century,
complicated as the intricacies of imagination.

Basics: your name and dates—just the years—
embellished with the Vajra brush
of Alex Grey's The Artist's Hand.
Symbols sandblasted into rock
like Indra's sacred thunderbolt blast
that ordained you with an artist's vision,
brilliant, clear, your diamond nature.

Standing at the Gate

I love the lavish bursts
of pale hydrangea Alice,
blooms arcing over a fence.
How does one live soft white
as it reflects sunlight

and know maya?

Day by day
varies the rhythm:
a vermillion raspberry,
a vanishing.

How else but to love
the profusion and the dying?

Practical Wisdom: Choosing a Home Funeral: What You Need to Know

The information I include below can help you begin planning a home funeral vigil, either for yourself or for a loved one. It is not comprehensive, so I highly recommend that you go to the National Home Funeral Alliance website (www.homefuneralalliance.org) and immerse yourself in all the resources and practical guidance available there. The workbooks published by the NHFA are invaluable tools for anyone wishing to create a home vigil. There are helpful how-to links, a You-Tube channel and videos demonstrating how to bathe and dress a body, how to close the eyes and mouth before rigor mortis sets in, how to work with dry ice, Techni-ice®, and other forms of refrigeration, and many more aspects of the actual physical care of the dead. There are also resources for rituals and sacred care of the dead and their families and communities. You can research the legalities of home funerals to find out what is possible in your state. You can find the nearest home funeral guide and advocate and how to contact them. You can contact the NHFA with any questions and concerns. So please make this resource your strongest support and ally.

I have chosen to focus here on what I feel are some of the most essential considerations for anyone wishing to care for their own dead, based on frequently asked questions about home funerals.

Is It Legal to Care for Our Own Dead at Home?

The simple answer is yes. Despite the fact that most people turn to professional funeral directors when someone dies, it is legal in every state and province for families to care for their own dead and to keep a deceased person at home until final disposition. There are nine U.S. states, however, where this innate legal right has been compromised, making it necessary to involve a licensed funeral director in some aspects of care. Those states are: *Connecticut, Illinois, Indiana, Iowa, Louisiana, Michigan, Nebraska, New York,* and *New Jersey.* Families can still participate in caring for their own in these states, but they should know and understand the laws and restrictions that will affect their decision to have a home funeral vigil. It is helpful in these states to find a licensed funeral director who is willing to work with you in supportive ways, such as completing the necessary paperwork and transporting the body, whether those are legally required or simply something you would prefer to outsource. For more legal support, please go to the National Home Funeral Alliance's "Quick Guide to Legal Requirements for Home Funerals in Your State" and the NHFA publication *Restoring Families' Right to Choose.* You can also refer to your state information in the book *Final Rights: Reclaiming the American Way of Death.*

Even though it is legal in every state, very few people are aware of this fact, including key personnel involved in death, such as doctors, medical examiners, hospital staff, law enforcement officials, even hospice. This is slowly changing, but it is still necessary to educate all those with whom you will be involved when caring for a loved one after death. This is where planning ahead for a home vigil is so important. (See chapter 10 for more details.) It gives you time to be proactive, and to inform everyone, including neighbors who might be concerned, what your plans are.

I have found that this proactive stance, which helps those in public and official positions feel respected and included in the decision, sometimes makes all the difference in a family's experience. It is often helpful to have a trained or knowledgeable home funeral guide/

consultant take on some of these tasks of informing others, as they are experienced in interfacing with the public, and speaking for everyone's innate right to care for their own. But if you are well informed, you have every right to educate and advocate for home vigils yourself.

What about Health Concerns? Is It Safe to Have a Home Funeral Vigil?

Many people are concerned about the safety and health issues of keeping a deceased person at home. There is still a pervasive "myth of contagion" in our collective psyches about dead bodies, a fear that the funeral industry aggressively marketed in the 1930s and has perpetuated to its advantage. The belief that embalming reduces the risk of spreading disease is part of the myth; in fact, only in the United States and Canada is embalming done routinely or required for infectious cases, which is counterintuitive and potentially dangerous. No state legally requires embalming, though many funeral homes have policies that require it for viewings in their facilities. According to the World Health Organization, the microorganisms involved in decomposition are not the kind that cause disease. And most bacteria and viruses that do cause disease are destroyed within a few hours after someone dies. (HIV can be an exception to this, but if necessary precautions are taken, this can also be managed.) Caring for our own dead is safe in almost all normal circumstances of death.

Bathing a deceased person and making sure they are clean after death, making sure the eyes and mouth are closed, and dressing them in fresh clothes also helps ensure that the body is in good condition for the vigil. Refrigeration methods (see below) help retard the rate of decomposition, so that there is rarely any smell or purging or problems in that regard.

In many states, one must legally "refrigerate" a deceased person within a certain time period after death, most commonly twenty-four hours. Some states do not recognize any other method than using a refrigeration unit in a funeral home. The use of dry ice or Techni-ice®, or even frozen ice packs or bags of ice, is considered legal refrigeration in most states, though the latter two melt and leak over time. Dry ice or Techni-ice® is most effective. It is important to place the ice beneath the torso of the person, to keep the organs cool, and at times on the top of the torso, depending on the condition of the person's body. Some practitioners place ice beneath the head as well, though I never have. This refrigeration ensures that the body is kept cool enough during the vigil. Find your nearest source for dry ice (in some states, this is not an easy task), and make sure there is plenty available, as you will need at least twenty to thirty pounds a day (three times that, if you are having a three-day vigil). Most dry ice comes in ten-pound slabs. Techni-ice® usually has to be ordered online and activated when received, which takes time and freezer space, so it is important to plan ahead if you are going to use this method. If you are working with a home funeral guide, she or he may have Techni-ice® and other useful supplies on hand. (See this chapter's Resource section for coolant information and suppliers.) The website of the National Home Funeral Alliance also has all the information you will need.

What Helps Make a Home Vigil Go Smoothly?

I always recommend that a family engage hospice if their loved one is dying at home and a home funeral vigil is planned. This streamlines the whole after-death process, provided the hospice staff understands your wishes and are on board. When a person dies, the death must be reported to legal authorities, and the death certificate process must be initiated. In some states, such as Washington, hospice staff notifies the doctor and medical examiner/coroner as part of their duties, making it unnecessary for family members to do so. The family can be left in peace, as no one has to come to the house, since hospice already has all the relevant medical information. However, if hospice is not involved, a family member must call the police or the medical examiner to report the death. Many times, this can start a whole series of events that might be chaotic and dramatic, making one's original wish to have a peaceful after-death time with a loved one far less likely. Police are required to come to the house to report the death, and often this can involve flashing lights and ambulances, and even paramedics who may feel obligated to do CPR. So if the death is certain, and you want to avoid such drama, make sure you work with hospice at the end. (See the Practical Wisdom section in chapter 10 for more information.)

Be prepared. I speak more about this in chapter 10 but will begin the discussion here. Home funerals work best when there is a team of family members and friends who show up and take on all the necessary tasks of making a vigil happen. Though some families work through their grief by doing everything themselves, most benefit greatly from having friends and community members take on tasks such as purchasing and replenishing dry ice, helping create the vigil space, being a spokesperson for the family, and making sure there is always enough food and comfort on hand.

Choosing a team before the actual death occurs is very helpful, as those people can be trained and educated about all that a home vigil entails, and people can self-select tasks that they feel most capable of handling. Having a team of people helps everything go more smoothly. It is also helpful to have one or two people act as "case manager" or leader, whose responsibility is to organize and help "hold" both the details and the larger picture. (See Appendix B for a description of that role.) The NHFA has published a wonderful resource: *Planning Guide and Workbook for Home Funeral Families.* I recommend having this workbook on hand, and filling it out long before you ever need it.

What about the Necessary Paperwork?

In all but the aforementioned nine states, families can legally act as funeral director themselves and can sign the death certificate in lieu of a funeral professional. In the states where the assistance of a funeral director is required, the funeral home handles the paperwork. If families are not utilizing the services of a funeral home, completing the paperwork is an essential part of the home vigil process.

Having the next-of-kin fill out the paperwork is possible and manageable. It often helps to appoint one person in the family who feels capable of handling this task. The next-of-kin must sign the death certificate, in lieu of the funeral director, unless the deceased has officially appointed a designated agent for disposition to handle all arrangements and has stated this in a signed document, giving the agent authority to sign the death certificate instead.

Again, it is very helpful to plan ahead and to familiarize oneself with the paperwork before the death occurs, filling out as many forms as possible beforehand, perhaps with the support of a home funeral guide who is familiar with the process. The demographic portion of the death certificate must be written in black ink with no cross-outs or white-outs. It's best to fill out a draft copy first.

The death certificate cannot be completed until after death, but in many states it must be filed before you can transport a deceased body in your own vehicle and before a person can be cremated or buried. In most states, families must have in their possession the burial transit permit (often on the back of the death certificate or attached to it, though some states separate the two) before transporting the body themselves. (Surprisingly, however, not all states require that you have the permit in hand before moving the body, so check your state's laws.) Once the final disposition has taken place, the permit must be filed with the town, city, or county, depending on local regulations. (Check with your local authority to find out what the time frame is for completing the filing of the permit.)

It is difficult or even impossible for families to file death certificates on the weekend and on holidays, so there may be times when it is necessary to hire a funeral director to help. The advent of the Electronic Death Registration System (EDRS) has also made it more difficult for families to file the death certificate, as only professionals have access to the system online and can file electronically. I keep a stack of paper death certificates for families to use. Home funeral advocates can ask their local registrars to always have paper death certificates on hand for families, and those preparing ahead of time can ask as well. *Keep in mind that the details of filing are different in every state, so be sure to check with your state Department of Health or Vital Records Division (usually part of the Secretary of State's office) for specifics.*

What Do I Need to Know about Transporting a Body Myself?

First, make sure it is legal in your state or province for families to transport their own dead. Second, have the necessary paperwork—the burial transit permit—in the vehicle before transporting a body (unless your state or province does not require the permit). It is also very helpful (indeed, required in many states) to place the body in a "rigid container" to ensure that the body is protected and that there are no leakages during transit. Often a family will purchase a cardboard cremation container, unless they are building a casket themselves as part of a vigil. This is a nice addition to a vigil anyway, as family and friends can decorate the container, and it serves as a natural holding place for people to send little gifts and mementos along with the person at the time of departure.

This means that if your loved one is being buried or cremated only in a shroud, you will need an additional container to transport the body. Sometimes you can obtain a gurney or "cot," as it is called in the funeral industry, though this means interfacing with a funeral home, which could be problematic. You can also purchase a wicker tray or other shrouding board, or a canvas carrier made especially for shrouded bodies, to use for transport and at the graveside. (For suppliers, see the Resources section of chapter 4.) These will be harder to obtain at the last minute, however, and more costly. *So plan ahead* for home funerals in general, and especially if you are doing the transport yourself. Please refer to the NHFA's "Quick Guide to Home Funerals by State" (see the Resources section) to discern what your state requires regarding transport. (This is part of the NHFA publication *Restoring Families' Right to Choose.*)

Community Care Groups

There is a growing movement to create volunteer teams of people who are on call within communities, and who can show up to assist the family in caring for the dead, creating vigils, arranging transport, and helping with all aspects at the end of life. This is a wonderful grassroots model for both secular and spiritual communities to follow. These care groups can form within specific spiritual communities, such as Buddhist sanghas or church congregations. It can also be very helpful for care groups to form that are not connected to any one religion or spiritual faith, but that are simply a group of dedicated, caring individuals who are called to care for the dead in their local community. Having such a group, if one is single and does not have family or even friends close by, can be comforting and supportive. Community care groups are a potent and successful way to reimagine ways to care for our own, as we used to do and are now reclaiming. See the Resources section for more information.

Taking the Fear Out of Home Funerals

All of this may seem overwhelming if it is your first time contemplating caring for your own dead, but take heart. At the end of the day, the paperwork is no more difficult than filling out any other forms if you know the answers; the process is logical and moves you along of its own accord. Most importantly, there are no funeral police. Do your best, call for help when needed, follow the process, positively engage the people who are there to assist you, and you'll find that basic common sense can be your truest guide. Best of all, doing it yourself in your own time and at your own pace, within the guidelines of the rules, gives form to what you are going through, without impeding your ability to be present. Completing paperwork and making your own arrangements are just other essential ways of caring for your loved one.

3

PARTNERING WITH NATURE WHEN WE DIE

... we have lost our sense of courtesy toward the earth and
its inhabitants, our sense of gratitude, our willingness to
recognize the sacred character of habitat,

our capacity for the awesome, for the numinous quality of
every earthly reality.

... our primordial capacity for language
at the elementary level of song and dance,

wherein we share our existence with the animals and with
all natural phenomena.

—THOMAS BERRY, excerpt from *The Dream of the Earth*

*W*e handle death more easily when we are resourced, or connected to something larger than ourselves. For many, a spiritual faith is this greater power, and that is a wonderful aid and

gift. But for all of us, as human beings, nature itself is an untapped wellspring of support and inspiration, offering us a place of holding and strength to face the end of life. Even if we have never had any conscious connection with the natural world, our bodies have, for we are nature, we are embedded and interdependent with all other forms of sentient life, and we rest in, indeed are held by, the earth in every moment of our days. If we can remember this as we die, we have a greater chance of awakening to our larger wholeness, to our true natures, and to the sacredness of who we are as human beings.

Such understanding is best received through our felt senses and imaginations, not through the musings of conceptual minds. (I will attempt that impossible task in this chapter's Practical Wisdom section.) When faced with the inexpressible, and we are here, my way is to tell stories, gleaned from my direct experience of what it means to partner or co-create with nature when we die.

I wrote the following vignette when my father was dying of cancer on our land in Alabama, nine years after Mama's dramatic departure. We were all home again, this time helping Papa "kick the bucket," as I heard him say to a friend on the phone, his voice catching, betraying his attempt to be light and buoyant about his own very imminent demise. As in my mother's time of dying, I sensed that the animals, creatures, and life of the land were actively engaged in supporting Papa as he faced his death. This is a true account, and I share it as a tribute to my father.

At the Borderlands

I think the bees knew that Papa was dying. In some strange empathic communion, one of our hives had developed a beetle infestation, and there were black masses of insects infiltrating the supers, at the same time Papa's cancer was spreading throughout his body. Our bees had been healthy for years—no disease or colony collapse, no problems to speak of. Now this. Papa was the beekeeper, the one whom the "ladies" knew and trusted with their honey and with their lives. It was as if this one hive had decided to accompany their friend in his suffering, even go with him across the veil.

We went down together to deal with the crisis—Papa in a cotton shirt that clung to his thin, emaciated body like a shroud—his slow, uncertain gait across the field so different from his usual pace; so sad. My brother Hal marched ahead in purposeful strides revealing a chronic impatience and masking the deeper unraveling going on inside him. Losing our father was a fierce and demanding task, one he could meet, but the toll was considerable.

The October afternoon sun was bright and warm—a mocking contrast to our mission of death—for we intended to burn the infested hive so that the beetles could not migrate over to the other supers nearby. I wondered what Papa must be feeling as he pulled on his bee suit and headgear. The bees were his friends, his constant companions since Mama's death years before. Perhaps destroying the beetles would be cathartic, giving him a sense of power to counteract his own futile longing to remain alive a little longer.

"I just want to live until the persimmons ripen, Lulie, and the leaves finish falling," Papa had said that morning, his eyes moist and his face so wistful. "Life is truly dear, isn't it? I'm sure gonna miss being here, miss being alive." "Here" was our Alabama land, in a mountain cove, at the end of a lane, up a steep stony drive, where old log cabins nestle in the woods as if they had always grown there. Though Papa really never retired from practicing law, he had changed his high-powered life being a trial lawyer in town, to spend his days cutting wood, growing a garden and canning food, driving the tractor across the bottomlands, making scuppernong wine, and giving honey away to all his church friends and family.

His was a good life, with a new woman companion from church, and days spent on the mountain, or driving into town to teach Bible classes about the Divine Feminine to all the old ladies in the little Episcopal church he helped start. This, after the diocese ordained women, an act he heartily disapproved of. And yet, after Mama died, the Feminine stalked Papa like a lover and, in his later years, he kept his hands in the dirt, and his heart open to her whispers and wisdom. My Southern, rather patriarchal father told me once that, in the early weeks of anguish after losing Mama, the only thing that really helped his pain was to go down to the garden and bury his face in the earth. His capacity to stretch and grow rather than stay frozen in older ways of being moves me to this day. Grief was Papa's agent of transformation. It cracked him open, and now it was helping him die. We all felt that his lung cancer, an illness often associated with loss and grieving, probably began in those searing weeks after Mama died.

Papa and Hal carefully dismantled the damaged hive, placing the supers, which were full of lethargic, struggling bees, in a row on the ground. I came closer and saw the black beetles swarming over the wax comb, wreaking havoc with the ordered and tidy kingdoms within. Hal told us to move back, stepping forward with a blowtorch. Without hesitating, he aimed the intense flame into the inner recesses of the boxes, so that bees, beetles, and comb were suddenly engulfed in acrid smoke and fire.

Papa stood under the tall cedar tree whose low branches served as a shelter for the hives—a shelter for him, too, in this moment. I noticed for the first time that the netting on Papa's headgear was black, not white like Hal's. From where I stood, I could no longer see my father's face; he was hidden behind a dark veil, hesitant, hovering at the borderlands. Behind him, the sky was achingly blue, and the air was filled with the humming of other bees in the branches. As I gazed, the sun's rays caught Papa's whole image, outlining his frail form with a bright halo of light. "It won't be long," I thought, witnessing this moment, this image of portending death. I sensed Papa's life force already loosening its hold and spiraling upward and out, upward and out, like the dark coils of smoke swirling and billowing forth from the boxes where his bees lay burning.

Later I went over to the workshop across the gully from the house to check on the status of Papa's cherry wood casket. Margaret's partner, Ray, talked to a local craftsman and got directions for building a simple box from wood Papa already had on the mountain—beautiful milled planks he had saved and cherished for years. Hal and a young man, Brian, who had been Papa's friend and co-worker, helped Ray build Papa's "little ship of death," as D. H. Lawrence called it.

Though our father loved woodwork and could have come at any time to view his casket, he never did, though he knew the men were hard at work evenings and weekends. I found this odd, though I tried to understand. I guess Papa loved living so much, he didn't want to contemplate being dead, which his own fine casket would insist he do. Just like he didn't want to talk about me putting him on dry ice during his after-death vigil in the dining room, though he was able to laugh and joke about being a flayed herring on ice—that being his name: Fish Herring. His real name was Harold, but people rarely called him anything but Fish.

When I opened the workshop door, Papa's bees were swarming everywhere. Someone had left the windows open to the honey room. The ladies had left their hives down in the meadows and made their way up the hill to confiscate their stolen treasure. That was to be expected. What I didn't expect was to see hundreds of bees circling Papa's casket, in a spiraling dance that was, to me, unmistakably focused and intentional. Old lore says that one must run and tell the bees when their keeper dies, and cover the hives with a black veil for three nights and three days. Just as the diseased bees seemed to know about and take on Papa's illness, these sisters were communing with and blessing the box that would take their keeper down off the mountain and away from them forever. Theirs was a dance of realization, acceptance, and honoring—their warm, steady humming a portent of all that was, all that had to be.

Elemental Wonderings

Nature showed up at the moment of death so powerfully when my mother died. The call of the wood thrush before Mama took her last breath. The sudden onset of fierce winds and bending branches, torrential rain, thunder and lightning breaking loose on our mountain within minutes of her going. The rushing waters that tumbled out of the spring, and the flash flood that surged over the top of our mountain like an errant river, never before or since appearing in such wild and boundless ways in our cove.

Such a strong elemental response at the very time of Mama's crossing remains a potent mystery, one that each of my family holds close in different ways. My way is to wonder—whether the storm and flooding were a co-creative effort on the part of my mother, the land, and exuberant elemental forces—all conspiring together to help Mama leave her body and her life—and granting my wish to keep her home and care for her after death. I will always ponder, too, if my daily invocations and prayers at the spring had anything to do with its eager, abundant response—a question that can never really be answered, and best laid reverently aside. Ask any of my siblings, and they will roll their eyes and give you a less "embroidered" explanation for the flash flood, and for all that transpired in the aftermath of the storm. This is right and good. We each brought our own lens and experiences to Mama's passage, and this collective truth is of course the most complete and compelling story in the end.

I do like to remind my family, however, that a similar storm blew up on our mountain a year to the day of Mama's death, June 4, at exactly the time Mama died, 5:20 p.m., in the late afternoon. This is my telling of that mysterious return.

Mama's Message

Our plan was to sit upstairs in the spot where Mama left the world, and light candles on the altar Papa and I had created on an old oak chest—with Mama's bronze angel statue, various photographs, her most loved books, and yellow roses. About 4:45 we opened the windows wide, as it was so sunny and beautiful, lit the tall white candles, and made ourselves comfortable: Papa in Mama's reading chair, I in the recliner, and Margaret on the rug with some pillows. I closed my eyes, listening to the lyrical drone of Papa's voice as he began reading passages from C. S. Lewis aloud and seeing again in sharp detail the scene from the previous year, when we had all gathered around Mama's hospital bed to lend support for her to fly away free.

I don't know how long it took me to realize that, behind Papa's voice, a wave of wind was weaving a tapestry of sound outside the window, tossing the branches of the trees back and forth. It had appeared suddenly, without warning, as the day had until that moment remained hot, cloudless, and still. I jumped up and looked out into the woods, marveling at what I saw. Gone was the clear, sunny day. A great bank of clouds had moved swiftly in and washed the blue from the sky. And, in the distance, thunder rolled toward us like a freight train gathering speed.

We looked at each other in amazement. Here it was, exactly 5:20 p.m., the moment Mama had died, and another big storm was making its way into the cove, with rain, and lightning and thunder, just as it had the year before. I was convinced then that the electrical charge of the storm had somehow helped ease Mama's consciousness out of her body. Was it bringing her back now for a visit? It was hard for me not to believe so, since, moments before, the day had shown no sign of the heavy, oppressive time that always precedes afternoon thunderstorms in Alabama.

A great gust of wind suddenly blew in, spattering us with rain, so we cranked the windows in a little, and sat there not saying a word. The storm's presence left us speechless. Within minutes, a torrential downpour descended, drumming on the tin roof like a militia band, sounding to me, in my ever-imaginative mind, as if all the percussion instruments in the world were there, announcing their most distinguished guest—Irobel.

Papa finally spoke: "How 'bout that, girls? This is something else, isn't it?" He had a big grin on his face, and his eyes crinkled up, as they did when he found life extremely dear. "Looks like Mama wanted to come be part of the ceremony, after all!" He picked up his book again and began to read, adding strength to his voice to compete with the driving rain.

I suddenly realized I was freezing cold. I had on a sleeveless shirt because it had been so hot, but now the atmosphere around the altar and the chairs was as cold as a walk-in refrigerator. Margaret must have felt the same, because she stood up and got each of us a blanket from the bed. We wrapped ourselves up tightly, shivering from the chilliness and the sheer strangeness of it all. I didn't say anything, but I remembered that frigid temperature that appear suddenly in rooms, are an age-old, accepted sign of a dead person's presence. It was hard not to recoil from the icy fingers of air, but I did my best, in case it really was Mama. I whispered "Hello" under my breath, and just sat there, trying to be as present as possible and sending her waves of love and welcome. It helped to send out energy, to meet the visitation head-on. I realized my effort to embrace the event, rather than recoil from it, actually changed my ability to stay present and aware.

I don't know how long we sat there, Papa droning on, Margaret lying on the floor with her eyes shut tight, and me trying to memorize the feelings I was having, knowing it might never happen again—that moment in time—when Mama could ride back in on a storm and penetrate the physical dimension enough to be there in the room once again. I think I was in a kind of shock; everything around me had that heightened, crystal-clear precision and detail often present during peak experiences and communions.

I was caught between never wanting it to end, because it was so alive and wondrous, and wishing it would dissipate quickly, because it was almost too much to bear. I—who often hang out in imaginative and etheric realms, and find such habitats very suitable and fine—suddenly could not tolerate the dreamy intangibilities of those kingdoms a minute longer. I was filled with an insatiable longing for the shapes and forms and sounds of my earthly mother. I wanted to see her standing in the room, brushing the dirt off her corduroy skirt, leaning over to stroke our dog Happy New Year's head, laughing at Papa with that amused little chuckle in her voice she often had when she was pleased with the way things were. I wanted her home. Period.

But such longings are always the ache of the ones left behind—the intolerable emptiness that will not be filled. Though I do wonder if dead people have longings too, to be back in the world of form for awhile, to eat ripe tomatoes off a blue willow plate, to hear the gulls screech above pounding surf, or to sniff gingerbread baking on a gray winter's day. I do wonder if this is so.

Papa stopped reading and looked up. The wind was a whisper, and the rain, only a drip, drip, drip upon the roof. As we listened in silence, the thunderclaps rolled away, their power muted by distance. A quietness settled on the eaves and the forest, and the cold air dissipated as quickly as it had come. I felt bereft with its going, and wanted to shout out for Mama to stay, but I hated to break the spell of silence that wrapped us all in its blessing.

Margaret suddenly sat up and, gazing first at Papa and then at me, said she had something to tell us. She looked a little sheepish, but she went ahead.

"When I called this morning and you told me you had left breakfast out for Mama [Papa and I had, as an offering], I didn't know what to think. So I asked Mama to give me a sign that she was really still around and could hear us speak to her. I told her I would really believe she still existed if she could make it rain, or something, thinking that would be quite a feat, since today was so hot and sunny." She gave us a funny little smile. "Well, I guess she did what I asked her."

I wanted to jump up and dance. This was just too good to be true. I had so wanted Maggie to believe Mama was not dead and gone for good, because she missed her so much and had been so depressed and lonely all year. What a lovely thing—to ask for proof and to receive it in such a specific and special way. Mama had not only made it rain—she had brought thunder, lightning, and wind as well, just in case Margaret had any lingering doubts on the matter!

Later that evening, Nancy called from Asheville, North Carolina. And guess what? A thunderstorm had happened there as well, right at the time of Mama's death. She had felt an enormous sense of comfort and was calling to tell us so.

―――――――――

I have heard many stories of birds, butterflies, and other phenomena, like the electromagnetic energy of Mama's storm, showing up as emissaries from the dead, especially in the first days and months after a person's crossing. Some will argue that it is wishful thinking on the part of the living, and imaginations gone awry from grief and trouble. So be it. Perhaps heartbreak opens our eyes to patterns and connections we were unable to notice before. Perhaps intelligences of the natural world are more attuned to us than we ever imagine or allow, enough to want to collaborate with someone newly dead and to bring a ray of hope and reassurance to the living. This is another story of such co-creation and love.

Evada's Gift

Evada was only thirteen when she died tragically in a car crash on I-5 near Mount Vernon, Washington. She was in her sister's car on the way to visit their father in Seattle. In Mali's attempt to avoid a vehicle that had drifted too close, her tire caught a soft spot on the edge of the freeway and her car flipped into the center median. Mali survived; Evada was killed instantly. She died one week before Michaelmas, where she was to portray Joan of Arc in her class play.

It was 1995 and none of us were actively involved yet in home funerals. But Evada's mother Heidi Kay and her stepfather Kent Ratekin were Anthroposophical and were part of the Waldorf community in Bellingham. They were determined to bring Evada home for a three-day vigil, following Rudolf Steiner's indications about how to care for a young person after sudden death.

In those days it was virtually impossible to get a hospital to release a body to the family, especially if the death involved an accident, with police reports and autopsies and a lot of red tape and hoops to jump through. (This is still true in many places, but the situation is slowly changing, thanks to the tireless efforts of so many in the home funeral movement, especially Lee Webster, past president of the National Home Funeral Alliance—see chapter 7.)

Kent's refusal to take no for an answer was admirable. He knew his rights, and he was not giving in. He finally managed to find a funeral director who agreed to go and get Evada and transport her body to a friend's Victorian house in Bellingham, where the vigil was set up in a small room at the top of the stairs. This was a coup in those days, and we learned that courage and conviction go a long way in guaranteeing our rights to care for our own dead, even after an accident. I consider Kent and Heidi early pioneers of the home funeral movement, and I honor all that they did to care for Evada during such a tragic and difficult time.

On the third day of Evada's vigil, I drove up with my friend Asha to sit next to the open casket, and to sing and be present with our young friend for awhile. We could not see Evada because she was wrapped in a body bag, but I will never forget what it felt like to reach out and feel the contours of her head and shoulders. Though the body was kept on dry ice for the three days, I could still smell the sweet odor of death, present because of the September heat and her condition after the accident.

This was my first visceral encounter with a dead body, close in, and it was a teaching for me. I remember vividly the wondering faces of Evada's Waldorf classmates and teacher, all packed into the room around the casket, sitting close and whispering, writing messages and tucking them around her, as if they knew their classmate needed such tickets of love and support for the long and unknown journey ahead. When their teacher led them in song, the young people's voices filled the room with life and enthusiasm, though many were singing through their tears. Such life forces fell upon Evada's still and broken form like a healing remedy. Steiner's teachings that the soul stays around for a time felt very real to me in those moments. I could feel Evada so strongly in the room, as if she were listening, even joining in. This idea was also substantiated in another magical way that became part of Evada's legendary crossing, part of her special gift to us all.

When Asha and I were driving up to Bellingham from our island, we stopped at a local farm stand to get flowers. We got separated and when we got back to the car, we smiled because we had both purchased big, golden sunflowers, thinking their bright boldness was a perfect offering for Evada. When we arrived at the house, Heidi opened the door and laughed out loud, turning so we could see the rest of the room. There stood vases of sunflowers—every kind imaginable. It seems we were not alone in our strong urge to bring what turned out to be Evada's favorite flower. Everyone else had as well! And the most compelling thing was Heidi's own story. The day before, she had walked out into the garden of the house where Evada lay in state, to be alone for a time. There, right in the middle of the rose garden, towered a huge, radiant sunflower, nodding at her in greeting. Heidi asked the woman of the house if she had planted the flower, or if it was a volunteer, and it turned out that no one had ever seen it before that day.

The idea that Evada could somehow influence us to buy sunflowers for her vigil, and that a tall sunflower could appear in a rose garden to greet and console her mother, is a fine example of the convergence and communication possible between human beings and nature at death's threshold.

Evada seemingly managed to penetrate the physical dimension one more time in my presence weeks later. Because she had been interested in Buddhism, my sangha practiced for her consciousness on the forty-ninth day after her death. Her photograph was placed on the altar, her dark, lively eyes gazing out at us like an invitation, even a dare. At one point during the Xitro practice, the photograph seemed to leap off the altar, tumbling to the floor. There was no gust of wind or movement of other altar objects to make it fall. We all just shrugged, laughed, and kept on with the practice, acknowledging Evada's audacious spirit, welcoming her presence once again, and loving and blessing her way.

All Creatures Great and Small: Animals and Home Vigils

It is often our relationship with animals, and usually our pets, that gives us the strongest experience of connection and partnering with other creatures at the threshold of death. Home funeral vigils are a natural container and opportunity for our animals to participate in our final days. In addition, many people are now creating home vigils for their beloved pets as a way to honor them and to have enough time to grieve and say goodbye. The following stories express these special ways of relating with our animals at the end of life.

My father Harold Francis was aptly named. He had a way with animals that always reminded us of Saint Francis, who tamed wild wolves and carried crumbs in the pockets of his robes for sparrows and hares and the stray dogs who followed him everywhere. Papa was the same. He laughingly tolerated squirrels gnawing through the window screens and brazenly bounding across his bedcovers. Once, when Nancy opened the lid of the compost bin in the kitchen and gasped in horror at the maggots crawling inside, he simply shrugged and said, "Everybody's gotta live somewhere, sugar." I remember my father tenderly carrying daddy longlegs outside and shooing the spindly creatures on their way; and many mornings standing in Mama's rock garden in his nightshirt, feeding the finches and blue jays and cardinals who flocked around him in the dappled forest light.

Dogs were Papa's dearest companions, in life and in death. When we set Papa's body up in the dining room of our log cabins, his dog Joy came in and lay down beneath the cherry wood casket. She kept vigil with her friend throughout the three days—her head on her paws, her eyes deep and sorrowful. Sometimes, though, she would forget and in the moment stay true to her name, thumping her tail with irrepressible energy, and sending messages of reassurance and thanks to her beloved one, lying in state above her.

On the third day, when we all gathered to wish our father farewell, the circle of our family stretched round the room. Four daughters and a son, spouses, and grandchildren there to honor the man whose life and loves were the reason we were all standing there. We numbered fifteen. Amongst us we had five more dogs, though they were roaming around in the kitchen, barred from the room for our ceremony, since the space was so close and small. Only Joy was allowed in, to keep watch in her normal place beneath the casket.

We read Papa's favorite passages from *The Book of Common Prayer*; Eliza and I sang "Wondrous Love"; stories were shared. I remember we spontaneously held hands and sang "Amazing Grace" to bring things to a close. As our voices rose in the room, the doors from the kitchen and hallway burst open, and all the other dogs rushed in, running madly around and around Papa, barking and howling with abandon. They were singing too, insisting that Papa's send-off could not happen without them. Indeed.

The men of our family lifted Papa up and carefully navigated the log cabin's low doorways, through the kitchen to the screen porch and out into the crisp blue of a November day. Branches in Papa's trees waved back and forth in the wind, and leaves fell all around us as we carried our father away from his home for the last time. I made my way to the van, for it was my job to drive Papa to town for his cremation. Some of the others would accompany me; some remained home to fix lunch and dismantle the vigil space.

As the men slid the casket inside the back of the van, Joy appeared suddenly from the kitchen, running down the stone flagged path, panting as if she might not make it in time. Though her legs chronically hurt, without a moment's hesitation she leaped up into the van and, climbing farther still, settled herself right on top of the cherry wood casket. Her eyes bright with purpose and determination, she wagged her tail and seemed to nod to me that I could now close the door. Thus it was that Papa's loyal dog Joy rode with him all the way to the crematorium, and only when we wheeled his body inside did she release her vigil and care.

Keisha

Keisha was a star child, a dog from another dimension. My friend Fanny and I always said so. She was first the pet of Fanny's ex-husband, and later her son. But Keisha and Fanny were fated to be together, so in time, Fanny found herself Keisha's keeper—a demanding but worthwhile adventure that spanned many years, many moves, many twists and turns together. Keisha was always by Fanny's side. They would carry on conversations, Fanny calling Keisha's name in her lilting Swedish way, like a song, and Keisha responding, her body shivering and dancing with delight.

One day I called Fanny to come visit, and she told me sadly that Keisha was ready to die, eager to return home to her world. Fanny was going to take her dear dog to the vet, but she wasn't sure about cremation. She thought Keisha would prefer burial, so a friend was coming by the next day to make that happen.

I told Fanny I would help her have a vigil, that doing so might really support her choice and ease the transition of losing her friend. Fanny had experienced vigils before with human beings, but never with a pet. She was grateful—eager to give this final gift to her loyal companion.

I was there when Fanny drove up, and we carried Keisha's heavy, lifeless body to the porch. Keisha remained outside while we arranged a small table covered in a beautiful cloth in Fanny's living room, beneath a gilded mirror that shone golden in the light of many candles. We brought Keisha inside and carefully placed her on her royal bed, surrounding her with bracken ferns and flowers from Fanny's abundant garden—buttery roses, purple rhododendron, and rosemary for remembrance. The room sparkled and shone, mirroring Keisha's bright effervescent spirit and love.

Fanny invited two friends, Philip and Brett, to join us in our ceremony, since they were both pals of Keisha's. While Keisha lay in the shimmering darkness, we four enjoyed Hungarian goulash and red wine and spoke of many things together. Afterward, we gathered around Keisha, some sitting on the floor, others in chairs pulled up close. Fanny began the ceremony by reading aloud emails of love and goodbye that many of Keisha's human friends had sent from afar. She had made all the messages into a decorated scroll, which she was going to keep as a special remembrance of Keisha's time here on earth. I sang a part of a Buddhist Xitro chant for the dead, imagining purifying light washing away any residue of pain or confusion Keisha might have picked up during her transition at the vet. Philip sang songs, funny ones he had sung to Keisha many times. Brett read Baudelaire's poetry in French and spoke of his gratitude to be able to share such space with each of us, and with Keisha especially. We basked in the warmth and generosity of our shared remembrances.

Keisha was pleased. We all knew this to be true. And so were we all. We left that night deeply nourished, grateful that we could create a vigil for Fanny's beloved pet, happy that Keisha received such a fine and fitting send-off to her land and home in the stars. The next day Keisha's body was buried beneath the lilac trees, where Fanny's rabbits hop back and forth over the grave, and hens cluck consoling little songs to themselves, missing their dear doggy friend.

Practical Wisdom: Co-Creating with Nature: An Exploration

The Practical Wisdom section of this chapter explores in greater depth some of the ideas in the stories I have shared here. The explorations are my own, and are part of my personal journey to answer the question: *What does it mean to partner or co-create with nature at the threshold of death?* They are offerings, not answers—open to each person's individual understanding of what it means to be human, and to live in relationship with the webs of sentient life all around us. I trust that you will find your own answers, your own insights and ways of knowing, ways that work for you. If my ruminations are not your "cup of tea," please just skip the Practical Wisdom section and move on to the next chapter about green burial and giving your body back to the earth when you die. But please read the following practical and essential section before you go.

Choosing a home vigil is partnering with nature, because we can be real and ourselves, and we can care for our dead in simple, natural ways. We use dry ice or other coolant materials to preserve the body instead of toxic embalming chemicals, and we let nature have her way, honoring that all living things die, all is impermanent. Spending time with the dead—touching, bathing, and dressing the stiff corpse of someone we love—can bring us to our knees, closer to our bodies and feelings, closer to one another, closer to the earth. We partner with nature in our willingness to simply be present with death once again, letting its power inform and guide us.

The other very important way we can partner with the earth and nature is to choose more ecological ways to dispose of our bodies when we die—ways that do not add to the toxicity and pollution of the environment, but contribute back to the cycles of life in organic and regenerative ways. Up until now, such choices have not been readily available, making it difficult to align our environmentally sound ways of living with choices we make for after-death care. Conventional burial, with its use of embalming chemicals, metal or endangered-wood caskets, concrete vaults, and lawn chemicals, is a practice that simply cannot continue if we are going to be sustainable in our ways of doing death. Even cremation, with its heavy dependence on fossil fuels, and its spewing of mercury and harmful dioxin emissions, sulfur, and carbon dioxide into the air, is not a viable option for a future where we are in the midst of climate change and the urgent need to develop different sources of energy.

Green burial, especially conservation burial, where we are protecting and restoring land that might otherwise be destroyed or developed, is a vital practice we are reclaiming today. More than 60 percent of people surveyed about natural burial said they would choose this option if it is available at the time of their deaths. And there are other, more ecological disposition options on the horizon as well, which I will explore in chapter 9. All these choices are restorative ways to partner with the earth and nature when we die.

My stories are portals of possibility: that nature is participating in our journeys at the end of life in ways we might not have imagined, and that we can call upon both the physical and subtle kingdoms of the earth to aid us as we navigate death's unknown and demanding territories. Our need to "come to our senses" and recover direct perception and experience, rather than live and inhabit only conceptual abstractions of our minds, is part of returning to more natural ways of caring for our dead, and learning to partner or co-create with nature and death itself once again. The following is my attempt to articulate further what this means to me.

I have so far used the word "partnering" more than the term "co-creating," as the latter is not one that most people have heard or can relate to easily. And yet, I explore "co-creation" intentionally here, as the concept invites a certain kind of relationship, one that sees the possibility of consciously creating with nature and the earth in new and emergent ways. This is a potent reimagination of what is possible in our lives and our deaths, and so worthy of inclusion here.

Such a view understands that the earth and the natural world are consciously aware and intelligent—capable of interacting and working with human beings, indeed doing so all the time, despite how oblivious most people are of this connection. To co-create means to craft together, to work and play as equal partners in manifesting something that might not happen without such collaboration. I will go further and say "without shared intention and love." In my experience, co-creation works best through an "I-Thou" relationship, where communication springs from love, respect, and communion, and where each separate consciousness views the "other" not as an object, but as sacred and essential to the shared task at hand.

I first encountered the idea of co-creation with nature in the late 1970s, when a book called *The Findhorn Garden* literally fell off a top shelf and hit me on the head in the stacks of a university library. I was twenty-three years old. Findhorn is a spiritual community in the north of Scotland where people seek to recover what native cultures and seers have never lost—the capacity to communicate with the intelligences of the natural world—with devas and elementals, with spirits of plants, animals, and land, in order to address the ecological and spiritual crises of our modern times. I remember sliding down to the floor in the stacks—my hands trembling, my heart pounding in anticipation, as if some part of me had waited all my life for that defining moment. And when I opened the book, I understood why.

People from all walks of life and places were joining together to explore a burgeoning wave of new spiritual consciousness surfacing collectively in the hearts and minds of many around the world. This was a planetary consciousness that saw the earth as a living being, with a biosphere of interactive systems that created a self-regulating, whole organism, Gaia. Our evolution was Gaia's, and we were being asked to partner with, to co-create with, the earth in conscious, intentional ways for the health and well-being of all. Though indigenous peoples had never lost this understanding, we were on a different turn of the spiral, an unknown emergent place that invited shared exploration and collaboration in the present moment and time. This was a collective knowing, becoming part of scientific circles for the first time—as the Gaia hypothesis, and later, when it was accepted, the Gaia theory. Sitting on the floor of the library stacks,

I knew, without knowing how or why, that I had found my tribe on the planet. It was as if a doorway opened inside and another part of me stepped forward, laughing and welcoming me home.

While I was at Findhorn, I was fortunate to spend time with Dorothy Maclean, whose work communicating with the devas—or the overlighting consciousness and intelligence of plant species, animals, mountains, and land—influences my life to this day. I also had the great blessing to connect with David Spangler and his body of teachings on Incarnational Spirituality, brought forward through the Lorian Association over the last fifty years. David and my fellow Lorians have given me the clearest understanding of what it means to be both a human being and a planetary being. Such understanding helps us be interdependent stewards, consciously working with the natural world and its subtle realms as partners and allies, and with the earth/Gaia as a living, loving consciousness with whom we are always in relationship and communion. (See the Resources section for further exploration.)

It is one of the cornerstones of David's Incarnational Spirituality that our human lives reach far beyond what we are taught or imagine. We are actually more an Incarnational Field—a multidimensional sphere of wholeness, woven from all the connections we have and are as human beings. Think of your life as a field of relationships—all that you came in with, your genes, your DNA, the kind of body you have, your ancestors, and your family. And then imagine all the relationships you have formed in your life, known and unknown, and add those to the tapestry. And all that you pay attention to, and spend energy cultivating with love—relationships with your job, your house, your garden, your pets, your community. These are all part of your Incarnational Field, your wholeness.

But there is more to our incarnations than meets the eye, so to speak. Our Incarnational Fields encompass what David calls the first and second ecologies of life on this planet. The first ecology is the intricacies and wonders of matter and the physical world, in all its complexity of forms and intelligence. The second ecology is the myriad subtle realms of energy and consciousness that interface with the first ecology, but are not often seen, recognized, or acknowledged as being an integral part of who we are. This way of understanding helps us see that, as human beings, we are both wondrously unique, particular, and individual, and at the same time interdependently woven within the collective web of all other sentient life, seen and unseen, on this planet. Buddhism shares this kind of perspective and view, as do other faiths, especially the mystical side of spiritual traditions. Scientists, especially biologists, ecologists, and quantum physicists, are making valuable contributions to these ideas.

My mother's death illustrates the idea of Incarnational Fields most clearly for me. Mama cultivated a vibrant and loving relationship with her mountain land for years. All the creatures and life of our home place, all the things she cherished and held sacred, all that she consciously cultivated and paid attention to, became part of her Incarnational Field: the log cabins she created; her wildflower garden with jack-in-the-pulpit, bloodroot, and ginger; the nature beings from the rocks and ridges; Christ and the angels she loved and taught about at her church. These were part of the potent and complex fabric of who she was. When Mama needed to leave her body behind, these relationships—the warp and weft threads of her unique life's tapestry (which apparently included thunder and lightning and wild elemental forces!)—all showed up and participated in her death in wondrous ways.

This idea of our lives being Incarnational Fields has helped me work at the threshold of death with greater understanding and clarity about all the different ways that we die, and about who and what shows up at a person's threshold. It gives me a context in which to view the interesting appearances from the natural world that occurred in the stories I have shared so far—like Papa and his bees, and Evada and her sunflowers. If we are paying attention, we can sometimes see these larger patterns in a person's life. And we can always affirm a person's essential wholeness, no matter how bleak and broken they may seem, or how hard their lives and deaths might be. We can observe and practice "holy listening," consciously seeking the sacred in all aspects of a person's life and death. This kind of awareness is very helpful when creating a home vigil or memorial service, for it guides us to create something that captures the uniqueness and authenticity of that person's life, in ways that are honoring and true.

I included this chapter because I feel each day how diminished our human lives are, and our deaths, without a living connection to the natural world. Though, as human beings, we *are* nature, so many people do not think about or cultivate this relationship consciously, nor do they view it as worthy of their attention and care. To have an "I-Thou" reverent connection with plants and animals and land is foreign to many people today. They do not understand such ways. Nor do they inhabit their bodies or felt sense of things, so that they are increasingly cut off from direct perception and experience, identifying only with abstractions and conceptual worlds within the mind. And, with the rise of technological innovation and virtual realities, this habitual pattern will only be strengthened in the future. Children of today are growing up with this kind of modeling, deprived of nature and direct experience, cut off from the very source of who they are as human beings. (Please refer to the Resources section for this chapter for books that support embodiment and a living dialogue with earth and nature.)

No wonder our deaths are difficult and traumatic. We are afraid, and we struggle, because we are not aware of the larger dimensions of our lives. And we have not cultivated a conscious and sacred relationship with our bodies and nature and all that can sustain and guide us when we die. Think of the stark and sterile ways most of us are dying, hooked up to machines and separated from all that could make our crossings more peaceful and bearable, more human.

So I always seek ways to remedy this situation when I can, and to help others do the same. It has been my experience that when nature is invited to participate, or is acknowledged and included in some way at the threshold of death, greater well-being is possible. Nature can be a leavening, balancing force within the hard, demanding labor always present in letting go. This can be as simple as opening a window to let fresh air and sunshine enter a stale and stuffy room. Or bringing a single green and growing plant to a person dying in a room devoid of life and comfort, as one of my friends knew to do.

I heard recently of a group of young people whose friend was hovering between worlds in a hospital and could not die. After failing to get permission to take the dying man outside on the grounds, where the air was fresh and cherry trees were blooming, the group persuaded a nurse to let them bring nature inside to him. They surrounded their friend with cherry blossom, cedar, and lichen and with rich humus from his vegetable garden at home. Within moments of receiving these gifts from nature, the young man came out of a coma, smiled, and took his last breath, letting go of this world, without any residue of his former struggle and pain.

We can insist that our mother be brought home to die, so she can be close to her garden and grandchildren. We can claim our brother's body from the hospital and bring him to the house for a time, surrounding him with all that he loved in life—apple blossom and aged cheese, his grumpy cat, his favorite flannel shirt, and voices from the kitchen, telling stories of his days. We can lay our only child in the ground and plant on top of her the salmonberries and huckleberries she loved in life, willing, praying that their roots grow down deep to keep her company there, and that the plants flourish and grow strong because our child can no longer do so herself.

Cultivating a living, loving dialogue with the natural world, and bringing that communion to the threshold of death, in whatever ways feel right to us, open many doors of possibility. We have seen this in the stories I've shared with you here. One wonderful potential is that we will discover a living, loving dialogue and communion with Death itself once again, so that we can live our lives closer to the bone, closer to the joyful heart of things, closer to the sacred wholeness of who we really are.

4

"BURY ME NATURALLY": Stories and Guidance for Green Burials

Take from me all earthly raiment and place me deep in my

Mother Earth; and place me with care upon my mother's
breast.

Cover me with soft earth, and let each handful be mixed

With seeds of jasmine, lilies and myrtle; and when they

Grow above me, and thrive on my body's element they will

Breathe the fragrance of my heart into space;

And reveal even to the sun the secret of my peace;

And sail with the breeze and comfort the wayfarer.

—KHALIL GIBRAN, "The Beauty of Death" XIV

*I*t is fitting that I open this chapter with a story of my first shroud burial, as it marks the beginning of my professional involvement in the green/natural burial movement. I had been part of simple burials in my community before that day, and active in helping our little local cemetery become "hybrid/green." But this was different. I was helping a family choose a shroud burial, as a funeral director within the industry, an option that was rarely available at the time. The experience my colleague Lindsay Soyer and I had that day captures so many elements of the beauty and gifts available when we reimagine how to bury our dead, and when we participate more creatively in natural dispositions once again.

A Shroud Burial for Theresa

It was a glorious morning when Lindsay and I drove up to the rural island cemetery where we were to hold our first shroud burial. We were funeral director interns at the time, for A Sacred Moment Funeral Services in Everett, Washington. The sun was shining, matching our excitement and taking the edge off chilly spring breezes that gusted off the water and over the bluffs. I was so happy to be able to show Lindsay the magnificent view that graced the old burial place.

To the west—the majestic Olympic Mountains, purple in the morning mist. To the east—Mount Baker, seemingly solitary and snow-capped, but connected to the Cascades range that fans out like an edge of lace beyond the rich earth of central Whidbey's farmlands. And Mount Rainier, or Tahoma-la, rising in the south as the great guardian spirit it is for the Puget Sound area. Below the bluff the Salish Sea, whose waves beat against the rocky beach, its cold waters catching the light and tossing it to the winds. We were thrilled to be there and to be part of helping Theresa have her dying wish—to be buried only in a shroud, in a simple "honoring the earth" green burial.

It was a good thing that Lindsay and I arrived early, as the grave was filled with roots that protruded far enough to snag a shroud being lowered into the ground. How we managed to remove those roots is a story in itself, one Lindsay and I still laugh about to this day. Suffice it to say here, we managed to remove the hindrances before the family arrived.

I was relieved when the car door opened, and the man who would conduct Theresa's Catholic funeral stepped out. We were expecting a priest who might not approve of Theresa's request to be buried only in a linen shroud, without the normal cement vault, or any of the fancy fittings a lot of Roman Catholic burials include. Father Thomas was a far cry from my expectations. He was dressed in a striking pink linen suit, and his face lit up in a smile when he saw the family and hurried over to shake their hands and hug those he knew. In one moment, everyone seemed to relax and rest in Father Thomas, including Lindsay and me, who just a half hour before had been frantically removing protruding roots from Theresa's grave and wondering if we were going to be ready before everyone arrived.

When Father Thomas came over to meet us, he was carrying two cast iron poles with little lanterns dangling from the tops. "I wanted to bring light to Theresa's day," he said, smiling. He was already doing that himself, with his brightness and enthusiasm. I knew then he was the perfect person to officiate at Theresa's green burial.

Theresa's body was still in the van, and there were a few details to attend to with the family. We wheeled her out on the gurney, and I untied the center knot of her linen shroud so that Theresa's daughter could place a nosegay into the little pouch that nestled next to Theresa's heart. Someone else presented a tiny teddy bear, and we retied the knot of the shroud with the bear inside. I invited everyone to gather round and tuck flowers in the folds of the shroud to add color and beauty. Some were shy about doing this. It was a new and rather startling experience to see someone wrapped only in linen, rather than enclosed in a casket. The contours of Theresa's body were so visible. There was no mistaking that we were adorning a dead body. Some people were unable to participate. Others joined in without hesitation, tucking red and pink carnations, freesias, daffodils, and daisies among the folds.

The men of the family were to carry Theresa's body to the grave, where four simple wooden planks lay across the opening. The body would rest on those planks during the service. The shroud was a natural linen, equipped with a backboard to support the body so it would not droop during carrying or lowering, with long straps sewn into the sides that would be unfurled to lower the body into the grave gracefully. (See the Resources section for the maker of these shrouds.) As the young men carrying Theresa processed slowly toward the grave, Father Thomas walked ahead of them, holding his Bible and holy water.

He told me afterward that he was filled with awe, and thought of Jesus when he first saw Theresa's shrouded body, and that he felt deeply humbled seeing the simple and stark figure resting on the wooden planks, with rich, dark, loamy soil below, and clover and grass creating a luminous green frame around the edges of her grave. "I knew then I had to speak about returning Theresa to our Mother Earth, in ways we used to know and are reclaiming."

Father Thomas kept his word and did speak of the earth as our Mother, and of giving our bodies back to her at death. It was healing for me to hear a Catholic priest honoring the earth—as if those few moments could transform centuries of denial of the body and of nature perpetrated by the Church. (I have since learned that the Catholic Church is leading the country in creating green burial cemeteries and promoting this more natural form of disposition. This is very encouraging.) Father Thomas's words were authentic and real. And they carried a sense of encouragement and acceptance that came from the man himself, and how he spoke and addressed the grieving family and friends. He was there for them in their sorrow, but he radiated a kind of confidence and conviction that all was as it should be. I remember watching an eagle fly over the bluff, its wings catching the midday light and reflecting it back to us all, its piercing cry echoing off the hills, honoring our sacred time together.

JAKE SENIUK'S LAST ART INSTALLATION

"Jake Lying in State at Home." Courtesy of Tristan Seniuk and family.

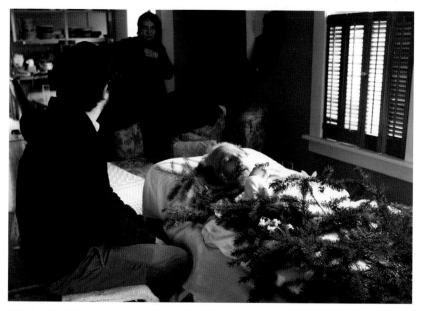

"Undertaking." Courtesy of Tristan Seniuk and Donna James.

PREPARING JAKE FOR NATURAL BURIAL

"Jake and His Mushroom Shroud." Courtesy of Tristan Seniuk and family.

"Sons and Friends Lowering Jake into Green Grave." The Meadow, Ferndale, Washington. Courtesy of Tristan Seniuk and family.

PAINTING CASKETS DURING HOME VIGILS

"Painting the Casket at Home." Courtesy of Olivia Bareham / Sacred Crossings.

"Boys Decorating Vahe's Casket." Courtesy of Olivia Bareham / Sacred Crossings.

ERIC IVAN FIELD'S HOME VIGIL

"Eric Home from the Hospital Hours after His Death." Courtesy of Eric Field's family.

"A Friend Built the Pine Casket and Then Word Went Out to the Community for Anyone to Come and Decorate It." Courtesy of Eric Field's family.

"Eric and His Son Loren."
Courtesy of Eric Field's family.

"Eric's Sacred Space near the Window."
Courtesy of Eric Field's family.

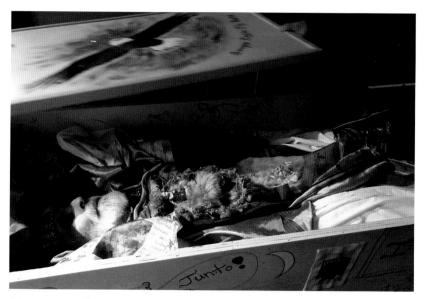

"Eric Was Dressed in Garments He Had Worn in Ceremony in Africa and Placed in His Casket with Messages, Sacred Items, and a Wreath His Wife Wore at Their Wedding."
Courtesy of Eric Field's family.

"Fanny and Keisha at Keisha's Home Vigil."
Courtesy of Fanny Porter and Keisha.

"Lisa and Her Beloved Dog Clover at Her Home Vigil."
Courtesy of Olivia Bareham and Lisa Schiavello.

JEANNE AND DOROTHY

"Jeanne Caring for Her Mother Dorothy at Home." Courtesy of the Lepisto family.

"Dorothy's Handmade Casket and Green Burial." Courtesy of the Lepisto family.

"Jeanne at Her Mother's Graveside Service." Courtesy of Deborah Koff-Chapin, artist/photographer.

LEONARD DANIEL HAMBY'S NATURAL BURIAL

"Leonard Daniel Hamby's Daughter Eliza-beth at His Natural Burial." Ramsey Creek Preserve. Courtesy of Dara Ashworth and family.

"Leonard Daniel Hamby's Shroud Burial." Ramsey Creek Preserve. Courtesy of Dara Ashworth and family.

"Hannah, the Family Dog, Died the Morning after Leonard 'Treat Man Dan' Was Buried. Kimberly Campbell of Ramsey Creek Kindly Buried Hannah next to L. Daniel Hamby So They Could Be Together in Death, as in Life." Courtesy of Dara Ashworth and family.

RAMSEY CREEK PRESERVE

"Entrance to Ramsey Creek Preserve, First Conservation Burial Preserve in North America, Established by Dr. Billy and Kimberley Campbell in 1996." Photo by John Christian Phifer / Courtesy of JCP and Ramsey Creek Preserve, Westminster, South Carolina.

"Ramsey Creek Natural Burial Headstone." Photo by John Christian Phifer / Courtesy of JCP and Ramsey Creek Preserve, Westminster, South Carolina.

PRAIRIE CREEK CONSERVATION CEMETERY/ HEARTWOOD PRESERVE

"A Shroud Burial at Prairie Creek Conservation Cemetery, Gainesville, Florida." Photo by Melissa K. Hill/Courtesy of Prairie Creek Conservation Cemetery.

"Metal Disc Used to Mark Plots in Grid System at Heartwood Preserve." Trinity, Florida. Photo by Andrea Ragan/Courtesy of AR and Laura Starkey of Heartwood Preserve.

LARKSPUR CONSERVATION/
KOKOSING NATURE PRESERVE

"Sapling Casket, Larkspur Conservation."Taylor Hollow, Tennessee. Courtesy of John Christian Phifer, executive director of Larkspur Conservation.

"Flower Pathway at Kokosing Nature Preserve Burial Ground, Gambier, Ohio."
Courtesy of Heidi Hannapel and Jeff Masten of Landmatters.

ESTHER SUTIN'S BURIAL/
ELOISE WOODS NATURAL BURIAL PARK

"Ellen Macdonald Reads Love Notes at Her
Mother Esther Sutin's Service."

"Love Notes around Esther Sutin."

"Grave Marker for Esther Sutin's Natural Burial."
All photographs are courtesy of Ellen Macdonald, owner of Eloise Woods Natural Burial Park,
Cedar Creek, Texas.

WHITE EAGLE MEMORIAL PRESERVE

"Shroud Burial in Winter." White Eagle Memorial Preserve. Goldendale, Washington. Courtesy of Jodie Buller and the Fink family, White Eagle Memorial Preserve.

"White Eagle Shroud Burial." Courtesy of Jodie Buller and the Fink family, White Eagle Memorial Preserve.

"Director Jodie Buller Making a Grave Beautiful before Natural Burial." Courtesy of Jodie Buller, White Eagle Memorial Preserve.

THE MEADOW NATURAL BURIAL GROUND

"A Procession with Shrouded Body on Caisson." Courtesy of Brian Flowers, The Meadow Natural Burial Ground at Greenacres Memorial Park, Ferndale, Washington.

"An Early Green Burial at the Meadow Natural Burial Ground." Courtesy of Brian Flowers, The Meadow Natural Burial Ground at Greenacres Memorial Park, Ferndale, Washington.

BIODEGRADABLE CASKET AND SHROUDS

"Biodegradable Wicker Casket/Hand-Dug Grave at Steelmantown Cemetery, South Jersey."
Courtesy of Edward Bixby, proprietor.

"Theresa's Shroud Burial (Cover of the Book)." Courtesy of Lindsay Soyer, photographer.

"Beautiful Shroud Burial at Eloise Woods Natural Burial Park." Courtesy of Ellen Macdonald, owner.

JUDY'S HOME VIGIL

"*Mother and Daughter, Judy's Home Vigil.*"
Courtesy of Lynn Hays, artist/photographer.

"*Judy's Goodbye.*" *Courtesy of Lynn Hays
artist/photographer.*

"*1,000 Paper Cranes from Judy's Elementary Students.*" *Courtesy of Lynn Hays,
artist/photographer.*

"*Painting Judy's Casket.*" *Courtesy of Shanti
Lousteneau, artist/photographer.*

I remember also, at the time of committal, that Father Thomas seemed strongly aware of the need to hold the family energetically, as some pulled the planks away and others hesitantly lowered Theresa's body down into the earth. He told me later how moving it was for him to see the tenderness with which the young men lowered Theresa down, and the sheer beauty of flowers and rose petals falling from many hands upon her silent form. (Theresa's shroud burial is on the cover of this book.)

It was quiet and peaceful after everyone departed. Lindsay and I waited for George the gravedigger to come down to fill in the grave. Part of our service is to make sure that a grave is closed properly, and I never leave until every aspect of that work is completed. We heard a loud engine start up and saw a huge backhoe, its shovel piled high with dirt, come rumbling down the hill toward us. I was immediately concerned. Theresa's body looked so vulnerable down in the grave. It just didn't feel right to dump a heavy mass of dirt on top of her all at once. I had never experienced a shroud burial before, and I was surprised how visceral my reaction was. It seemed so brutal, unlike when a body is surrounded and protected by a closed casket. I suddenly wanted to fill in the grave by hand.

But the backhoe was almost upon us, and I didn't feel I could ask George, who is getting on in years, and his son Casey to spend hours helping us fill in Theresa's grave ourselves. Plus Lindsay and I had to get back to the office that afternoon. It wasn't realistic. So I didn't say anything when the gravediggers got out and made their way over to where we were standing.

"George and Casey, since you've never seen a shroud burial, have a look. It's quite something, and so beautiful with all the flowers," I said, moving away so they could have a closer view. I wanted them to understand through direct experience what it was like to have a natural burial, without the concrete vaults and heavy caskets they were used to handling.

Both George and Casey just stood there, peering down into the grave for the longest time. Neither one of them said anything.

Finally George said quietly, "This is the way they did things with Jesus, having a shroud and all."

I nodded, wishing I could seize the moment and ask if we could fill in the grave by hand. But I knew it was too much to ask.

Then, to my amazement, George voiced the thought himself: "Let's fill in the grave a little bit ourselves first. We can't do the whole thing, but at least we won't be dumping that big pile of dirt on her body right away. Casey, go get those shovels we've got in the back."

I discovered a whole other side of my crusty old gravedigger friend that day: a sensitive, tender side and a felt sense that told him bringing his big backhoe in right away wasn't the best way to go about things after all. These men—the gravediggers and Father Thomas—helped me know that caring for our own dead in more simple and natural ways is an instinctive capacity we still have within us. Choosing green burial can help us awaken that innate wisdom once again.

Where Have All the Flowers Gone?

My next story is in deliberate contrast to Theresa's. It illustrates the difference between natural and conventional (modern) burial practices, and the environmental oblivion or blatant disregard present today in many cemeteries, and within the funeral industry as a whole.

I got to the cemetery early to meet with the sexton and assess where family members should park. As far as my eye could see, there were row upon row of graves, all with flat square markers that looked like pathways of white stepping stones across a trim and manicured lawn. A sprinkler was shooting water and pesticides over a chosen area of the cemetery. I knew this because the workers trimming the hedge were wearing masks and there was a faint odor drifting toward me in the morning breeze. I was glad that my family's plot was nowhere near that area.

When I arrived at the designated plot, a white tent was already set up on one side of the grave, and metal chairs were placed in rows so the family members could sit during the service. The grave did not look like a grave, more like a mechanical contraption that was there to mask the true purpose of the gathering. Artificial plastic green turf outlined its edges, supposedly to mask the rough cuts where the backhoe had dug; but if that was the purpose, it had an opposite effect on me. This sounds harsh, but it really did look like a cheap framing job on a badly botched project. That, coupled with the metal lowering device that hovered over the grave like a cage, made the entire scene feel strange and unreal—the opposite of a natural burial, where it is so clear that one is there to bury a loved one, because the grave is open and bare and waiting, no concealment or pretense present, just the reality of what is.

The most shocking thing was the vault the family had chosen. The top was lying off to the side, waiting to be put on after the graveside service by the cemetery maintenance crew. I walked over to examine it more closely. It was bronze, or some semblance thereof. Its ruddy tones shone in the sunlight, glinting like a newly minted penny. Only this vault was not purchased with pennies. It must have cost someone a fortune. The rest of the vault had already been lowered in place. Its fine features seemed so incongruous with the rest of the grave, highlighted in plastic and the lowering device's worn and tarnished metal. I thought for a moment of the eons of time that bronze vault was going to stay in the ground, supposedly keeping its person safe and protected from nature's ravaging, decomposing armies of bacteria, insects, and who knows what other dangers.

It was actually the outer fortress for the person being laid to rest. The inner one was the casket itself, soon to arrive to be placed on the lowering device. The family had chosen a stainless-steel, rubber-gasketed casket, meaning that their mother, Patsy, was sealed inside, surrounded by polyester white lace and velvet. The rubber sealing was an additional effort to keep Patsy's body safe and unharmed within.

Before everyone arrived, I spent some time working with my aversion to this type of conventional burial. It would not do for me to stand there with the family with any vestige of criticism or judgment in my heart. They were making choices that were entirely right for them. I knew that, having met with them. They were a wonderful clan who adored their mother and were honoring her wishes. Patsy had planned her whole funeral and burial, and these were the choices she had made. She had done the same for her husband a few years before; now it was her turn.

The ceremony was beautiful, and I found myself wishing I had known the woman who could imagine her own graveside service so vividly and write it down in such detail for her family and minister to follow. That took foresight and courage on Patsy's part, and made everything easier for all concerned. It was admirable. I loved the poetry she had chosen and the music. The whole ceremony was elegant and moving.

When the final benediction and blessing was said, the family stood up from their chairs and moved out from under the tent to speak with others who had gathered round. There were tears and laughter, conversation and hugs. Everyone seemed very pleased with the way things had transpired. I was pleased too, for them. And for Patsy, whose vision and plans and financial means had made it all possible.

It never occurred to the family to remain present during the closing of Patsy's grave. That was the job of the cemetery staff and the funeral director. I promised to remain until the end, as I always do. That closing was such a stark contrast to the natural burial I had experienced only a few weeks prior, where the family lowered their father's wooden casket down themselves with straps, then filled in the grave afterward, shovelful by shovelful, their voices filling the air with stories and song.

A huge crane lifted the bronze vault lid and dropped it into place, hiding Patsy's shining steel, rubber-gasketed casket forever. Then the dirt came, landing on the vault lid in heavy thudding sounds, the screech of the machines slicing the still morning air into fragments—or so it felt to me. I spent my time tearing all the plastic wrap off the bunches of flowers people had brought, and removing the packets of plant food inside, also plastic, knowing all would be taken shortly and thrown into a landfill somewhere.

After the maintenance crew finished, and headed off to lunch, I couldn't help but arrange all those flowers in a lovely mandala on top of Patsy's grave. The brilliant hues of freesias, lilies, carnations, daisies, and delphiniums splashed a ring of brightness and beauty on the barren dirt. It was my gift to Patsy and her family. Then I too took a break. When I returned to make sure all was well, my mandala of flowers was already gone.

—————

Most people are shocked when they hear the statistics of what actually lies beneath the ground in our cemeteries. We bury 827,060 gallons of toxic formaldehyde embalming fluid, enough to fill an Olympic swimming pool *each year;* 2,700 tons of copper and bronze and 90,272 tons of steel from caskets, enough to build a Golden Gate Bridge *each year;* 1.6 million tons of reinforced concrete from burial vaults, which could construct a highway from Denver to St. Louis *each year;* 20 million board feet of hardwoods for caskets—the equivalent of 77,000 trees, many of which are from endangered species of wood, *each year.*[1] Though this sounds extreme, in essence our cemeteries today are toxic landfills, even the ones that are beautifully kept and peaceful and serene on the surface.

I insert these statistics in the midst of my storytelling as a kind of wake-up call.

But I do not want to break up the flow of stories here to delve deeper into a discussion of green burial versus conventional practices.

———

[1] Statistics from Lee Webster, "Green Burial by the Numbers," in *Changing Landscapes: Exploring the Growth of Ethical, Compassionate, and Environmentally Sustainable Green Funeral Service,* ed. Lee Webster (Ojai, CA: Green Burial Council International, 2017), 99.

I will continue this exploration in the Practical Wisdom section, offering ways that people are reimagining how to bury the dead, and reclaiming and discovering new ways to contribute back to the earth and environment, rather than continue to pollute the ground with harmful, toxic, and unsustainable practices. Please feel free to go to the Practical Wisdom section at any time in your reading.

I return to telling stories—this time to illustrate how home funerals and green burials at times need to happen together, to have the best and most seamless experience. This is an important teaching tale for anyone who is thinking about green burial but has not considered the fact that one's body has to reside somewhere until interment can happen. If one wants to avoid being taken to a funeral home, it might be best to plan for a home funeral and green burial together.

In Joy's Way

Margaret's end-of-life plans were all in place—had been for two years, since she was first diagnosed with cancer. But it was Roger, her husband, who suddenly began to decline. Both had purchased green burial plots in our local cemetery. Beyond that, there were no details in place for Roger. I remembered my friend once saying to me that he wasn't that interested in his body being cared for at the house, not knowing how his family would take to the idea of a home funeral. So I had those clues to go on. The trouble was, though, he also did not want to work with any funeral home. This was an interesting dilemma.

Without a home vigil, I was going to have to find somewhere to keep Roger's body while the paperwork was being handled. No one can be legally buried until the doctor signs the death certificate, and it is completed and filed with the local registrar. And until the burial transit permit is obtained, which must be present in the vehicle transporting the deceased to the place of final rest, and given to the cemetery staff before that person can be lowered into the grave.

I knew I could always call upon the services of A Sacred Moment, where I was working at the time as a licensed funeral director. But this was not Roger's first choice, since he liked the idea of family acting as licensed funeral director instead. This meant the family, with my guidance, would be handling the paperwork, which was going to take longer to accomplish—at least one or two days after Roger's death, and maybe longer if he expired on a weekend. So what to do with Roger in the meantime if he could not stay at home?

Again, A Sacred Moment's removal staff could come and get Roger and take his body to our care facility and morgue down in Kent, south of Seattle. But Roger's house was only a few miles away from the cemetery, so this didn't make any sense at all from a practical and ceremonial perspective. Nor from an ecological one, and this was the most important consideration. Roger was a man who had worked closely with nature and subtle worlds all his life, which is why he wanted a green burial.

It would certainly not be "green" to transport his body across the water on a ferry, and battle Seattle traffic, just to keep him for a few days at our morgue before bringing him back through Seattle traffic, and back across the water on another ferry, to deposit him at a cemetery that was located only a hop, skip, and a jump from his home. No, I was going to have to figure something else out, and do so soon, as once Roger turned toward death, he seemed quite eager to get on with things. I sensed it would be only a matter of days before my friend would be making his way onward.

I need not have worried. Roger's daughter Susan Jane, his brother Terry, and Terry's wife Caroline saw immediately that keeping him at home for a time after death was a sensible solution. Susan Jane had been caring for her father day and night anyway for two weeks. Continuing to do so for a time afterward would only add to the profound experience she was having. And she was grateful not to have people outside their circle care for Roger's body. Terry felt the same. And Margaret was happy to go along with whatever the rest of the family decided. Once they understood that it was legally possible and that I would be able to guide them in the process, everyone relaxed and began imagining immediately how to make Roger's send-off a special and creative experience. Margaret had already chosen a shroud for her green burial, but she remembered Roger saying he wanted something a bit more substantial, so we settled on a cardboard container that our friends Carole and Marty Matthews blessedly braved the ferry lines to go and purchase from A Sacred Moment. I suggested that Margaret's four young grand-children paint and write messages to Roger on the container, an idea they loved and enthusiastically agreed to do.

Roger died on an April spring morning, only two days after our family meeting. Margaret was by his side. There was a deep peace in the bedroom when I arrived. I brought the first grape hyacinths and narcissus from my garden and placed them by Roger's bed. Soft light fell on his face from the window. A dear friend, Cynthia, held sacred watch over the family and me as Roger was dressed and tenderly laid out on his bed. Terry, a strong environmentalist himself, liking the idea of a green burial, fully embraced the home vigil as well, helping dress his brother and tidy the room with practical and caring hands.

Though it had not been part of the original plans, Margaret let her closest friends and community know that Roger was holding court at home, and she invited them to come by and keep him company for a time. This is the beauty of home funerals. We have time to be ourselves and to tune in and know what would be most comforting and helpful to us in the moment. Having friends knock softly on the door and enter, bearing forsythia and tulips, Roger's favorite wine, and good food to feed the family—this bolstered Margaret's flagging spirits and kept her going all that day. Having people sit beside Roger and meditate and sing and carry on conversations with him, making merry and mourning in the same moment—this was community at its finest.

The day of Roger's burial dawned blue and sunny and clear. I went to a forest on retreat land that Roger and Margaret loved and supported, and I gathered the freshest fiddlehead ferns, their tops still curled inward, as if bowing, and bracken with long, graceful fronds. Roger was strongly with me as I traipsed the paths and found the most luminous, green, growing life to adorn his grave. I felt a deep companionship with him, and with the trees towering above, and the sturdy new nettles and gentle violets springing up all around me.

Though I worked very hard that day, making sure the grave was marked and dug on time, setting up the lowering device, helping the grandchildren with the decorating of the container, transporting it to the house, and so on, I felt a grace carrying me, giving me strength and putting me in "joy's way," something Roger would have loved. He would also have found it satisfying that the family could simply arrive at the cemetery whenever they felt ready, rather than having to show up at a certain prearranged time and interact with strange funeral directors with schedule pressures and agendas.

I saw again how helpful it was to have a home vigil, *because* Roger had chosen green burial, and how easy and peaceful it turned out to be, weaving together these two ways of caring for our own. People gathered round Roger one last time and toasted him, clinking glasses of fine wine, telling stories, and sharing memories. The children proudly brought in their creation—a box with orca whales leaping and diving on the cover; musical notes to honor Roger's love of the symphony; flowers and bright colors and words written well. The strongest among us carried Roger's body out into the living room, and settled him comfortably inside his special box. Then, calmly and without fanfare, we carried him out of his house for the last time.

It was late afternoon, but no matter. No one was at the cemetery waiting for us. I would text George to meet us there, so he could fill in the grave afterward. We took the back roads so that we could be a procession and go slowly and feel our togetherness. Upon arrival, Roger was carried reverently to the grave; and his orca whale box, sitting on the lowering device, made everything feel festive (at least to me). Susan Jane created a lovely ceremony, despite how difficult it was for her to commit her father's body to the open ground. I remember the late-afternoon light settling on Roger's casket like a gentle goodbye. The children wanted to turn the crank to lower Roger down, and I gave thanks that they could do so, with no official person telling them they were too young or it might be improper or dangerous. Roger was respectfully laid to rest that day, and Margaret, even though she was living in Idaho at the time of her death, now lies peacefully beside him.

How Margaret's body ended up with Roger is another green burial family story, too long to tell fully, but wonderful enough to include in a brief way here. Margaret's son Marty and his wife Durenda, after moving to Idaho, cared for his mother until her death. Margaret had given them permission to cremate her, and to put her cremains in with Roger, since Idaho was a long way from the island, and it might be too much trouble and expense to get her body home. But Marty knew Margaret's truest wish was to be buried in her linen shroud next to Roger, and not be cremated. As a way to work with his grief and challenges, Marty designed and built a completely biodegradable pine casket, with no metal—only pine wood joinery. In his words, "The on-the-fly project helped keep me reasonably composed." He called to ask how he could legally transport his mother across state lines and bring her to the island cemetery himself. I told him that it was not something most people attempted, but that it was legal in every state to do so, except Arkansas and Alabama, which required (for no proven reason) embalming before a body could be taken over state lines. I would back him transporting Margaret and would be available if he needed help in any way. (Visions of the film *Little Miss Sunshine* did cross my mind.) I learned later that a local funeral home was very helpful with all the needed paperwork, which is encouraging for future families.

Jim, another of Margaret's sons, flew to Idaho "to help with the drive in the trek across the white tundra" (Marty's words again). I gave Marty the gravedigger's number so the grave would be ready, and I suggested he not drive through Oregon, as the funeral industry had made things harder there for home funeral families. Oh, and if he were going to use dry ice, he had to be willing to drive with the windows open, even though it was January, because the carbon dioxide from the evaporating ice in a closed-up car might be harmful.

So Marty and Jim drove the long roads from Idaho back to their mother's beloved island (presumably with the windows down!), took the ferry across, and brought Margaret quietly to the cemetery themselves. All four children were present that cold, wintry day, with spouses and most of Margaret's thirteen grandchildren as well. I was not there, but I can imagine how free and unencumbered they must have felt, being able to have the cemetery to themselves, and to lay their mother/grandmother to rest, in the tradition and manner most important to them all.

So Margaret got her wish to lie next to her dear Roger, in the green meadow where robins visit regularly and the owls call in chorus at twilight. I too visit regularly, and every All Souls' Day (November 2), when the cemetery is open in the evening for people to light luminaries and place them on the graves of those they love, I bring my friends two white bags, glowing with light, and set them side-by-side between their graves. Seeing those luminaries shining out into the darkness, so like the two of them, always makes me smile. Perhaps somewhere Roger and Margaret are smiling too.

———

In all the green burial stories I have shared with you so far, the graves were dug with a backhoe and were ready when the family arrived. I have experienced one unique and beautiful green burial where the family hand-dug the grave themselves and slowly filled it in after the service, making such care an integral part of their goodbye. This was a death in my island community, and it stands out for me as a perfect example of how home funeral vigils and green burials can weave seamlessly together and provide a complete participatory experience for the family and community, as well as for the person whose body is being returned to the earth.

For Robin

Robin Adams died of melanoma on a bleak January afternoon. His wife Judith and family were there to accompany him in the last hours of his life, and their friends and community were ready and waiting to help create his home vigil and assist with his green burial in our little local cemetery. When I arrived at the house, just one of many coming to honor Robin and comfort Judith and their children, I was struck with how warm and inviting it felt walking into their home. Robin's spirit was there still, seeming to open the door and usher us inside with his distinctive South African voice and polished manner, offering us food and drink and a respite from our own feelings of loss and sadness. Of course, the actual welcome and sense of deep hospitality radiated from Judith, who decided to open Robin's vigil all three days to anyone who wished to come and participate in the awe and beauty unfolding there. Judith's quiet strength and creative vision, and her willingness to make caring for Robin after death a rich and nourishing community event, moved me deeply. It was a kind and generous act, on Judith's part, in the midst of her own pain and sorrow. It was inclusive, spacious, full of grace. The bright warmth generated from that choice did so much to help all of us reimagine what is possible when someone dies.

Judith was clear that she wanted Robin's grave to be hand-dug, rather than have a mechanical backhoe do the job. She said the backhoe was simply "too violent." But it was also part of her creative vision to have the community join in. I came early to the cemetery to be there for our friend Marilyn Strong, the home funeral and green burial guide who was holding Robin's vigil and graveside ceremony. The grave was prepared, quietly waiting in the morning mist. Its potency was startling.

In a grave dug mechanically, the soil is shaved away suddenly and abruptly by the great metal shovel of the backhoe. The job takes an hour at most, so there is a feeling of efficiency and rapid completion, and that energy often remains around the grave for me. The sides of the grave can look a bit rough and torn, and I always want to "soften" them somehow by bringing ferns and moss to line the edges. George, who has dug most of my families' graves, is an artist in his own right with the backhoe. Watching his skilled handling of the machine is inspiring. Yet Robin's grave—dug intentionally and with love by their son and friends over six or more backbreaking hours—his was a different art entirely: a thing of beauty and soul.

The sides of Robin's grave were not rough or broken in any way. They were crafted and sculpted, one shovelful at a time, by caring and loving hands. The curve of the shovel, thrust over and over into the dark earth, formed an intricate scalloped design that reminded me of a creation by Andy Goldsworthy, the British sculptor whose art is shaped outside from the elements of the natural world. The grave was not straight-edged like a backhoe creates, but more rounded and soft, and it was lined on the bottom with layers of vibrant, plush green moss and cedar and evergreen boughs. It was truly a work of art. But it was more than that. It was alive, exuding a tangible energy that came from the bodies, hands, and hearts of the humans who had shaped the sides, shovelful by shovelful, in a spirit of camaraderie and support, together there in the falling rain. The grave Robin and Judith's son and friends created for him was their gift—a living container of love.

Judith is a gifted poet, our community's own cherished poet laureate. She has written a poem especially for this book about the home vigil and green burial journey she and Robin experienced together:

And We'll Adorn His Body

Do not take him away with
shining shoes of strangers
to a somber black display.
Leave him and we'll adorn his body.
Let the musicians come.

Sit among flowers, candles and the
voice that remains in the room.
Let the ones he found so hard to leave
linger in exalted calm as
winter mist hovers in the garden
while the heron flies
close to the chimney and
under the moon birds hush in
dripping calligraphy of branches.
Wrap him in a saffron shroud and
include in the pocket a poem.
Lay him in majesty.
There is nothing more noble than death.
The widow sings a requiem,
the door opens and closes as a temple,
villagers arrive with stories and
laughter and feasting.
Friends with shovels approach the grave
the young doing most of the work
the old digging in a half rhythm
for their own transition.
And in the downpour amazing grace
to bring him from his
worldly house to the place
we speculate to be this or that.
In the slow largo of descent
upon boughs of cedar,
white flowers from New York
thrown into his arms and across his body.
Shakespeare would describe
such a gathering in the final act,
an assortment of characters
close to the mystical bridge.

—*Judith Adams*

Practical Wisdom: Natural and Unnatural Burial Practices

When we physically lower a corpse into a grave ourselves and feel its weight and stillness, we have a felt sense of what it means to be dead. When we contemplate the depth of the grave in terms of how rapidly our loved one will decompose (such efficiency an actual goal, rather than something we are trying to prevent), we come up close to the stark reality of what happens to our bodies after death. There is no way that we can avoid this encounter. It gives us a direct experience of truth; what simply is, and will be for all of us.

Such experience is a powerful gift, a reckoning, and a return. When we creatively engage in rituals and ceremonies that give something back to nature, there is often a tangible sense of wholeness and completion, and a kind of peace that seems to come from the earth itself, and the cyclical webs of life welcoming our loved one home. Such experience can be a potent remedy for the fear, avoidance, and denial so many of us carry about death today.

Here are the essential principles of a natural burial:

- There are no grave liners or vaults of any kind in the green section of a cemetery or in a natural burial ground. Vaults are often standard policy in U.S. cemeteries, though not required by federal or state law. This is often a maintenance issue, as vaults keep the ground from sinking, making mowing and upkeep more efficient and cost-effective. In a green burial cemetery, a person is placed directly in the earth in a biodegradable container or shroud to decompose naturally.

- The depth of the grave is 3.5–4 feet rather than the traditional 5–6 feet normally dug. This ensures the most efficient decomposition of the body, as more oxygen is present in the first 3–4 feet of soil, and therefore is the place of greatest aerobic activity. This depth also harbors more bacteria,

fungi, and insects that will help with decomposition. Bodies
buried deeper will decompose much more slowly, making the
chances of generating greenhouse gases a more likely possibility. Most importantly, 3.5 feet is the depth where most
roots of trees and shrubs grow, so that a body will be con-
tributing its nutrients more effectively to the soil and to life
in this more shallow grave.

- The deceased person cannot be embalmed with formaldehyde
  and other toxic chemicals. If such a procedure is necessary or
  desired by the family, nontoxic embalming based on essential oils must be used. Many people choosing green burial
  also choose home funeral vigils, where the body is cared for
  naturally and preserved with dry ice, Techni-ice®, or other
  cooling methods before disposition.

- The burial container must be biodegradable and the dece-
  dent clothed only in materials that will decompose naturally.
  Acceptable containers are: biodegradable shrouds; unfinished
  hardwood caskets with no metal handles or screws; cardboard
  or untreated fiberboard containers; caskets made of biodegradable bamboo, wicker, or other easily renewable sources.
  No endangered or treated hardwood caskets are accepted.
  Ideally, a family would find a container locally, to minimize
  the carbon footprint of shipping products long distances.
  Nonbiodegradable objects should not be placed inside the
  container with the person.

- The use of headstones is discouraged and in many natural
  and conservation burial grounds is not allowed. Natural
  stone native to the burial ground can be used, or graves can be
  located by GPS or a plat system of the grounds. Some burial
  grounds advocate for communal memorialization, where
  names are placed together on one marker in one place, rather
  than having individual and separate site commemoration.

- The use of native plants, shrubs, and trees is encouraged and is required in some burial grounds to maintain and enhance the local ecosystems. Conservation burial grounds are linked to conservation easements and organizations whose job is to protect and manage the land in perpetuity. Such designation can help conserve land and ecosystems that might otherwise be lost for the future.

Conventional burial is the opposite of natural burial, for this standard industry practice is actually designed to delay the inevitable decomposition of our bodies for as long as possible. This kind of burial is also a strong source of pollution and toxicity and is not a sustainable practice for the future.

- Often the deceased is embalmed before burial, with formaldehyde and other chemicals and disinfectants toxic to the environment and to funeral director staff.

- Caskets are usually elaborate and ornate, crafted from steel, metal, and endangered species of wood. Most caskets are hermetically sealed, as "protection" for the body (as if sealing someone away is going to prevent their dissolution and decay). In fact, this set of circumstances creates slow, anaerobic decay, rather than natural decomposition, which integrates our organic matter with the earth. Neither the external nor the internal materials are biodegradable, but are often very toxic, both in makeup and manufacturing. The distribution, shipping, and manufacturing of parts and caskets span the globe, creating a huge carbon footprint that is wasteful, unnecessary, and unsustainable.

- Grave liners or vaults made from concrete, plastic, fiberglass, or even bronze are placed in the grave before the casket is lowered. These liners are like a box and have a lid. Combined with the casket, this means that there are two barriers between the body and the earth. Funeral homes speak as if vaults provide greater protection for the deceased; however, the vault's main purpose is to keep the grave from sinking so that cemetery staff can mow the lawns without impediment and keep maintenance costs down. Plus, vaults add a great deal to the burial fee.

- Many conventional cemeteries today have manicured lawns, using fertilizers, herbicides, pesticides, and a large amount of water to create monocultured memorial parks. This is very different from natural burial grounds that strive to actually create vibrant, biodiverse ecosystems and proper land use for the future.

No doubt many of us have experienced or chosen the kind of conventional burial described above, as it is by far the most accepted practice today. I have kin who, even though they might be aware of the financial and environmental cost of their decision to be buried in such a way, will still choose all the elements that the funeral home suggests. Such choices are aligned with their lifestyle, values, and spiritual customs, and they will find a sense of comfort in doing what is "always done" and fulfilling the wishes of the deceased. Caring for our dead in ways that are authentic to each of us is a vital priority, and I know and honor this, from my training as a funeral director, and from being an interfaith minister and celebrant. At heart, there are no right or wrong choices when we are dealing with death and the loss of those we love.

The purpose of this writing, however, is to help readers be more informed about the environmental and social impact of conventional burial practices (and of cremation, which I will address in chapter 9). This is part of reimagining death—being able to understand every aspect of one's decision, and choosing from a place of wholeness rather than partial awareness of a situation.

A Brief Look at the Natural Burial Movement

It is important to remember that natural burial was the traditional way we always buried our dead before the advent of the modern funeral industry—meaning we simply dug a grave and buried a person straight into the ground, without cement grave liners and fancy caskets. Many old historic and rural cemeteries in the United States still allow natural burial, though this is changing, especially when corporate funeral homes move into a town, buy up local cemeteries, and require very different and environmentally harmful policies.

It is important here to also honor Jewish and Islamic cultural and spiritual customs that have for centuries discouraged or prohibited unnatural burial practices, advocating for a simple pine box or shroud, without embalming. And many indigenous cultures have never changed their burial practices, believing that returning the body to Mother Earth and allowing it to nourish new life in cyclical ways is the most sacred and reverent way to honor the dead. People of these cultures and faiths have been guardians of green burial practices all along.

The Natural Death Centre in Great Britain, founded by Nicholas Aubrey in 1991, was one of the first organizations to make the public aware of the importance of natural burial. The NDC is a social and educational charity that, free of charge, helps people with all aspects of dying, bereavement, and consumer rights. They support home vigils, which they call family-organized or DIY (direct-it-yourself) funerals, and all green and environmentally friendly funeral care. They have helped natural burial grounds become a household term and be readily available in Great Britain today. There are more than 270 natural burial grounds in the United Kingdom, and more are being established yearly. The NDC created the Association of Natural Burial Grounds in 1994. Members have to comply with the association's Code of Conduct, which provides standards that the public can rely upon. The ANBG also assists individuals in the process of establishing new natural burial grounds and provides guidance to and networking for all members, representing them as a whole.

Dr. George William (Billy) Campbell was working on the idea of conservation burial in the United States as early as the late 1970s, when he was a biology/ecology student at Emory University in Atlanta, Georgia. His experience reading Jessica Mitford's book *The American Way of Death*, and his own father's death in 1985, which cost the family as much as purchasing five acres of land at the time, convinced Billy that something had to change in the way we were "doing death." Already deeply committed to land conservation, he had a lightbulb moment of realizing that natural burial could actually finance the purchase and preservation of land and ecosystems. He was writing and speaking publicly about this idea as early as 1987 and was working on creating scientific standards that would be guidelines for those who might create such conservation burial grounds.

Billy and his wife Kimberley established Ramsey Creek Preserve in 1996 in Westminster, South Carolina, and began burying people naturally, without embalming, vaults, or fancy headstones. Their preserve is arguably the first of its kind in the world—certainly in North America—and has served as a model and inspiration for everyone in the green burial movement. In our conversations, Billy said that, for him, conservation burial was at first simply a utilitarian method to save land, but that over the years, doing the actual work of helping families bury their dead changed him and "informed how [he felt] about the transformative potential of conservation burial."

Several years later, in partnership with former Jesuit lay minister and communications specialist Joe Sehee and his wife Juliette, the Campbells helped form the Green Burial Council, a nonprofit 501(c)(6) organization, with a board of leading experts from the fields of restoration ecology, conservation management, sustainable landscape design, law, and consumer affairs. This board created scientific and ethical certification standards for natural burial cemeteries in North America. A system was devised whereby various levels of conservation cemeteries were recognized, including hybrids (those existing on conventional cemetery land), natural (those dedicated to natural burial exclusively), and conservation (where land is held in partnership with conservation agencies, and burials provide a revenue stream and support conservation goals above ground).

One important aspect of the work of promoting the concept of green burial is raising awareness of the public to "greenwashing," a term coined by New York environmentalist Jay Westervelt in 1986 to describe products and services that appear eco-friendly on the surface, but that carry an environmental or carbon footprint that offsets any positive gains. Caskets made from wicker or grasses, for instance, are biodegradable but may have traveled from Great Britain or Indonesia, and may have been made by child labor, or may not have been part of fair trade agreements. In the funeral industry itself, funeral directors who offer "green burial" packages may be selling suspect products and not have a green cemetery within a workable distance, leaving one to wonder what is truly green about it.

One of the strongest contributions of the GBC has been to engage diverse and often disparate people—land trusts, park service agencies, educational institutions, government agencies, religious organizations, and death care providers—to work together in shared intention. Their common endeavor is to continually evolve practices to dispose of our dead in more ecological and sustainable ways, and to conserve land, wilderness, and natural resources while doing so.

Establishment of the GBC was an important historical step in the evolution of green burial consciousness in the United States. As of this writing, 2018, the next innovative and exciting development will be within the conservation burial ground movement, and in educational endeavors to inform the public of ways they can be part of protecting and conserving land, and also developing places where humans and nature can co-create together for the benefit of all. (My honoring and gratitude to Lee Webster for helping me write this section.)

The Idea of Successive Burial

Successive burial, a practice in some natural burial grounds, deserves discussion as part of reimagining after-death care. Successive burial means that graves are eventually reused after a certain length of time has passed—say, fifty or seventy-five years. For a nation like America, where land has always been plentiful, being able to purchase one's own permanent "real estate" for burial is an unquestioned right for those who can afford it. This is true in Canada as well. Sharing one's grave with another human being is not something North Americans have had to consider, and the idea remains controversial.

People in Europe and other parts of the Western world have dealt with land scarcity for centuries, so the practice of allowing a body to be buried for a set number of years, and then be removed to make room for someone else, is a far more commonplace and accepted practice. Family members can be buried in the same graves over time, which at least keeps successive graves more personal. With explosive population growth and land being snatched up for development, as well as the unknown elements of climate change, migration issues, and political unrest here in the United States, the idea of successive natural burial grounds is an increasingly important part of reimagining ecological after-death care for the future.

The Importance of Conservation Burial Grounds

We are truly giving back and co-creating with the earth and the natural world if our deaths and burials actually help conserve, restore, and protect endangered ecosystems and the biodiversity of life for our children and future generations—and if the places where we are buried create or preserve either wilderness or tracts of land where human beings and nature can co-exist (co-create) together in mutual, life-giving ways.

Conservation burial grounds (some of which are represented in the insert of color photos in this book) have the potential to transform the very way we speak about caring for our dead. Kimberley Campbell told me recently that we need to reimagine the very language of death care itself. This thrilled me, for it resonates so deeply with my intentions for this book. (I would add reimagining the language of death as well.) For example, the word "cemetery" may not even exist in the future if there is no more land available for people to "own" plots and have their bodies lie undisturbed forever. The challenge to reshape our very thoughts is an exciting one.

People in the conservation burial movement are consciously grappling with the reality of overpopulation, and are seeing the wisdom in creating nature preserves where our lives and deaths are interwoven. We can bury our mother and protect a tributary of water or an endangered species of orchid at the same time, and go with our children to have picnics and take nature hikes every time we visit a mother's final resting spot. These are ways many people can be lovers and stewards of land and place, in a time of ever-shrinking green spaces, and when we so desperately need balance and reconnection in our increasingly nature-deficit lives.

In a recent essay for the journal *Conservation Letters*, Matthew Holden (a mathematician studying conservation at the University of Queensland in Australia) calculates that, given the size of the average burial plot (and this could be more, since natural burial plots tend to be larger), if every American chooses to have a conservation burial, two square miles of land would be saved every year for wildlife and the environment. Holden also calculates the potential revenue that could be designated for conservation efforts if everyone refuses to pay for burial practices that harm the environment. If all Americans who opt for embalming, standard caskets, and concrete vaults choose conservation burial instead (and I would add green and natural burial as well), then out of the $19 billion spent on death and burial every year, $3.8 billion could go to protecting the natural world.[2]

Wilderness is essential to our souls. It is my conviction that without having a living relationship to sovereign land—and by sovereign, I mean land left untouched for the most part by human hands or only lightly stewarded and protected in respectful and noninvasive

---

[2] Matthew H. Holden and Eve MacDonald-Madden, "Conservation from the Grave: Human Burials to Fund the Conservation of Threatened Species," *Conservation Letters: A Journal of the Society for Conservation Biology*, October 30, 2017.

ways—we as a species might not survive. Or if we do, we will be shades of ourselves, cut off and separate from all that really nourishes and sustains life. As David Spangler and others have said, we need to be more embodied, more incarnated, more co-creative with the natural world. Conservation burial is a way to manifest that intention. Here in North America, we are blessed to still have large tracts of public land. But that gift is being threatened on all sides by corporate and foreign greed, and the reckless decisions being made by our own government and those who do not understand or care about the consequences of their actions. And, if we are to be honest and realistic, because the population of human beings is only going to increase, we are all a major threat to the natural world, and to the preservation of the environment. The idea that we might be able to conserve nature and wild spaces and biodiversity by creating more intentional conservation and nature preserve burial grounds is a source of great hope. To me, it is one of the strongest and brightest reimaginations of death and how we can care for each other and the earth when we die.

5

"YOU'RE DEAD. NOW WHAT?"

Humor and Laughter at the Threshold

If you feel that you're not ready to die, never fear. Nature will give you complete and adequate assistance when the time comes.

—EDWARD ABBEY

No book on home funeral vigils and green burials would be complete without a chapter dedicated to laughter, even joy, in the midst of mourning. I have seen humor shift the energy in a room full of grieving people within moments. It's harder to stay closed off and frozen if we are smiling, even if it's through our tears. Laughter (and crying) help us to naturally let go of tension—our guarded posturing; hunched shoulders sheltering broken hearts; shallow breathing held in for fear of breaking down entirely. We breathe more easily when we are amused and feel more relaxed and buoyant for a time. Suddenly things seem a little less terrible, a little easier to bear—especially if we are sharing this experience with others. Even death feels closer in—more intimate, less scary somehow—because we have let down our defenses and can actually feel and be real together.

There are plenty of opportunities to find humor and levity in death, especially when we are upfront and personal with the dead body, as we are in home funeral vigils and green burials. There's no buffer against the flotsam and jetsam of our direct experience when we are the ones caring for the dead, rather than giving that job to others in the funeral industry, and no end to the interesting and wonderful things that can happen along the way. Such experiences bind us together and create marvelous tales and adventures to be told.

In this chapter I share a story of laughter and love—trusting it will entertain as well as teach, since there is also information in the telling that might be of use to you someday. A T-shirt I saw somewhere says, "Let's put the fun back in funerals." When we are cut down by shock and loss, unable to inhabit any landscape but grief and despair, this could be an inappropriate and offensive thing to say. Yet there is a message there whose truth often arises naturally when families say "yes" to being more involved in the after-death process.

Families and communities who are reclaiming this kind of care often find that their heavier perceptions and thought forms about death are changing in subtle but powerful ways. The searing pain and sorrow are there—perhaps even more so, as they are allowing themselves to truly feel. Yet there are more ways to find solace and comfort, and we have greater room to breathe and simply be ourselves—creating a far greater lightness of being all around. This collective transformation of how we hold and view death—our reimagining—is one of the greatest gifts happening in the natural after-death care movement. It is part of healing the circles, part of creating and knowing wholeness in our lives and in our deaths once again.

A Red and White Tablecloth for Helen

It was early morning when the phone rang beside my bed. My friend Linda was calling to tell me her mother Helen had died in a nursing home on our island. Could I come and help her create a vigil there in the facility, and could I also help her bring her mother's body back to Linda's house that afternoon? Her sister Carol and brother-in-law Steve would be arriving from Minnesota, and her sons and nephews needed to get there from Seattle to tell Helen goodbye. Linda wanted to have a home funeral for her mother—probably for two or three days—before Helen was buried in the family plot in a cemetery on the mainland.

I had hoped to go to the nursing home before Helen died, because I knew it would be necessary to ask permission for what we wanted to do. It's always helpful to be proactive in these matters, as institutional staff normally have had little or no experience with families caring for their own dead. Our requests would be viewed as highly unusual and perhaps create anxiety and resistance on the part of the management, and a stressful situation for Linda and her mom. This was what I wanted to avoid.

I told Linda to go ask the managing director if her mother could remain in her room for a few hours. This would allow more time for Linda to just be present with Helen and to bathe and dress her if she wanted to do so. It would also give me time to work on the paperwork and get a death certificate for Linda to fill out and sign. (She would be acting as licensed funeral director, something families are legally able to do in all but nine states in this country.) This death certificate, if filed that day, would also give us a burial transit permit, which would allow us to take Helen in a van home to Linda's farm, Heartsease, for the home vigil.

As long as Linda was in possession of that paperwork, transporting her mother from the nursing home herself was perfectly legal. But hardly anyone knows this is true, so I was going to have to educate the staff and the director right away about our wishes, since the normal procedure was to call the local funeral home soon after someone dies and have them come to pick up the body. I had my work cut out for me; meanwhile, time was ticking away, and Helen was lying up there in her room, probably wondering what in the world her crazy daughter and friends were trying to do with the body she had so recently vacated.

When I got to the nursing home, Linda had already filled the room with lilacs, echinacea, lavender, and rosemary from her garden. For "remembrance," she said, coming over to give me a big hug. The scent of flowers and herbs and the bright hues brought to an otherwise stark and utilitarian room a quiet comfort for us all. The staff were gracious in allowing Helen to remain in the room and seemed quite interested in what we were doing. (We were fortunate because Helen had no roommate, and there was not an immediate need for the beds.) Linda and another friend, Gaea, had bathed Helen and dressed her in her favorite frock. We spent time lighting a few votive candles on the dresser (something else we needed to ask permission to do). The room held a tangible peace, and several nurses commented on it. One said she had no idea it was possible to care for someone after death in this way, but she knew now she wanted to do something similar when her own mother died.

Meanwhile, I went off to deal with paperwork, which thankfully wasn't a big deal, as the nursing home was near the public health department and vital records office. This was during the early days of my work, but I was already befriending the local registrar and educating her about families' rights to care for their own, so she was on board with my request that day.

When I returned to the nursing home, I knocked on the managing director's office door to break the news that we were transporting Linda's mother away from the facility ourselves rather than using a funeral home. I could tell she was shocked, but after listening to my information and seeing the paperwork, she admirably agreed to support us.

I was acting so professionally, but inside I was wondering what in the world I was going to do when it came time to actually pick

Helen's body up and get her in the van Linda had borrowed from another friend. I knew we could lift up the sheet under Helen, make a kind of hammock, and carry her out that way. But that meant we would have to ask the nursing home to give us their sheets. Plus Helen would be lying on the hard floor of the van, and she might even roll around, which was unacceptable. Also the management might be horrified. I knew I needed a stretcher or cot of some kind. And the only place I knew to get one was from my friend Char Barrett, who had completed the home funeral training with me and had gone on to become an alternative licensed funeral director. But she was on the mainland far away. I shared my thoughts with Linda, who happily realized that her nephew Joe M and his partner Joe B were coming over to the island and could perhaps go get the cot from Char and deliver it to us at the nursing home later on.

Thankfully, that's exactly what happened. The lovely Joes arrived a couple of hours later, full of excitement that they could be the bearers of the most important item needed for our wild endeavor. They immediately jumped in to help in all ways: measuring Helen's body, the width of the door, and the length of the van, meanwhile chattering on about how fascinating such a venture was and how thrilled they were to be a part of it all. I doubt the nurses had ever witnessed a more ebullient family gathering around a recently departed loved one, nor a more intriguing one. Several of the staff kept making up excuses to come by the room, peeking in and adding tidbits of advice. The atmosphere was becoming decidedly party-like by the time we were ready to put Helen on the cot.

It was just as well, I suppose, for at that moment we needed to remain upbeat, having remembered we had nothing to wrap Helen in. We could strap her on the cot, but she would be terribly exposed for her departure through the halls and out into the sunshine and the waiting van. Joe B asked if purging and leaking of bodily fluids were likely to occur, and didn't we need something plastic in case; and the other Joe exclaimed that Helen was far too much of a lady not to be wrapped in something elegant for the journey.

"I know," Linda said. "I have a tablecloth in the back of my station wagon. Maybe that will do." She came running back in with a red and white checkered plastic affair that made all of us raise dubious eyebrows and then shrug in acceptance; for really, what other choice did we have? The tablecloth didn't quite go all the way around Helen's body, but it covered enough of her to make her look presentable. More than presentable. She actually looked festive in her attire, like a lovely picnic table on a bright summer's day. "Perfect," we said, congratulating ourselves. Never mind that all the way back to Linda's house, the sides of the tablecloth kept slipping down, and Helen's face would suddenly appear, gazing up at the windows as if making sure we were taking all the right roads and doing all the right things to get her home.

By the time we arrived at Linda's house, we had been working for hours. We were exhausted and in need of lunch and a strong cup of tea before we prepared a place for the three-day vigil. We piled out of our cars, going around first to check on Helen. In our weariness, we left the back door of the van open when we trudged up the steps and went inside. We were all sitting around Linda's kitchen table when the doorbell rang. Who in the world could that be? Linda and I both went to the door to see, and when we opened it—there stood the UPS man, his face ashen, his hands shaking as he put down his package and handed Linda something to sign. And there right behind him was Helen, lying in state in the open van, the sun shining on her dead face, and the cat pacing back and forth beside her.

We did our best to keep straight faces and to act as if nothing out of the ordinary was going on. Linda signed for the package and thanked the UPS man in a kindly way. But there was no mistaking the giggle in her voice, and I could hardly contain myself. I stepped into the hall so my contorted face wouldn't make matters worse. When I glanced around the corner, the poor man was backing away, refusing to look anywhere near the direction of the van. He navigated the steps and literally ran to his truck, climbing in, revving the engine, and driving off very fast. We all collapsed in peals of laughter, imagining what he would tell his boss back at headquarters or his wife at the end of the day. We couldn't stop guffawing, but we did go shoo the cat away and close the back of the van.

Very soon after, we rescued Helen and brought her into the dining room, where we arranged her cozily on a massage table draped with beautiful tapestries that Linda had collected over the years from her travels. We also surrounded Helen with all kinds of herbs and flowers from the farm, lit candles whose flames flickered in the mirror on the piano, and put on a CD called *Graceful Passages* in the background, with music and spoken words from different spiritual traditions to guide the dying and the dead across the threshold.

When Carol and Steve arrived later that day, they opened the dining room door very cautiously and peeked inside. They had been hesitant about Linda's plans, wondering what wild schemes she had in mind. But the sheer beauty of the vigil space helped them relax a little and breathe. Carol actually came right up to her mother and took her hand, a look of gratitude flooding her face in spite of herself. "Oh, Linda, thank you," was all she said. But it was enough.

The vigil was special. Linda's son Max, arriving from Seattle, joined in enthusiastically with the dry ice care, fetching it from the fish department at Payless and helping us with that sacred task. He was grateful, as he got a chance to be with his grandmother in ways he would never have experienced had she been taken immediately to a morgue.

And healing moments happened, ones that may never have surfaced if the family had gathered in a funeral home instead. Linda and Carol had chances to voice their regrets about Helen's care at the end of life, and to figure out comforting ways for Carol to be the main organizer of Helen's graveside service after the vigil. Steve also warmed to the idea of having Helen at home for a three-day vigil, remembering that this was the way his extended family had once cared for their dead. During the three days, people stopped by to pay their respects, and to play music and sing for Helen and the family. Strains of hammered dulcimer and guitar filled the rooms.

There was good conversation, nourishing meals, laughter, and tears. Chicken soup, chardonnay, and love flowed freely, and Helen was toasted and honored, surrounded by those who held her close in their hearts.

On the third day, I telephoned the corporate funeral home that had recently acquired the cemetery where Helen was to be buried. We asked if they could come and get Helen's body, since the casket Carol had picked out was being purchased from them. The funeral director quoted Linda some outrageous price—$800 just to drive over on the ferry and pick Helen up, not to mention almost $4,000 to open and close the grave and have a funeral director simply stand there at the graveside service. This didn't even include the cost of the plot or the elaborate casket Carol had insisted on purchasing. We were stunned.

I knew we could drive Helen ourselves since we had the burial transit permit. And we still had Char's cot and the borrowed van. What were we thinking? I called back and told the funeral director we would be bringing Helen ourselves the next day. There was a potent silence on the other end. "Are you sure?" he stammered finally, his voice hardly audible on the line.

"Oh, yes," I said. "We'll be there at two o'clock tomorrow. Where should we bring her?" The man gave me some directions—to go around back to the morgue door and to make sure we did not drive up to the front steps, implying we should in no way create such an unwanted scene in front of other customers. I agreed to do as he asked, grateful to save Linda's family some money, given they were shelling out thousands already.

When we drove onto the ferry the next day, a wind was whipping the water into whitecaps, and the boat rocked back and forth. We had strapped Helen securely to one side of the van, grateful to have Char's professional cot. But the body was still quite visible to anyone peering in. We joked that if the ticket man tried to look in the back windows of the van, he too would go home with bizarre stories to tell. Luckily, however, there was no passenger charge on the island side, so we didn't have to ask if dead passengers had to pay just as much for a ticket as living ones did. I realized then that, in the future, I would recommend that families transporting a loved one at least purchase a cardboard cremation casket or build something themselves. That way, the body would be easier to handle, and more sheltered and contained.

I'll never forget the look on the funeral director's face when we drove up behind the fancy columned building, honoring his plea for us to take the little back service road instead of driving Helen up the long, curving drive to the stately entrance in front. We were tempted to disobey, for it would have been such a rich teaching moment to haul Helen up the marble steps, throw open the great wooden doors with brass handles, and deposit the cot ceremoniously on the thick Oriental carpet in the entranceway. Other families would have immediately known there were alternative ways to take care of the dead! But Linda said Helen hated hoopla and drama and would not want to be singled out as an example for others. So we drove meekly around the building, and I backed the van up to a metal door that was shut and locked like the entrance to a secret scientific laboratory. We rang the buzzer and heard it echo deep within. An intern finally answered, looking at us quizzically but going to get the funeral director.

When I lifted the van door, the director gave an audible sigh of relief to see Helen strapped to a cot, a familiar item of his trade, so welcome in the strange and alien situation he found himself in that day. Who knows what he was expecting? We said our loving good-byes, but we did not tarry, as the man seemed hell bent to get Helen out of sight as soon as possible. The last thing we heard him say to the intern as he wheeled Helen inside was, "At least they thought to use plastic."

We did indeed: red and white checkered plastic, in fact. A well-used tablecloth. Just in case Helen needed to be reminded of all things dear in life—family and picnics, good food and fine wine, parties and presents—and most of all, laughter and love.

Practical Wisdom: Helpful Field Notes

- There are more steps to handle if your loved one dies in a nursing facility or adult family home, and you want to take the body somewhere for a vigil, or simply have more time at the facility before calling a funeral director. It is helpful to be as proactive as possible and let the manager and staff know your wishes before the death occurs. This prevents any surprises and could pave the way, with less stress and confusion, for everyone to understand how best to proceed at the time of death.

- If you wish to transport your loved one to another place for a vigil, as we did with Helen, remember that, in most states, you must obtain a death certificate, file it, and have the burial transit permit with you in the vehicle that you are using. This could be simple or difficult to accomplish, depending on your circumstances. It is helpful for you to already have a hard-copy death certificate in hand, with your section completed. (See the Practical Wisdom section of chapter 2.) You should also determine which doctor will sign the death certificate, and let that person know beforehand that you are acting as licensed funeral director (if you are in a state where this is possible) and that you would like him or her to work with your family in this way. You may need to educate the doctor that this is legally possible, as many medical staff are not accustomed to such requests.

- Obtaining hard copies of death certificates is more difficult nowadays, since many vital records offices file death certificates electronically, and only authorized people can use this service. But it is still possible, so don't give up if you really want to transport your loved one. Again, having figured this out before the death can make all the difference in being able to complete the paperwork yourself. After getting the doctor to sign the death certificate, file it with the vital records office in the county where your loved one has died. The registrar will give you the burial transit permit at the time of filing. This is the paperwork you need to transport your loved one's body legally.

- If you feel that doing the paperwork yourself is too much without some help, you can contract with a home funeral consultant/guide, as Linda did with me, and she can walk you through things. Alternatively, you can ask a funeral home to help you, but you need to work with one that is open to and supportive of families caring for their own dead.

- If you know beforehand that your loved one is going to die soon, you can arrange to obtain some kind of container in which to transport your loved one. I recommend purchasing a cardboard container from a local funeral home. Or ask a home funeral consultant how to find workable ways to bring your loved one home.

- The hours we had with Helen in the nursing home were very special. For many people, this will be enough time to say goodbye, without also taking their loved one home for a vigil. I recommend taking the time you need, and trusting your own knowing and wisdom about how long that should be. It also depends on the facility, and whether they are open to having a deceased person remain in the room after death. For the best outcomes, look at all your options, follow your heart, and communicate with all involved.

- If final disposition of your loved one is with a funeral establishment or crematorium or cemetery that does not know about or support families caring for their own, it is helpful to talk to staff beforehand to let them know what your plans are, the legality of what you are doing, and how you plan to work with them. I have found that being calm and informed yourself, and respectful of the organization, and their concerns and needs, goes a long way toward creating the right conditions for a successful endeavor overall.

———————

It is challenging for most of us to think about death and about our bodies someday becoming inanimate corpses in need of disposition. We are learning to talk about dying a bit more, thanks to the efforts of end-of-life educators, hospice workers, and those advocating a more "death positive" movement today. Talking about "being dead," however, often still evokes some level of denial and avoidance, even in people who are committed to living as consciously and intentionally as they can. It's for the most part unconscious. It is as if our very bodies rebel, on some deep, primal, somatic level, when faced with the idea of not existing someday; and this rebellion can affect our ability to stay alert and present and focused about after-death care considerations.

This is why the phrase "You're dead. Now what?" can be so useful at times. People tend to laugh first when they hear me say these words, so there's a moment of openness and engagement that might not be there if I had simply started with "What are your after-death plans?" or "Have you thought about whether you want to be buried or cremated?" Laughing and taking the whole thing more lightly often make it easier to continue our conversation. Our bodies are more relaxed and less defended, so the whole inquiry about death can be less encumbered, more spacious and free.

This is a good thing, because having such a conversation and getting our wishes and plans in place way before we need them can be so liberating and helpful—for ourselves and for all those who will be taking care of us when we die. I will explore Advance After-Death Care Directives in greater detail in chapter 10. Meanwhile, remember how helpful it can be to approach all this with a greater sense of humor and fun, and a commitment to yourself and others to lighten up about all things death-related, if possible. Who knows? Being able to look in the mirror and say to yourself, "Okay, you're dead. Now what?" could be the start of a fascinating, even fun-filled inquiry into the nature of being and not being alive.

6

SACRED CARE OF THE DEAD

Be kind, oh be kind to your dead

And give them a little encouragement

And help them to build their little ship of death . . .

Oh, from out of your heart

provide for your dead once more, equip them

like departing mariners, lovingly.

—D. H. LAWRENCE, from his poem "All Souls' Day"

I found the poem "All Souls' Day" late one afternoon during one of those liminal days up on the mountain helping my mother die. It was a quiet time, sitting next to Mama. She was sleeping, her gaunt face finally peaceful after a morning of unresolved pain. My sisters had gone to town for groceries, and Papa was digging in the garden to ease his soul. I was fretful, knowing I was going to have to let go of wanting to have a home funeral and to build Mama a beautiful little boat for her journey, since no one could agree on anything. I tried to meditate, thinking that might help me let go of my attachment, to no avail. So I moved restlessly over to the bookshelves where Papa kept all the volumes of poetry and biographies of poets. My hands landed on *The Complete Works of D. H. Lawrence*, and, without any conscious intention, I opened to "All Souls' Day."

It felt like a sign, of course, telling me to stay on track with my wishes to care for Mama after death. Why else would I randomly open to a poem that urges the reader to "be kind to your dead / And give them a little encouragement / And help them to build their little ship of death"? No, it was definitely an omen—perhaps Mama speaking to me from her soul in that moment, as she slumbered. You know the rest of this story: Mama did get her "ship of death" in the end (though it was certainly not little!) and, thanks to the land and the storm, we managed very well to "equip her lovingly."

D. H. Lawrence's poem continues to inspire me in my work as a home funeral guide and especially as a minister and practitioner at the threshold. Home vigils are a special way to better "equip" our loved one, both physically, with loving care of the body for a time, and spiritually, by using the vigil time to be with the soul in our thoughts and hearts, in ways that are right for that person.

When someone we know dies, we instinctively hold that person in our awareness and, if we have a faith tradition of some kind, in our prayers and practice. This is part of being human. Of course this kind of companionship can be offered no matter where a person's body ends up after death. Offering our presence and love across the veil certainly does not require a home funeral vigil, or being present with the body. Home funeral vigils simply give us more intentional space and time away from our normal hectic lives to focus on caring for a loved one. They also bring back to Western people the awareness that the time right after someone dies—in that interim gap between having a body and not having one—can be a powerful opportunity to connect with the departing consciousness and lend support and guidance, if that feels appropriate and possible.

Some Eastern and Western spiritual teachings claim that a person's consciousness often remains nearby for a time, especially for the first three days, and that the transition out of a body can sometimes be disorienting and a struggle, especially if the death is sudden and unexpected. Buddhist teachings claim that our emotions are seven times stronger on the other side, as we no longer have a body to buffer us from those powerful waves of feeling. Apparently those who have died are clairvoyant and clairaudient as well, so part of sacred care could mean being careful about what we do and say in the presence of the dead, and in the weeks afterward. It is helpful if we can focus on being companions and a source of strength and reassurance for the soul while it acclimates to the experiences it is having in the bardo or postmortem realms.

There are many ways to explore what sacred care of the dead means. But I will start first with a story from a culture that has never lost its understanding of how to care for the dead, and has much to offer people of the Western world—we who are so often uncertain about what to do or how to be when someone we love dies.

I have had the great privilege of helping traditional Tibetan Buddhist families in the Seattle area support their dead with prayers, rituals, and practices they have always followed but have not been able to do within the limitations of the American funeral industry. Char Barrett and I, along with all the staff at A Sacred Moment Funeral Services, have helped make it possible for faith communities to once again be able to care for loved ones in traditional sacred ways at home. We were one of the first funeral homes to make that part of our mission and vision. My story of a Tibetan woman, Pemala, exemplifies how valuable this kind of support can be for spiritual practitioners and their families and communities—and for me, I might add. My time with Pemala and her family was a great gift and teaching in my life, one for which I will always be grateful.

Treasure Teachings from the Threshold

I was the only one still at work when the phone rang, and I heard a frantic voice on the other end: "My mother has passed away in the hospital, and I heard you support home vigils. We are Tibetan, and my mother was a very devoted practitioner. We need to find a lama so we can do the rituals and prayers from our tradition. We want to bring my mother directly home. Can you help us?"

The perfection of the moment did not escape me. I had picked up the phone, and I was the only practicing Buddhist on staff. I contacted Char, who had just left for a much-needed vacation, but I was already setting things in motion. I asked the women of my sangha to alert Kilung Rinpoche, who had a center on our island and could possibly be of help. I arranged for the other staff members to meet me at the hospital, and contacted our removal team to transport Pemala to her home.

It turned out Rinpoche was boarding an airplane for Denmark, and so was unable to come to the house, but he said he could still help from afar. My sangha friend had mistakenly told Rinpoche that the deceased was a man. Rinpoche corrected her and said no, it was a woman, and her name was Pemala. What a gift: Rinpoche had already contacted Pemala's consciousness in the bardo, even though he had never met her in life. I knew I could reassure Pemala's daughter, Dachen, that her mother was in good hands, spiritually and practically, now.

It was evening when my colleagues Jan and Chris and I reached the hospital and found our way to Pemala's room. We spent a few moments discussing what we could and could not do. I wanted to focus on minimal disturbance of Pemala's body, because, as a Vajrayana student myself, I know how important it is not to touch a practitioner if at all possible right after death. This is part of Tibetan Buddhist teachings. Dachen's instructions to the hospital staff and to us about using the sheets to move her mother's body, rather than touching Pemala anywhere, verified my intentions. When I told Dachen that our Rinpoche was a Vajrayana teacher and would be helping from afar, and that I knew the practices for the dead, we both marveled at the synchronicity of things. "It's my mom," Dachen said. "She's orchestrating everything." I had to agree.

Standing next to Pemala, I sensed she might need as much support as possible, because her death had been sudden and unexpected, and in a hospital setting, away from familiar surroundings. It was important to keep her undisturbed as much as possible, even though we would be moving her home. This conviction helped me stand strong when Matt, the removal man, arrived and balked at my request to lift Pemala with the sheet under her, so as not to touch her directly, and to use the quilt we had brought, rather than zip her into his plastic body bag.

Dachen explained that, in their spiritual tradition, the ideal death is for the consciousness to exit out of the top of the head; the body below the waist should not be touched, especially the feet, in case it draws the departing consciousness down to exit another way. We managed to get Pemala on the gurney without touching her lower extremities; we covered her body with the quilt; and we only used one strap, buckled loosely, rather than using the three tight straps Matt would have preferred. Someone came forward and covered Pemala's face respectfully with a white silk kata. Everyone was speaking Tibetan, so Dachen translated for us along the way.

Geshela, Pemala's brother, came forward with a silver box of sacred relics that came from Lhasa. Dachen explained that this box, which had an image called a Sipa Ho engraved on it, would dispel all obstacles and must precede Pemala through every doorway and threshold as a protection, and that Geshela would walk in front of the gurney holding the box. He also asked to accompany Pemala in the removal van. Although Matt didn't usually let family members ride with him, he agreed. Matt seemed as moved as I was at the reverence and ritual unfolding before us.

There were lots of cars already at the house when we arrived. Warm light poured from the big windows, and someone opened the door for us, ushering us inside. The rooms were full of Pemala's Tibetan family and friends. We met Pemala's husband Tsetanla and, with Dachen's help translating, tried to reassure him that all was well; and Dachen's daughter Chukyi, whose quiet and steady presence seemed so supportive for her mother, and for her grandmother Pemala, arriving home. Votive candles had already been lit on the altars and mantelpiece, and the house was full of beautiful Tibetan thangka paintings and statues. The richness of color and warmth comforted me and gave me strength.

Matt was waiting outside with Pemala and Geshela, so we had to act quickly to create a space for Pemala in the crowded house. Dachen and I decided to clear out the family room, and she had several men move a sofa and set up the massage table that Chris had brought from work so that Pemala could lie in state for her vigil. We carefully covered the table with cloths and transferred Pemala, using the sheet the hospital had given us. I tucked the used sheet under her body as best I could, and Dachen covered her with a fresh white cloth.

Though I couldn't understand all the Tibetan being spoken around me, I realized that many family members and friends were shocked that Pemala was allowed to come home and that she would be able to stay there while all the elaborate rituals and prayers of their tradition were carried out for her. I felt so grateful to be part of a new funeral home that was supporting families and communities to reclaim their right to care for their own dead, and to follow the spiritual traditions of their culture instead of worrying about the rules and regulations of the funeral industry.

I also sensed that holding this vigil wasn't going to be easy. Dachen had already told me Pemala's cremation couldn't happen until the proper astrological readings were requested, and prayers from lamas and monasteries in India, Tibet, and Nepal were done. That could take days. "How many days?" I asked quietly. "Maybe a week," she said. Inwardly I gasped, but I reassured Dachen all would work out, while silently praying to Pemala and all the deities to remove obstacles and create an auspicious passage that could help make my promise a reality.

Perhaps those prayers were heard, because my cell phone rang shortly afterward, and my friend Jeanne was on the line. She couldn't believe it, but Rinpoche's flight had been canceled. A volcano had erupted in Iceland, the flight's first destination, and no planes could land there. This, on the very day Pemala had left the world. What an auspicious sign for Pemala, as Rinpoche could come the very next day to the house. I hurried to tell Dachen, and she and her uncle Geshela shared the good news. Smiles of joy broke out on so many faces. To have Rinpoche come would be a gift and blessing.

Late in the evening, I sank down wearily on the couch in the living room with Chris and Jan. People brought us plates piled high with food, and Geshela carried a pot around, filling everyone's cups with warm tea. People were so welcoming and kind. At one point Dachen came and sat beside us. I asked her how her family came to Seattle. She told me that in the 1960s, Professor Turrell Wylie founded the first Tibetan Studies program in the United States, at the University of Washington. Supported by the National Defense Education Act, Professor Wylie was able to bring Geshela, a notable scholar, to Seattle, where he taught colloquial Tibetan for thirty-seven years. Students came from all over the world to study there. Dachen and her mother Pemala joined Geshela and Seattle's growing Tibetan community in 1968.

What a gift, to be present with this special family, and to be caring for Pemala, whose body lay quietly in the next room. I felt so privileged and honored to be there, and to help create the right conditions for a devoted practitioner to complete her sacred transition from this world. That sense of privilege and honor served me in good stead when, in the days to come, I was challenged to my core in my role as home vigil guide and funeral director. Somehow I had to translate intricate, elaborate requests from the family and Rinpoche into practical and legal actions that the modern system of caring for the dead would understand and be able to accommodate. It was a fascinating and humbling journey.

And it took everything I had to actually pull it off. The actual time of Pemala's cremation depended upon astrology readings from various countries. Then there was the challenge with time zones and, more importantly, how Tibetans and Westerners differ in ways of understanding time itself. It was impossible to be efficient, so I gave up trying. I settled for creating a boundary based on the crematorium's availability, and I hoped and trusted that divination dates would magically coincide. Fortunately, it all worked out. Again, I felt Pemala's influence in everything that emerged.

The atmosphere in the house changed when Rinpoche finally arrived. His presence was so kind and calm and confident. It settled everyone down. People stopped chatting and went and found chairs so they could participate in the prayers and practices. Books from a local monastery were passed around. Someone lit more incense and butter lamps, and the drone of muttered mantras began.

The main focus for Rinpoche and Dachen and Pemala's family was to care for Pemala's spirit and consciousness as she found her way through the bardo between death and rebirth. The *Bardo Thodol* was read aloud for this purpose. The astrology reading said that the sungdhu must be read, so a pecha Tibetan holy book of the sungdhu was found within the Tibetan academic community, providing the needed loose pages of text, which could be divided up and read aloud by three friends and Geshela in the days before the cremation. Dachen continuously played a recording of the *Bardo* readings by Nyoshul Khenpo Rinpoche (Chukyi's grand uncle) and burned sur, an incense fire offering for the three days, as the Tibetan view is that a consciousness traveling through the bardo can still hear and smell, and can be nourished and guided from the physical world.

Prayers and practice would continue for forty-nine days, with a focus every seven days at the time of Pemala's death. Every decision prioritized arranging and making offerings to lamas and teachers at many monasteries to do spiritual practice and burn butter lamps for Pemala in the days ahead, and this remained the most important intention throughout. All else was secondary. I found myself imagining how different our death care in the West would be if we also made care of a person's spirit right after death a main focus and priority.

Though the spiritual care was paramount, the details of physical care were very specific and rigorous too. I learned that no one born in the year of the Dragon, Sheep, or Pig could handle Pemala's body at all, or her rebirth could be compromised. Thank goodness my birthday falls in the year of the Horse! And we had to find someone born in the year of the Rabbit to sweep the house after Pemala's body was removed. Luckily, a family member from Vancouver was born in the year of the Rabbit and gladly performed this task. I took notes on all these details and requests, because they might come in handy for other Tibetan home vigils later on.

The date for cremation was finalized. Pemala needed to leave her home at dawn on Friday, four nights and three days after we had brought her home from the hospital. Perfect. It was a blessing that the crematorium was willing to accommodate us at an early hour and on a day they didn't usually do witnessed cremations. Thursday night, we checked off all that would go with Pemala on her journey and planned to meet in the hushed darkness before dawn. When I arrived at the house Friday morning, the air was crisp and clear and charged with hidden light. My heart was full. The first birdsong began as I knocked on the front door and made my way quietly inside. Geshela greeted me with hot tea and gestured toward a table laden with food.

We had secured a cremation container sturdy enough to hold Pemala's body and all the items that would accompany her on the journey. Dachen came from the warm kitchen carrying a pitcher of blessed water and burned incense with frankincense and juniper. She sprinkled the entire container with this elixir. People gathered around Pemala, and Dachen placed the Sipa Ho that Rinpoche had given her carefully on Pemala's heart. (Rinpoche could not be present.) This Sipa Ho would serve as a map and blessing for Pemala's consciousness to be guided in the bardo and in the next stage of her transition.

Men grasped the sheet beneath Pemala one last time and lifted her body reverently into the container. Dachen placed a cooked leg of lamb and a pair of cotton shoes at Pemala's feet. Because Pemala's main practice was Vajrayogini, she was covered with a red cloth with three lines, the top one broken on her heart/chest, and a green cloth with the same three lines covering her face. Family and friends brought white silk katas and placed them around Pemala's body, adding the scent and beauty of roses, lilies, and other flowers and ferns to bless her way.

Tibetan tradition gives specific instructions for taking a person for the last time from her home. The deceased must depart first from a west door, feet first. We found a west door and symbolically took Pemala through, as the container would not fit through that opening. Once more I was especially moved by the attention given to thresholds. Geshela did the honors again, carrying the special silver box with the engraved Sipa Ho image to dispel obstacles, and preceding Pemala at every doorway as support and protection for her journey. Pemala's body was taken out the north door of the house and into the van, then out of the van and through the big door of the crematorium, all the way to the opening of the retort itself. Such care created a tangible field of guardianship and holding.

Dachen, Tsetanla, Geshela, and other family members, along with a Khenpo, recited prayers and bardo readings before and during the cremation. Everyone refrained from crying because it is believed it will disturb the recently deceased. We set up votive candles, flowers, and sacred cloths in the little room whose window overlooks the retort. Incense was burned. Already, books were open and everyone was reciting the practices out loud together. I had paperwork to attend to with the staff, so I slipped in late. The drone of chanting generated a vibrant field of presence and care, and I imagined Pemala resting in that energetic field as her earthly form disappeared. The chance to remain for an hour or so while the cremation was in progress offered a perfect time to do spiritual practice and to be together as family and friends.

This is the gift of witnessed cremation. If being with a loved one every step of the way after death is important, then being present for the final disposition can often bring a sense of deep completion and blessing. A Sacred Moment is a funeral service that offers families this opportunity. Many other funeral services do the same now, as more and more people feel that taking part in this final stage is important and is part of caring for one's own. This is particularly true of families who have kept a loved one at home for a vigil, and who wish to accompany that person through to the end. But other families who release a loved one to the funeral home right away can still schedule a witnessed cremation and be present at the time, as a final act of tribute and goodbye.

Practical Wisdom: Discovering Your Own Way

What to Know about Witnessed Cremations

If you choose a witnessed cremation, it is important to be proactive with the crematorium and to ask ahead of time, because accompanied or witnessed cremations, where family and friends are present, must be scheduled, often as the first cremation of the day. If a funeral home is working with you and doing the transport, they can help with scheduling. They will have to expedite the death certificate so it is complete within two or three days, so there will probably be an extra charge for that service.

If you are transporting the body yourself, call the crematorium as soon as the death occurs and tell them you want to come with family in three days' time, or whatever you decide. Keep in mind that you need to keep the deceased at home for as long as it takes to get the death certificate filed, as you will need the burial transit permit to transfer and to hand off the body to the crematorium staff before the cremation can occur. The crematorium may also charge an additional fee for a witnessed cremation. Being prepared beforehand streamlines the process for everyone concerned.

Afterlife Explorations

I have told Pemala's story to pay tribute to all the Tibetan people who understand so deeply how to care for the dead in sacred ways. It is important to remember that each of us will have our own way of caring for the dead, our own customs, and these certainly need not be so elaborate or steeped in ritual as the Tibetan Buddhist practices are. In fact, there will be those reading these words who do not even believe that individual consciousness continues after death, making the whole question of how to best care for a person's soul in sacred ways afterward unnecessary.

It is obvious from my writing that I am a person who feels our consciousness continues after death, and does so in an individual personal way, at least for a time. But I want to honor each reader's imagination of what happens to us when we die, and to speak in a manner that remains relevant to you in your exploration of more healing and natural ways to care for your dead. I therefore encourage you to pick and choose from this chapter only what has heart and meaning for you.

As a spiritual seeker all my life, and a student of the nature of consciousness and mind, I remain curious about the afterlife. I am cautious of "beliefs" in general, and I try just to be present and open and interested in dying—about its mysteries and wonders—rather than resting in any certainty or knowing. I'm learning to inhabit the questions that arise at each death, rather than the seeming answers, for inevitably any answer has subjective elements and may or may not be helpful to another. Just as there are infinite ways to manifest being human in the physical realm, there are probably infinite ways to continue on (or not!) after we die.

It is entirely possible that what happens to us after death will mirror the ideas we believe in life. After all, our lives are a manifestation of our thought forms and the lens through which we view the world. Why would this not continue to be true after death? If consciousness continues after we leave the body, it makes sense to me that those who believe that they will "go to heaven" just might find themselves there, as their minds will create that reality. And those who believe that there is only oblivion when we die may find themselves in that kind of cessation and void. It's also possible, even probable, that we are astounded after death, all our preconceived notions disappearing in the face of powerful direct experience we could never have imagined while we were alive.

I am influenced by my immersion in Buddhist perspectives on death in my musings above. I have learned how much the Buddhist teachings and understanding of death can help anyone who is experiencing the seismic shifts of dying or losing someone they love. Because Buddhism is a repository of thousands of years of study about what it means to live and to die as a being of consciousness on this planet, the wisdom and understanding available in those teachings is invaluable. And it is accessible to anyone if seen from the perspective of having practical and concrete ways to help ourselves and others at the threshold of death.

David Spangler's teachings on death and dying also speak to me, mainly because they center on the person who has died, and not on any one spiritual path or belief. These teachings provide a frame of reference that honors each person's personal and individual way of being human, and his or her unique connection to the Sacred. (I use that word to encompass all ways of being alive and in relationship to the seen and unseen realms of existence.)

We are a three-part act, according to David's understanding of what it means to be human and incarnated in a body here on earth. Our incarnation is not just the time we spend as an individual person on the planet, but also includes a pre-birth existence, as well as experiences in what David calls the postmortem realms. This means that before birth, my soul was already engaged in being Lucinda this time around, and after my death I will still be Lucinda, at least for a time, just without my physical form. Whatever I do in the postmortem realms will be an essential part of who I am as Lucinda, until I am ready to move on to become another incarnation entirely.

When I share this way of thinking about the afterlife with others, many feel deeply comforted to imagine the person they love simply off on a further adventure on the other side of the veil. I know I did, imagining my mother gardening near a little cottage and hob-nobbing with some of her favorite luminaries—George MacDonald, Elizabeth Goudge, Madeleine L'Engle. David's subtle contacts from the postmortem realm have told him that we might work on a project in the third stage of our incarnation—one we longed to accomplish in life but were unable to finish. I love thinking of my mother being a scholar and teacher. She had a fine intelligence and discerning mind, and in some ways these gifts were not fully tapped in her life as a homemaker and mother of five children.

Interestingly, this view of the afterlife dovetails with the Buddhist idea of the "karmic bardo of becoming." This is the state of consciousness most of us fall into after death, if we do not recognize the clear light, or the ground luminosity, or the sacred wholeness of who we really are. (The last term is from David Spangler's Incarnational Spirituality teachings.) According to Buddhist teachings, for most people this opportunity to "wake up" to our true natures, or wholeness, flashes by in an instant, and we enter instead a time of unconsciousness, and then the karmic bardo of becoming. In this bardo realm, we take up our former habitual tendencies and inhabit mental and emotional bodies once again. The landscape we then experience is molded by how we lived our lives before. This is also where we experience the "life review" so often spoken about in many other traditions. (The Buddhist ideas are paraphrased from Sogyal Rinpoche's *The Tibetan Book of Living and Dying*, page 287. See the Resources section.) So one can see the similarities between a Western perspective like David Spangler's and an Eastern one from Tibetan Buddhism.

I include this exploration here, for I have found that such perspectives have been very helpful to people who have no tangible interest in spiritual teachings, but who are desperate to have some kind of framework within which to view either their own deaths or the loss of those they love. Rudolf Steiner's teachings of Anthroposophy are also very helpful, and they are included in the Resources section.

As you know from my writing, it is important to me to share any ideas that might help ease the shock and trauma of death and loss, for the living and the dead. As an interfaith minister, and especially now as a funeral director, my work brings me in contact with many kinds of people and their perspectives on life and death. Though these perspectives differ widely, deep down we all have a longing to remain connected somehow to those we have loved and lost, or at least to keep their memory alive. This is the strongest, most universal emotion I encounter working with others at the end of life. This longing is a force field that exists on both sides of the veil, in my experience. The dead also long to remain connected to those they knew and loved in life. They need us, and we need them. That is my felt sense, my understanding from working at the threshold of death. (Please see Rudolf Steiner's book *Staying Connected: How to Continue Your Relationships with Those Who Have Died.*)

Over the years I have collected useful tools and perspectives from different spiritual faiths and traditions, in order to offer comfort and understanding to others at the time of death. These tools can also help those who long to stay connected to the dead, but do not know how. It is my hope that these ways can help strengthen the communication between the living and the dead, for those who wish to explore this kind of co-creation. This is a subject that could be its own book, so I am including only a few generic suggestions here, ones that have helped me most in feeling a living connection to the dead. (For more information, see the Resources section.)

I. David Spangler's ideas that there are postmortem subtle realms, which we inhabit as a continuing part of our incarnation, appeal to many people, at least as a useful and powerful imagination that can bring comfort and solace to those left behind. This view also leaves the doorway open to the possibility of the dead continuing to interact with those they knew in the physical dimension, and perhaps maintaining a sense of partnership with the living still. My ongoing experiences communicating with my father after his death strengthen this way of looking at the afterlife for me. It certainly keeps my dialogue with him, and others who have passed on, more current and alive.

2. Rudolf Steiner has written many books on staying connected with the dead. The Anthroposophical suggestion of reading to the departed as a way to stay connected has inspired many people—some who do not pursue Steiner's teachings, but who simply like the practice of reading out loud to a loved one still, as a way to reach out intentionally. There are compelling accounts of souls on the other side depending on these readings for their continued well-being and evolving journeys. My father read to my mother many times after her death, sitting in her favorite reading chair. In the days after my father died, when I set the intention to read to him, he guided me to certain books, and specific paragraphs he had underlined in life, which became a way we could communicate for a time. I try to read to my father on every anniversary of his death, October 30—enjoying the quest to find books and passages that might support and inspire him still.

3. One of the Buddhist practices I like to share with others is that of praying and connecting to the dead for forty-nine to fifty days, or seven weeks after a death, each week at exactly the day and time the person died, if possible. Such a rhythm can be deeply intentional and comforting for the living, and, in my understanding, an energetic invitation to the dead to return at those times as well, to receive love and prayers as they journey onward. One need not be Buddhist to try this

way of connecting. It has helped many people I know to cope with the rawness and intensity of the days and weeks immediately following their loss.

4. It is fascinating to see how many people are now drawn to the Mexican tradition of the Day of the Dead (November 1), especially here in America, where we are bereft of traditions and customs to honor our dead in an ongoing way. It is deeply satisfying and comforting to create a beautiful, vibrant altar, filled with bright colors and candles, and the photographs of family, pets, and important people in our lives—all those who now dwell on the other side, but who are invited back each year to be wined and dined and celebrated again. I especially love the custom of putting the departed's favorite food and drink out, to entice them back across the veil for a little sustenance and nourishment. These customs are creative and soulful, weaving joy and sorrow, life and death, together as one.

How Home Funerals and Green Burials Support Sacred Care of the Dead

The idea of keeping someone's body at home or in a designated special place for up to three days after death is a common practice throughout the world, and spans many cultures and traditions. It is a tangible way to bring sacred care to the living and the dead, no matter what we feel happens to us when we die. If you are someone who feels that a person's awareness stops when the body does, the home funeral can become even more of a gift—a time-out-of-time opportunity to spend additional precious moments with a person you will never see or communicate with again.

You can still "equip" that person "lovingly" by creating a beautiful space for her to lie in state, be dressed in her favorite clothes, and be toasted and celebrated for a time; or by providing her a cardboard

or wooden "little ship of death" to journey to the cemetery or crematorium in style. This physical care of the dead can be just as
important to reclaim, as we have seen, within death practices that
rarely offer the kind of comfort and closure we really need. It nourishes the family and friends left behind, and it is, in itself, an act of
sacred care and love.

If families are more held and supported in coming to terms with
a death, as they often are with home vigils, and they can find ways
to grieve and let go in healthy ways, then perhaps the person departing can move on with less worry and concern for those left behind,
and less hindrances and obstacles for his journey. Helping families
with their stress and pain is also helping the one leaving. This too is
sacred care of the dead.

The concept of taking three days to care for someone after
death has both practical and spiritual origins. If you keep watch
over someone's body for three days, you are more certain that they
are well and truly dead, and there's less chance of burying the person
alive. In times past, when this was harder to discern, this was a vital
consideration. Perhaps the idea that it takes three days for a person's
consciousness to fully leave the physical form was also a bodily felt
sense, so that people instinctively kept a person at home for that
time in the past. Watching over the body and doing prayer and practice for three days is an important part of many spiritual traditions,
and is an age-old and valid reason for having after-death vigils.

I have found in my home funeral work, however, that the full
three days are at times not necessary. This is a relief to some families
who wish to take a little time, but cannot sustain the full three days.
We kept my mother home for less than twenty-four hours, and that
was enough. I later read in the book *Mind of Clear Light*, by His Holiness the Dalai Lama, that "the most subtle consciousness usually
remains in the body for three days, unless the body has been ravaged
by disease, in which case, it might not remain even a day. For a capable practitioner, this is a valuable opportunity to practice" (Dalai
Lama, 2003, 150). Because my mother had been ill with cancer for

so long, she probably did not need the three days I was pushing for. The time she did get was no doubt perfect for her, since she was not a Buddhist practitioner, and had her own experience to follow once she entered the postmortem realms.

The numbers of people who want a one- to three-day vigil after death are increasing, for many reasons—one being that it simply feels more natural and healing to be cared for at home by those we love. There are many people now whose spiritual practice includes the belief that having more time at the moment of death and afterward helps one fully leave the body in more peaceful and resourced ways. It also strengthens the chance of waking up to one's true nature or wholeness, one's ground luminosity, as Buddhist teachings would say.

So spiritual practitioners are including home vigils in their Advance After-Death Care Directives, and are specifying in detail the spiritual practices they wish family and friends to do for them after they die. As we saw in Pemala's story, her three days at home enabled her family, the community, and Rinpoche to carry out the prayers and customs that were part of her tradition, lineage, and practice, thus supporting her consciousness more effectively as she traversed the bardo state. This is sacred care of the dead.

And what about green burial? How does that offer sacred care for the dead?

I remember talking with someone whose mother died a firm agnostic and who wanted nothing done for her after death. The daughter was suffering from the bleak emptiness of this demand, and she knew she needed to sanctify her mother's death in some way, for her own sake. She didn't need to have any spiritual "woo woo," as she called it, looking at me mischievously. She just needed to know her mother's death had some kind of meaning, and she needed a way to remember her.

When I suggested that she choose a natural burial for her mother, the woman's whole face lit up. Her mother had loved nature, and so did she. Helping her mother rejoin the cycles of life, and replenish the earth in her death, was all the meaning the daughter needed. She wrote me later and said that she has an abiding sense of peace and well-being, a sense of the Sacred, whenever she visits her mother's grave. And she can't help feeling her mother's presence still, in the rich soil and the native blueberries thriving there.

It is helpful to remember that anything we do out of the goodness of our heart is, in itself, sacred care of the dead. I believe that the dead respond to such energies of intention and love, and benefit greatly from our simply being ourselves and showing up in the most real way we can. I love what David Spangler offered while I was writing this chapter. In his words: "The whole practice of caring for the dead, whatever form it takes, is a form of womb-building for the individual's birth into a new state of life. Just as the physical womb holds, protects, nurtures, and prepares the fetus, so the loving womb of celebration, loving thoughts, prayers, etc., can hold the person newly born and emerging into the afterlife. Though biologically different, the two wombs really perform much the same function. That, I think, is a simple way of looking at it. It's empowering, blessing, and enabling the soul as it moves to whatever form its ongoing destiny and life take it."

Part of reimagining death, for me, is opening to the possibility that the veils between being alive and being dead—between the physical and subtle dimensions of life—are much thinner than we imagine, and these veils are ever shifting and changing in this time of upheaval and transformation on the planet. Increasingly, I feel the presence of the dead in my work at the threshold, and it seems there are those who wish to share their wisdom, and to co-create with the living to help usher in the "Great Turning," as Joanna Macy calls this time of uncertainty and potential.

I do not know if this is true. It is an intuition, a potent imagination, one I find important not to abandon. In the end, it remains a question, perhaps unanswerable, but worthy of asking all the same.

It is part of my other inquiry, the one about co-creating with nature and the earth at death's threshold. Are we also being called now to co-create with the dead and other subtle dimensions of life to help humanity, nature, and the earth in our shared evolutionary journey? Not only to survive, but to thrive, in healthy, sustainable, ever-renewing, ever-hopeful ways.

I leave you with these quotes from Rudolf Steiner's book *Staying Connected*. In his words: "The dead speak to the living out of the space woven by the feeling of community (or solidarity with the surrounding world), … from the feeling of universal gratitude … the feeling of never, never losing hope in life is the feeling that enables us to experience a right relationship between the living and the so-called dead."[1] And from Christopher Bamford, editor of Steiner's writings in the book: "… this trust in all life and in humanity and the earth provides the basic medium whereby the dead can communicate with us."[2]

---

[1] Steiner, 1999, 192–200.

[2] Ibid., 193.

7

WHEN WE DIE IN THE HOSPITAL:
Field Notes for
Finding Our Way Home

One of the greatest challenges to home funeral families whose
loved one has died in hospital is overcoming body release
policies that are either counter to the law or nonexistent.

—LEE WEBSTER, *Building Bridges along the Death Care Continuum*

The number of people who will die in hospitals or other institutions is still greater than the number of those who will die at home in the United States at the time of this writing. For that reason, it is very important to consider what a hospital death can mean for families who wish to bring their loved one home for a vigil—either themselves or with some other transport aid. As Lee Webster states in the quotation above, even in states or provinces where the law gives custody and control of a deceased person's body to the next-of-kin, the hospital where that person died may have policies that directly hinder the release of said body to the family.

In many hospitals, there is no policy that even deals with releasing a body to the next-of-kin, as such an idea has never even occurred to the policymakers, based on the assumption that everyone will automatically be calling a local funeral service.

I will discuss this challenge to home funeral families further in the Practical Wisdom section. But I begin first with a story. This one was written by a home funeral practitioner and guide, Shelley Sherriff, who kindly agreed to write about her experience with dear friends Eric and Candace, and how Candace, with Shelley's wise, in-the-moment guidance, managed to get Eric home from the hospital for a special three-day vigil. The beautiful photographs of Eric's home funeral are included in the color insert of this book.

"Bringing Eric Home" by Shelley Sherriff

In British Columbia, Canada, where I live, private citizens are entitled to transport and care for a body without engaging a funeral director. However, there's a bit of a catch, because the transportation part requires a special permit, which can be obtained, after the death, only during regular weekday office hours.

This means that when someone dies in a facility at night, or on the weekend, the delay in getting that permit will likely mean that bringing the body home privately just isn't feasible. But it's still possible to bring our dead home, if that's our wish. Of course having a plan helps, but sometimes things happen too quickly for that!

My friend Eric was diagnosed with multiple myeloma several years ago. With various treatments, his symptoms were quite well managed for most of that time, and the progression of the disease seemed gradual. However, the time came when that changed; the cancer was spreading quickly, and treatments were now hurting more than helping. He decided to stop them and let things unfold as they would.

In early November, his pain grew much worse, and he spent about ten days in the hospital, getting that under control before returning home. Knowing that he wouldn't be with us much longer, a small group of very close friends were trying to plan when we might gather together with Eric one last time.

We live in various places in Canada and the United States, so finding a time that worked for everyone to travel was tricky, as always. We knew the situation was urgent, but just how much so was impossible to gauge with any certainty.

Eric's wife Candace is a physician, so we turned to her for a most likely time frame. While knowing from experience that death's arrival time is unpredictable, based on all available information she thought he likely had several months. So we friends were looking at gathering in early January, while Eric's family planned to come up from California in mid-December.

Eric remained at home, using a hospital bed set up in the living room, with Candace increasingly caring for him as he became frailer physically and mentally. She asked me to come over to Salt Spring Island, where they lived, from my home on nearby Vancouver Island to discuss end-of-life arrangements, which I assumed would include a plan for having Eric's body lie in honor at home after his death. We were going to do this the second weekend of December.

But by late November, Eric had become very weak and remote. He wasn't participating much in conversations and, when asked, said he felt "weird" but couldn't elaborate. On December 1, he returned to palliative care at the hospital. In his confusion he'd been insisting on getting up in the night and walking around, so caring for him safely at home had become impossible.

Around suppertime on December 2, which was a Saturday, Candace popped home from the hospital to make some calls. Eric was clearly slipping away faster than previously expected, and she wanted to let his family know they should try to come sooner than planned. Before long, she received a call from the hospital telling her Eric's condition had changed and she should get back quickly.

Candace did, and she sat beside Eric reciting the end-of-life prayers that are an important part of their Buddhist practice. Shortly after midnight, he died peacefully. And so it was that Eric died in the hospital, in the wee hours of a Sunday morning, with no plan yet in place for how we would transport his body, and no chance of getting the paperwork to do it ourselves until sometime on Monday.

After spending some private time with him, Candace began making calls. She called me at about 2:30 a.m. to figure out how to proceed. She'd already talked with a funeral home on Vancouver Island that's associated with the Memorial Society she belongs to. But they didn't want to make the trip over on Sunday, and especially not just to transport Eric's body back home. I hunted up the number for the one funeral home on Salt Spring Island, and she called them. They'd never had the request before to simply drive the deceased home. Although they were initially reluctant, they eventually agreed to come at 8 a.m.

A young man from their Buddhist community who loved Eric joined Candace at the hospital and stayed with her to help. He found someone to give them a big bag of ice, which they placed around Eric's body to start cooling it. Following my advice, Candace tied a cloth around Eric's face to hold his mouth closed.

The funeral director arrived with his van, and back at the house helped lay Eric out on the hospital bed in the sunroom. Taking the first ferry over, I arrived at 10 a.m. and we began creating a sacred space around Eric, where he would lie for three days.

In their Buddhist practice it's very important to disturb a body as little as possible during that time. So, rather than dressing him then, we simply placed pads and flattened bags of ice under him and draped a beautiful cloth on top. His favorite head bandana discreetly covered the cloth holding his jaw closed. We lay fresh cedar boughs alongside him, and put flowers, meaningful objects, and candles along the window ledges. Windows ajar and a curtain across the doorway assured that the room would stay cool and private.

Soon others began to arrive, and were able to sit peacefully with Eric in that liminal space. On Monday, his adult children and their mother arrived from California. At first, they were very apprehensive about seeing him and didn't go in where he lay. But, knowing that they had time and privacy, they were able to take it slowly and gently, and each in their own time did go in to be with him when they felt ready. After that, they spent lots of time with him, coming in and going out freely, taking pictures, crying, laughing, talking to him, and gradually taking in that he had died.

A friend built a beautiful box for Eric that we set up in the studio, along with art supplies. We invited the community to come and decorate it however they wished. Over those days, people covered the box inside and out with poems, prayers, love letters, paintings, and photos.

On Tuesday evening we washed Eric's body and dressed him in his favorite ceremonial garments. Family and friends gathered for a beautiful, intimate home funeral and farewell. Early on Wednesday morning the funeral director came with his van once again, this time to carry Eric's body to the crematorium on Vancouver Island. With great respect, he guided us in carrying Eric's body out of the house and placing it in the coffin. Although this was a new experience for him, he was gracious and encouraging. Eric's son Loren carefully fastened down the coffin lid, and we slid it into the van. Then we drove in a convoy to the ferry, and just at dawn we crossed the water all together on Eric's last earthly journey.

Practical Wisdom: Navigating Hospital Policies

Candace, Eric's wife, and their friend Shelley have graciously allowed their story and photos to be part of this book, as a teaching tale, and one from which I can work in this section to help you understand all the considerations you need to think about if your loved one dies in a hospital setting, and you wish to bring the body home for a vigil.

As you can surmise from Shelley's story, Eric's death was sudden and unexpected, on some level, even though everyone knew he was dying. Candace and Shelley had not met yet to plan for Eric's home funeral, so they were not prepared with different ways to get Eric home. And Eric's death happened late on a Saturday night, when there was no chance for the family to handle the paperwork.

Candace and Eric were fortunate that they were in a small island hospital that would accommodate their wishes for Eric's body not to go to the morgue. (This is a request from many Buddhist practitioners.) The hospital staff even helped Eric and Candace's young friend procure a big bag of ice to start cooling the body. And Eric died in a single room, a practice Shelley said hospitals in her area try to do when it is obvious a patient is dying.

In a larger hospital, it is possible none of this kind of support would have happened. Many times, when I was working at A Sacred Moment, we would have to speak for families who did not want a loved one to go to the morgue, when hospital staff were insisting that they needed the bed or the room. In most cases, having our removal staff take the body right away and transport it to the home was the only solution. (I have also found that hospital staff can be very kind and accommodating, and often try to find another single room where a loved one's body can be moved if the family wants and needs more time.)

It was a wise decision for Shelley to recommend to Candace to call the local funeral service. Again, fortunately, the funeral director, although he had never encountered a family wanting to bring a loved one home, agreed to come as soon as he could the next morning, and to provide transport and paperwork. Note that the other funeral service was not willing to do this. Families wanting only transportation and paperwork services may run into difficulties finding a willing funeral director to help them with only these simple services, especially if the request is an "at-need" one, as this one was.

Because Eric died on a Saturday night, it was not possible for family and friends to transport him themselves. But what if he had died on a Tuesday? Shelley and I discussed this question at length. Because the family was not prepared to transport Eric themselves on a Saturday night, no one ended up asking what the hospital policy was, and whether they would have agreed to release Eric's body to Candace, rather than to a licensed funeral director. And it is not known if staff would have allowed Eric to remain in the hospital room and not be transferred to the morgue while the family completed the necessary paperwork in order to transport Eric's body themselves. It could have taken the family at least two days. Again, perhaps the Salt Spring hospital would have worked with Candace, but in a larger hospital this would be far less likely.

The other challenge Candace, Shelley, and friends might have had, if they had wanted to transport Eric's body themselves, was the necessity, stated by law, that the body be transported in a "rigid container." Families do not normally have a rigid container on hand nor do they have access to cots or gurneys, as funeral homes do. (This was the case in my story of trying to transport Linda's mother home from the nursing home in chapter 5.) I suppose it is possible to come up with something, as families are wont to do, like a wide board, to place the body on. But the body would still need to be wrapped in something (remember Helen's red and white tablecloth) to contain supposed leakages. (This is one of the main reasons a rigid container is required by law in some states and provinces.) This home-style solution could, however, make the hospital staff even more reluctant to release the body to family members. So this has to be taken into consideration. *If one has time to plan ahead, the family can purchase a cardboard container from a local funeral home, to have on hand for when the death occurs. It is, of course, necessary to have a van or truck standing by as well.*

One might easily conclude from this discussion that the best course of action, should a loved one die in a hospital, is to call a local funeral home to help transport the body home, or to contact some kind of transport agency that is willing to help. Shelley and I agreed that this would often be the best choice to make, especially for those who are sensitive about a loved one being in the morgue for a time. Or when a loved one dies suddenly and unexpectedly, on a weekend or holiday, when there will be a delay in the paperwork if a family does it. Or if a family discovers at the time that they simply don't have the bandwidth or help to take on all the paperwork and transportation themselves.

It is very important, however, to continue to work to change hospital policies so that they reflect the actual legal right families have to take a loved one's body home from the hospital without having to engage the services of a funeral home. I believe that more and more families and communities will want to transport a loved one home themselves if possible. This is why it is so helpful for home funeral advocates to educate staff in hospital and other institutional settings, about a family's legal right to have a body released to them, rather than to a funeral service. Advocates can help those hospitals change their thinking, their language, and their policies so that families do not have to deal with the added stress of arguing and wrangling with staff at the time of death.

Be prepared and be proactive. Lee Webster, former president of the NHFA, has kindly given me permission to include her very helpful checklist for families who wish to transport their dead home from a hospital setting. This is from her book *Building Bridges along the Death Care Continuum.* (See the Resources section for chapter 2.)

"Hospital to Home Funeral Blueprint" by Lee Webster

When a death occurs in a hospital, the possibility for removal of a body by family may depend on a variety of factors, such as the cause of death, organ donation, autopsy, and many other considerations. This list of steps to take when asking for an exception to an existing policy can't cover every eventuality, but here are some key items that may be addressed should a family request to remove a body themselves or ask for additional time with the body. Keep in mind before asking for a policy exception that it is well within the hospital's rights as an independent business to enforce their policies in support of their staff and other patients. The key is to find neutral ground where your family can voice their concerns and describe their intentions respectfully, with an eye to a positive outcome for all.

Here are some suggestions for families looking to bring a loved one home when there is restrictive policy in place.

- Ensure agreement with the home funeral plan with all family members prior to approaching hospital personnel.

- If possible, obtain the hospital's Body Release Policy in writing. If it is compliant with the law to release to the family, the hospital staff should be versed in assisting families with appropriate paperwork completion and the removal.

- If the Body Release Policy does not clearly state the right of family to remove, ask to speak with a social worker, nursing supervisor, or other staff with policy authority.

- For this conversation, have with you (and hope not to need):

- Completed written advance directive regarding after-death care, including a signed and witnessed designated agent form if someone other than the next-of-kin is chosen to be responsible, if one exists.

- Identification documents (license, passport, etc.) and proof that you are the legal next-of-kin according to the law in your state.

- Confirmation of your right to have the body released to you according to specific statutes that give next-of-kin the right to custody and control of the body in your state.

- Legal statutes that describe the limits to legal authority for hospital personnel after completion of the time of death on the medical portion of the death certificate.

- Legal language that indemnifies the staff members from responsibility after release of the body to the legally designated person with custody and control, whether that is the next-of-kin, a hired funeral professional, or a designated agent.

- Consider enlisting the aid of clergy, a social worker, or a home funeral advocate to help negotiate the release.

- Inform the hospital personnel of your plans to bring the body home as early as possible.

- Invite hospital staff to help with bathing the body, washing hair, or assisting in completing the medical portion of the death certificate by obtaining the physician's signature after completing cause of death.

- Because hospitals may not have the capacity to hold a body for long periods of time, there may be pressure to remove the body before there is adequate time to get the paperwork processed along typical routes. You will need a transport permit to remove.

- Determine if your state issues provisionary transport permits without full death certificate registration, and from whom.

- Ask medical personnel for help in expediting the completion of the medical portion of the death certificate.

- If immediate removal is required and you are unable to obtain the paperwork, ask for assistance in locating a transport company that will charge only for paperwork processing and transportation to the home.

- Call funeral directors to request similar services.

- If an autopsy has been performed, there may be reluctance to release the body back to the family. The Medical Examiner/ Coroner will be the person in charge of making decisions, so appeal directly to him or her if possible.

- If organ donation has occurred, the harvesting care team will be in charge. You will need to assure them that you are capable of and willing to cope with the results of the procedure.

Depending on the organs donated, you may require assistance in body care and moving the body.

- If the person died of a contagious disease (not necessarily an infectious one), removal to the home will depend on what precautions will need to be followed, what medical agencies are involved, and other considerations, such as local and state health department protocols. Ask for assistance in understanding the particular needs and ways of dealing with them in a home setting.

8

CONSCIOUS DYING:

A Death with Dignity

The fear of death follows from the fear of life.

A man who lives fully is prepared to die at any time.

—MARK TWAIN

Some of the most valuable experiences in life arrive unexpectedly, unbidden. When Char called me into her office to say that we would be handling a Death with Dignity case, and that it would be a home funeral vigil as well, I was intrigued, as I had not encountered someone yet who was consciously choosing to end his or her life. But when I looked at the case file and saw the name, I felt only shock and sadness.

Julian Riepe. I knew this person. He was my friend. Long ago, he and his wife Laurie and children Annie and Jackson were part of my family festival work. That was nineteen years ago, and sadly we had lost touch with each other. Now another of life's thresholds was calling us—this time, for Julian, and it would be his final one, the end of his days. As I stood there, my hands shaking, I knew without a doubt that I would be supporting this family—and that it was meant to be; perhaps had been part of the deeper pattern of our connection all along. Such recognition filled me with grief, but also with awe and gratitude. Life in that moment felt very dear.

Feeling gifted and grateful stayed with me through all the days and weeks Julian, Laurie, and I worked together. And I know that many other people who were with us felt the same. My friends had a large and caring community who were by their side from the beginning. By choosing a Death with Dignity, and a home funeral vigil, Julian, and Laurie as his partner in these choices, pioneered a new and intentional way of embracing death. They reached a level of awareness, a reimagination of what it means to die that few of us will ever know, and they did it with grace and courage. Together, Julian and Laurie consciously embraced death and, in doing so, became sacred teachers for us all.

I have asked Laurie to tell their story here. Her writing is real, truthful, and vulnerable. She expresses from the inside out what it means to be the one left behind, the wife who stands with her husband in his choice to die, but has also to experience the bone-shattering ramifications of that decision. I write of my own experience with Julian's passage, and hopefully convey how helpful a home funeral vigil can be for all those involved in a Death with Dignity choice. Just giving everyone more time and space to come to terms with such a decision can make all the difference in being able to integrate what has happened. As conscious as Julian and Laurie were, actually carrying out their plan was daunting. Laurie's story reveals how much she needed all three days to even begin to tell her Julian goodbye. I think Julian knew this would be so, and why he asked for a vigil after his death.

It is our hope that receiving both Laurie's and my perspectives on those days can be clarifying and useful. Laurie's is the offering of a broken-wide-open heart, her intimate and sacred witness of Julian's departure from this world. My lens is one of a friend and guide, to help make the vigil and witnessed cremation possible, to support Julian on his journey, and to aid Laurie, family, and friends in finding some semblance of comfort and holding to ease the raw anguish and shock of those first days. I like to think that the stories are a tapestry of what is possible, offering a new imagination of what it can mean to consciously die.

"The Long Conversation" by Laurie Riepe

We were the couple who talked about everything. But, in 2010 we stopped talking. Right when we needed conversation, words failed us.

A year before, Washington State voters were the second in the country to pass the Death with Dignity Act—allowing terminal patients with fewer than six months to live to legally receive lethal medication. We didn't canvass for the initiative; when it passed in the general election, we didn't celebrate as though our sports team won. We tucked the information away. In February 2010, my husband's cancer was growing in ways we couldn't dispute. After six years of illness, Julian was given six months to live. He decided to stop his efforts to extend his life. He entered home hospice and was given a morphine pump. But still we didn't talk about death, not directly.

Instead, in May we went away for the weekend. We chose a place on Whidbey Island where we'd been for our tenth anniversary. I didn't like the unfamiliar silence developing between us. Waiting in the ferry line, I pressed a point about death and talking, how we should talk about what we didn't want to talk about. He pressed back from his position: "Let's just enjoy this, what's happening now." He didn't have to say *please*. I heard him.

He'd heard me, too.

In the middle of the night, I awoke and burrowed toward him in the king-sized bed. Julian wasn't there. Opening my eyes, I saw the breeze blowing the drapes where the glass door was open. I grabbed my sweater and stepped into the doorway. He stood naked, facing the black nothingness of Puget Sound. The silhouette of his morphine pump rested on the railing of the deck. He raised his arms and face—an orchestra conductor holding the note at the end of a symphony. I walked out, my eyes following his gesture: stars.

Feeling me behind him, he said, "It's so beautiful." He was crying. I walked up beside him, under his right arm where I fit best. Putting my hand on his back between his shoulder blades, I could feel he was cold. He'd been out here awhile.

"I don't want this to end." He was referencing everything.

I looked at the hanging splinter moon. Below us, the water captured and threw back starlight in a sheet of inky reflection. An even-darker void loomed across the water where I knew the Cascade Mountains stood.

A moment later he added, "How could I ever say *no*?" Now he was asking the Everything.

He brought his arms down, wrapping me close. I didn't answer him. I didn't know either.

Julian couldn't control the timing and progression of his disease. But he could control whether and how to have the conversation I'd pushed for on the ferry dock. Two days later, Julian told me he was looking into Death with Dignity. He wanted the option to end his life, if it came to that. I was relieved he was taking his death on directly. He was speaking the unspoken, shaping the narrative about how he would die.

Julian's decision began a monthlong process—formal and measured—of legally required conversations with doctors and pharmacists—conversations with protocol as exacting as peace talks between heads of state: he requested the means to end his life in the ways he was required; they asked if he was sure about his choice, as they were required to do. He was required to assure them. Nothing was required of me. Not yet, anyway.

The day he received the prescription for Seconal in the mail, Julian and I walked our old yellow lab the five blocks to the pharmacy, following another legal requirement: hand-delivering the handwritten prescription. We made the walk our own. We held hands and we walked slowly. We let Edgar sniff each patch of grass. We didn't talk about death. Having the prescription meant we didn't have to; instead, we talked about the sweetness of the day, not quite spring and not quite summer.

A week later I picked up the medication at the pharmacy and put it in our lock box. I felt Julian relax.

I also felt him watching me. I was struggling with what I was losing. One August afternoon in the garden, he under the crab apple tree and I in the sun, I placed my feet in the coolness of his lap. "I'm never going to find someone who understands poetry the way you do," I sighed.

He looked up at the roof with its three layers, the uppermost as old as our marriage of twenty-seven years. I followed his glance— the curling edges, the mounds of furry moss. Looking back, I could see him calculating the cost of replacement. His expression shifted. Now he was calculating the timing of his joke.

"Yeah, well, maybe he'll fix things." Julian always had a smug smile and uptick to his voice when he was delivering his line. I groaned, letting him know it had landed perfectly.

This is how we talked about what was coming.

Having the pills in our lock box helped Julian know that if things got too bad, he wouldn't have to endure just for the sake of endurance. Having the means, though, didn't help him know what to do next. How could he maximize his life and still be able to administer the pills himself, another legal requirement? How would he calculate the timing of this? An impossible question. So we played cribbage. While we played, we talked about concepts like autonomy. We circled around ideas—quality of life and self-determination. Julian seemed excited he had a way to be in relationship with his death, that he wasn't just sitting, exposed, big game in an open field. For my part, I liked the circular conversations—as though we were going nowhere. But it cost me, too, waiting for what I didn't want.

Right before Christmas 2010, we met with our therapist. We discussed Julian's fragility and its impact on our marriage.

"You've got to let her go." When Julian heard this, something happened in him: a contraction in his center, an involuntary spasm, then he started sobbing—uncontrollably. This is the way grief talks: guts and viscera and connective tissue first. It reaches in with its mysterious syntax, and it doesn't let go until you're fluently dreaming in grief. Now it was my turn to watch Julian struggle with what he was losing. I sensed I would come to know this new language, later.

When I heard Julian's crying, I saw something. His question about saying goodbye to the Everything was becoming a simpler question, simpler and harder. How could he say goodbye to me?

After the meeting with the therapist, something changed in Julian. He'd been waiting to figure out what was left—what more he needed from his life. When he saw it had to do with letting go of me, he finally knew what to do. He picked a date for his death—the second Sunday in January.

At noon on the Friday before, I finished working in my basement office and came upstairs. Julian's twin sister Jane was cleaning my kitchen, yellow vinyl gloves and soft, hurt eyes. Our daughter would fly in from California in a couple of hours, my brother from New York later that night. I felt my panic, finally. I went to find the one person I always turned to when I saw something I hadn't quite seen before.

"Julian, I have to get out of here. Can we go somewhere? Away?" I was imagining Mexico. "Lunch?"

After the gourmet tomato soup and the fancy grilled cheese, favorites at our favorite restaurant, I sat back in the cushy booth and said, "I felt bad before I ate, and I feel bad now that I've eaten."

He looked me in the eyes. "Laurie, you're going to feel bad for a long time."

I didn't know, not then, how much it would mean to me to have him say that, how much I would need to know later that he'd seen what was happening to me.

The conversations we'd been having shared a quality of standing together on a high hill and watching the storm build and roll toward us. These were conversations of gesture—a knowing look, fingertips brushing, sighs. They were sweet and close. I felt safe. But there was a final, unsafe conversation that Julian needed. Turns out I needed it, too.

The thing I didn't want was for Julian to die. The thing he needed me to do was to let him go. He needed me to let him know that I was ready.

On the afternoon he took the lethal dose of medication, Julian fell into a coma. He was snoring lightly, but he wasn't dying. Until now we'd had a map, of sorts, the protocols leading us. Now I was in unknown territory; death still had its way with mystery. It was taking a long time, longer than we'd thought. The time that it was taking was hurting me, making me want to cling. I didn't know where the words came from, but finally I knew what to do, what was required of me.

"Honey, you're causing trouble here," I teased in that way we had.

I paused. His chest rose and fell. I could hear the snow swooshing as it slid off the skylights. I held still, listening.

The pattern of his breath. The too-wet snow, unable to hold onto the roof. I used my voice to reach him. "When you're released, I'll be released."

His response was immediate. Julian stopped his breath. He ended his life.

When I didn't see his chest rise again, I looked at his face. A hint of a smile. It reminded me of how he timed his jokes, how they landed so perfectly. As if he were saying, "That was simple, wasn't it?" and "You only had to ask."

DAY ONE: DYING DAY

I'd never seen a dead body before.

As soon as my mind figured out that Julian was gone, my body took over. My mind went somewhere else. I lost my mind.

There was the silence of his body stopping, a silence that can't be described. And then there was the noise my body made: a whole-body noise; a deep, guttural, high-pitched, completely unfamiliar/familiar sound. Keening. I wish that keening sound had washed over me in my childhood. I wish I had known the old women who filled the world with that unfamiliar/familiar sound, that ancient body sound. I wish I had seen those women collapse and go to bed. I wish I'd seen them eventually get up and wander in the ghost world. I wish I'd seen them find their way to the window to sit in front of a day that wasn't theirs. I wish I'd seen those women find their way back.

Something was dying in me. I didn't know something would die in me and that I wouldn't feel, well, like me. Looking back, I see now that on that first day I was in an altered state; that the disequilibrium was anchored only by the activities that were necessary—activities Julian had planned. His sister washed his body with a sea-sponge and lavender water. I cried.

The men, whom Julian had asked, carried his body downstairs— using an old comforter as a gurney, the ends bunched up to make handles. They took him out the back door and down the steps through the basement entry. I went crazy with grief. My friend Carol lay on my bed with me and petted my head, making sounds like the sounds she must have made in her youth to her horse, Dooner, when he was afraid.

A week before his death, Julian had gone through his closet and bagged up most of his clothes, everything except what he'd need for that last week. Seven pairs of underwear, seven undershirts—some jeans and his favorite sweatshirt from Annie's college bookstore. Baseball caps. In his enthusiasm, he sent the clothes in which he wanted to be laid-out and cremated—the yellow linen shirt and the chinos—to the thrift store. Like Keystone Kops, our friends made a mad dash to Granny's Attic to plow through other discards and find our particular black plastic bag. Julian's death clothes lay nestled inside, as though they were waiting to be returned, as though they were cocooned by the jumble of other people's losses.

Once they got him downstairs, the men placed him on a little platform they'd built, draped with purple cloth and cushioned with dry ice. Someone put the sky-blue cap I had knitted on his head. He was ready for his vigil. Or we were ready for his vigil. Or we were ready for our vigil that Julian had planned for us. It's hard to figure out the right language.

But still, I hid upstairs and went crazy. I walked the dog in the middle of the night and felt like when I was a teenager, a little high on pot and uncertain of the world. I noticed that everything was electric; there was an aura around or in the people as they offered me food, and around or in the trees as I walked the familiar path. I was surprised by happenings—my friend Sheri suddenly arriving from Vancouver, BC. I hadn't known that she'd known Julian was dead (or was going to die). Time was so slippery that day. We'd been young together, and she'd known me when I first knew Julian, and it felt right/wrong that she was here in this time, which seemed conflated with all the time of my life with him.

Oh, that was another thing. Right as he was dying, I saw Julian, clearly, as a baby—how he must have looked when he took his first breath. I saw the beginning in the end of the man.

DAY TWO: GETTING USED TO IT

I did go downstairs. I marveled at him—at the him-ness of him. At the sheer beauty of him—the miracle of him. I was grateful and in awe and quiet when I was with him, laid out on his low platform, draped and dressed, with his blue cap.

Our children, Annie and Jackson, and I went together at times. We brought the dog; we went alone. There was music he'd chosen. There were candles that were watched and replenished by people whom he'd asked to be on duty. There was a cardboard "coffin," sitting on sawhorses in another room, that neighborhood children and nieces were decorating with glue and phrases cut out from magazines and pens and crayons.

There was food upstairs. Lots of food and lots of people.

Through the day and night, there were people coming to sit with him, coming to meditate and pray and sit shiva. There were people with prayer shawls and others with hippie malas. There was a Tibetan singing bowl that at one point got placed on his chest so that he looked like his heart was a big open font echoing the sky.

At 5 a.m. I wandered from my bedroom to the living room in my bathrobe. The basement door opened, and there was my friend, snow dripping from the shoes in her hand; she'd come by to sit with Julian before she went to teach her early-morning yoga class.

People slept all over the house: the kids and their friends, some I'd known since they were toddlers and others I'd never met before. They camped out together in back bedrooms downstairs, smoking cigarettes, furtively blowing smoke through the windows. My brother slept in my son's old room. Jane took a sleeping bag and slept in the room with Julian's body.

I slept in the bed I'd always slept in, the one I'd slept in with Julian. But I moved to his side of the bed. I tricked myself, without really knowing what the trick was. Later I realized I hadn't wanted to feel the lack of weight where there should have been weight. I didn't want to have a sense of the absence of his presence.

I seem to have a way I like to try to cheat death.

In those three days, though, whenever I got too crazy with my attempts to finesse my way out of the loss of him, I was brought back to the rightness of all the wrongness. By being with his himness, with his body. The thing that my mind grabbed onto was how alive he seemed, how animated he still was in his inanimate state. He seemed to be breathing. It looked as if his chest was rising and falling. A lot of people saw it, and we marveled together: optical illusion? shared wish? something about the way consciousness lingers? or the nature of change?

I found myself thinking that maybe how we become dead isn't like a switch turned off, but more like the light changing at the pivot points of the day. First it's just light, then less light, then color that is related to light—color like pink. Then the color changes, and shades of blood come in, shades that hint blue then imply iron and eventually simply say gray.

We watched and we marveled at the thing Julian had made—this vigil, the orchestration, the artistry.

DAY THREE: HOLDING ON AND LETTING GO

Something got going in me on the third day—a sense that I didn't want Julian to leave, that I wanted his body to stay. It wasn't in words that I thought this. It was something in the way I felt. The jut of my jaw. The way I said no. The irritation I was beginning to feel at people's generosity. The way I was trying to hide my irritation. I got tighter and quieter. Somewhere early in the third day a plan (a very ill-conceived plan) hatched and stuck in me. The plan went like this: I won't.

So ill-conceived was my "I won't" plan, by the middle of the day all I could do was helplessly miss my cues in the artistry of Julian's vigil. I couldn't make decisions about when (today or tomorrow?) to go to the crematorium. Or how to get there (rent a van or a hearse?) or who should go (everybody or a few?). I got more and more paralyzed. Late in the day I tried to make it about me—grieving widow and all that. But something seemed hollow and wrong.

So I went back to his body. I noticed something.

There wasn't so much him-ness anymore. There wasn't so much wonder, awe. Things were more static—thing-like. His stillness was more still. There was also a feeling that he was over there—that I was separate. There wasn't so much pull and feel of the weight of him.

DEPARTURE

The next morning, I had to get up early. It was no longer a house party—now the gathering felt like an assemblage, a contingent, or maybe a delegation—something vaguely militaristic. We had come to the limit of Julian's vision, and we were kind of on our own now. Lucinda had arranged to get Julian to the crematorium by 9. It was way down south, and there was a process to get him out of the house, people to organize. We decided we would bring the dog, too. But before all that—before the campaign of getting Julian to the funeral home—I had something I needed to do.

Even though I'd been touching Julian at times while he was laid out downstairs—resting my palm on his chest, for example—I hadn't really handled his body after he'd died. But my witchy-Wiccan naturopath friend, Robin, suggested to me that I should close Julian's chakras using essential oils before he was taken to be cremated.

This made sense to me.

While everyone else was trying to get dressed and make coffee and grab toast, I went downstairs and closed the door. It was just the two of us.

I unbuttoned his yellow shirt and pushed the panels aside. Then I unbuttoned his chinos and unzipped his pants.

I started where Robin had told me to start. I moved my hands under his underwear. So familiar. Gently, I placed the vetiver oil at that soft fontanel behind the scrotum. I thought about having said yes to each other for such a long time.

Next, I slid my hands so that one was at his hip and one at his shoulder, and I rolled him onto his side. His back was ridged, cold from the dry ice—and the skin was mottled where the blood had pooled.

Resting his weight against my thighs, I put sandalwood oil at his sacrum, tracing the triangle at the base of his spine. I gently placed him back, laying him flat.

Right where the ribs flair, at his diaphragm, I dripped five drops of helichrysum. I cried as I touched him. I had never felt so tender, so open, so grateful. I was moved by how fast and full his life had been—how sweet loving him had been. There would be times in the future when I would feel how wrong it is that Julian is gone; but tending his body that morning—his life, his death—was right, in the rightest way that things can be right.

Then I put oil at his heart—where the breastbone is—rose oil in that little dip.

And at the hollow of his throat, rosemary.

I looked at Julian's face and I allowed myself to place my hand on his cheek—resting it there. I looked at the tumor on the other side of his face; it had caused him so much pain.

I pooled the tulsi oil in my left palm, and using my right thumb I stroked in a circle at his third eye, between and above the brows, as though he had a headache, as though he needed soothing.

Finally, I slipped the sky-blue cap off, dripped five drops of frankincense onto my palm, and massaged it onto the top of his bald head. The room was quiet. It was quiet between us. I sat back on my heels and rested.

When I was ready, I straightened his clothes, drawing the curtain of his shirt, buttoning. I placed his cap back on.

Before I went, there was one last thing. In my palm, soft and fragrant now, I placed my collection of baby teeth from Annie's and Jackson's childhood. I held the small jumble, and I looked at Julian's face—the sweet angles. Then, I placed the little teeth in the pocket of his shirt. It was right for him to have them.

There was more that happened that morning. Poems were read, roses laid, jazz played. There was confusion and hilarity and forgetting. At one point, we all had to wait while the mortician down at the crematorium worked to get Julian's ring off to give to me—a kind of backwards wedding. Looking back, I see me struggling with a rising feeling of brokenness.

NOW, TODAY

I still feel the weight and pull of him. Sometimes I crawl over to his side of the bed. Sometimes I don't know what happened to me when I lost my husband in 2011.

There's something, though, that I do know. Julian had a good death.

And there's something else, too. We had a good goodbye.

"Julian's Festival" by Lucinda Herring

Julian and Laurie's living room was filled with people—their daughter Annie and son Jackson, Julian's twin sister Jane, a whole community of loving friends there to learn about Julian's plans. I don't think anyone in that room had ever been asked to schedule a death in their calendars. Show up on January 9, for that's the day Julian was choosing to die. I felt an element of shock in the circle, and I knew one of my tasks would be to help people understand more what we wished to do—hopefully relax, feel safer, and be reassured.

Julian held court from the beginning, introducing me lovingly as the person who would help them create his "festival" when he was gone. We smiled at each other, but it was hard not to tear up. He led so naturally, orchestrating his own funeral, to the surprise and awe of everyone in the room. Who would be in charge of food and sustenance? Who would do the phone tree? Who would like to supervise the neighborhood children in painting his casket and writing poems? Julian was concerned that he was a big, heavy man, and he asked me to work with all his men friends to set up and even practice the best way to transport his body to the meditation room downstairs for the vigil. It was remarkable—his clarity and courage, the rare combination of humility and power he carried, sitting there on the sofa with Laurie.

I was moved by the two of them. Though they were suffering so much, Julian and Laurie were still able to hold space for their friends and family to come to terms with this difficult decision. People had a chance to express their feelings, and they did. I was there to listen to concerns and offer ways people could feel more comfortable when the time came. What a privilege it was, to share what I knew. But the greatest gift was experiencing Julian and Laurie, and their conscious leadership and love.

I remember Julian throwing a big arm over one of his friends whose face was stricken with grief, pulling the friend up to stand beside him. In that moment, Julian towered over us, his face radiant despite how disfigured the tumor made him look. This gesture was so caring. I realized how much Julian was empowering us, how benevolent and giving he was to others, even though he was the one ill and dying.

This would take everything, Julian acknowledged, and that was what he wanted. He wanted it all, and we mustn't forget to laugh and celebrate as well. Yes, there would be tears and pain and challenge. It would be fierce and raw, unbearable. He also hoped that things could feel normal, ordinary, as natural as possible. Death in life; daily life; life in death. This we must try to do. For Julian, there seemed to be less and less difference between living and dying. It was hard to believe his forceful spirit wouldn't still be with us after death.

Julian, three days dead, lay in state in the meditation room downstairs. The tumor on his face was quiet, hidden in beautiful silks. He wore his favorite knitted cap. His bearded face had grown younger and younger each day, as the cares and stresses of his illness fell away. He was magnificent. People commented on it often, and called him King. He looked like King Arthur—a huge, burly man full of love and vitality, even in his death.

Every day, I felt Julian's consciousness like a radiant sun, coming to warm and sustain us. Resting quietly in the room between my duties, listening, I sensed his suggestions in my heart. He was still orchestrating, my friend, only now from the other side. He seemed to understand that I was holding a lot: the care of his body/tumor, the emotional needs of others, education of a community of people—many who had come to experience a death in this way for the first time and wished to talk about it, to know how they too could have home vigils for their loved ones. I felt Julian's collaboration and support across the veil.

At the end of the vigil, a good friend and I found an electric-blue van that would play satellite jazz for Julian, since that was his favorite music. We filled the back with helium balloons and flowers. I would drive the King to the crematorium—the "kiln" as we were calling it, since Julian was a potter. Laurie would sit beside me. I felt so honored. Even in her dissolution, Laurie was such a powerful presence—Julian's sovereign partner in their journey.

On the morning of the departure, Laurie donned an electric-blue vintage coat that matched the van perfectly. All the men walked

solemnly down the walk, carrying the King to his awaiting cardboard "boat." It was wild and boisterous and beautiful—covered
with bright paint and drawings and messages of love and farewell.
The children in the neighborhood who wrote poetry with Julian had
written him poems and placed them in the casket to accompany him
on his journey. In our closing ceremony, some children stood and
read their poems aloud into the hush and beauty of a dawning day.

It was my job to drive my friend's body in rain and snow all the
way to the crematorium. I trembled at the responsibility. But Julian's
spirit called upon mine. He asked me to keep expanding, keep getting bigger. So I did. At one time on the highway, I realized I was
driving as slowly as I would have in a cortege or procession, because
I was carrying the King. Cars were rushing by us, but we were in a
sacred time and space of our own creation. We chuckled and sped
up, jazz spilling from the speakers to lighten our way.

In the big, industrial back room of the crematory, we gathered
together. A child, Julian and Laurie's niece, was so attentive and curious, so present. In a whisper, she asked me if we were going to
"cook" Julian now. I nodded that we were. Solemnly, her sister rang
a bell three times as we prepared to slide our friend inside the "kiln."
Someone tied a yellow Smiley Face balloon on his cardboard boat.
It bounced up and down and all around our King, as the oven doors
closed. Julian's last message: Don't forget to smile. We were laughing
through our tears.

Laurie stood with her daughter and son and calmly pushed the
button that would set her Julian on fire. Though she did not know
this herself, her presence warmed the stark concrete surroundings.
I felt how the love and conscious marriage Laurie had shared with
her husband fully flowered at the time of his death. It is one of the
most powerful gifts I have received in this work—experiencing the
rich intentional Love between my friends, how that Love seemed to
only grow stronger through its final transformation.

There was such deep humanity in our journey. It was unbearable,
but we bore it. We bore it together.

Since Julian's death, I have taken part in a number of cases where someone chooses to take lethal medicine to end their suffering. Several times I have been called as a funeral director to a home where the family felt distraught about their loved one's decision, and this negativity spilled over to the people coming to remove the body from the house. If the medicine does not work right away, a level of stress and confusion can become part of the journey for those left behind, and at times for the person trying to die. I have also experienced very peaceful, even joyful, transitions after a person takes the medicine—where the family was accepting and content because the loved one died on her own terms, her autonomy and dignity intact.

Laurie and I have offered presentations together—she sharing her story, and I talking about how helpful home funeral vigils can be to families and friends needing more time and opportunity to come to terms with a loved one's conscious choice to die. As a psychotherapist, Laurie now works with clients interested in conscious dying. She also runs support groups for families of people who have chosen Death with Dignity, based on her own needs and experiences after Julian died. Laurie and I have discovered that the Death with Dignity topic is truly an edge for many people, and it has been challenging to be on the front lines, sharing our perspectives. Yet we know the inquiry is a needed and important one to explore. It is clear to both of us that conscious dying is the next frontier waiting for our creative engagement, understanding, and love.

Practical Wisdom: Making the Choice: What You Need to Know

Death with Dignity laws allow qualified terminally ill adults to voluntarily request and receive a prescription medication to hasten their death. As of January 2019, California, Colorado, the District of Columbia, Hawaii, Oregon, Vermont, and Washington State have

Death with Dignity statutes. In Montana, physician-assisted dying is legal by State Supreme Court ruling, although there are few guidelines for doctors to work with this change in law at the present time.

To qualify for a prescription under physician-assisted dying laws, a person must be:

- a resident of California, Colorado, the District of Columbia, Hawaii, Oregon, Vermont, or Washington State; and

- eighteen years of age or older; and

- mentally competent, i.e., capable of making and communicating his or her health care decisions; and

- diagnosed with a terminal illness that will, within reasonable medical judgment, lead to death within six months; and

- able to self-administer and ingest the prescribed medication.

All of these requirements must be met without exception. A person will not qualify under aid-in-dying laws solely because of age or disability. Two physicians must determine whether all these criteria have been met.

Persons with dementia or Alzheimer's do not qualify, as they are not considered mentally competent to administer their own medicine. The only option for someone diagnosed with these conditions is to choose VSED—voluntarily stopping eating and drinking. The challenge with this is that persons must be able to personally choose and then carry out such a decision themselves. This often means making such a choice in the early stages of a diagnosis, which can be a very difficult, if not impossible, task for most people to manage.

In states where Death with Dignity laws exist, no doctor is ever obligated to assist with such a death. It is important to ask one's personal doctor if he or she supports such a choice, and find other doctors who are willing should one's personal doctor refuse. Remember that a person must have two doctors sign off on the request.

Currently, it is not possible to acquire a list of supportive doctors, though this may be a policy that changes in years to come.

It is important to know that the application process can take two to four weeks to complete. Often, as death draws near for someone, the ability to make clear and lucid decisions is compromised. In such cases, it is probably already too late to initiate the process. Those who are interested in obtaining the prescription medicine are advised to begin the application process early so that all is in place when the medicine is needed. Many people have reported what peace of mind they have, knowing the medicine is present and available, even if they never choose to use it.

It is helpful to engage hospice and to die at home if possible, as hospitals have different policies about supporting the Death with Dignity option, and most do not allow a person to ingest the medicine on the premises. End of Life Washington has a chart on its website documenting which hospitals support Death with Dignity, and which do not, and the different ways such institutions work with patients and families wishing to make this choice at the end of life.

Death with Dignity advocates strongly emphasize the right choice of words when speaking of a person's option to take lethal medicine to end his or her life. This wording is taken from a document found on the End of Life Washington website: "… the term, 'physician-assisted suicide' is inaccurate when talking about the Death with Dignity Act. The correct term to use is 'aid in dying.'" The California, Oregon, and Washington State laws clearly state: "Actions taken in accordance with [the Death with Dignity Act] shall not, for any purpose, constitute suicide, assisted suicide, mercy killing, or homicide, under the law." The Washington Death with Dignity Act did not legalize assisted suicide in Washington State. RCW 9A.36.060 states that "A person is guilty of promoting a suicide attempt when he or she knowingly causes or aids another person to attempt suicide" and "Promoting a suicide attempt is a class C felony." Assisted suicide is still illegal in Washington.

Families who have had a loved one use Death with Dignity experience something no other family does. This makes their grieving an uncommon journey, one that needs a certain kind of awareness, support, and care. It is highly recommended that families connected through a Death with Dignity choice find each other and create a support group if possible. Laurie Riepe, whose powerful story is told in this chapter, is a psychotherapist facilitating such groups now in her work, focusing on conscious dying.

9

REIMAGINING THE
FUTURE IN ECOLOGICAL
AFTER-DEATH CARE

If we surrendered to the Earth's intelligence
We could rise up rooted, like trees.

—RAINER MARIE RILKE

*T*here are ideas and technologies right on the horizon that have the potential to radically transform the funeral industry and our existing options in after-death care. Some of these visions, like Promession, began appearing, like collective seeds, about the same time communities were beginning to reclaim home funerals and the right to care for their own dead, in the 1990s. These paradigm-shifting ideas are all focused on disposition that either is patterned after nature or is at least less toxic and destructive to the earth and the environment. Although the first two projects shared are not

available yet to families, they offer compelling alternatives to cremation and conventional burial.

New Imaginations for Our Bodies after Death

I begin with a story—one I wrote for my friend Katrina Spade,
whose Urban Death Project, now called Recompose, has been an
inspiring endeavor I have supported since its beginnings in 2014.
Recomposition, a process that "gently converts human remains into
soil, so that we can nourish new life after we die," is still in its imple-
mental stages but is moving steadily toward manifestation each year.

Recomposition

I remember walking into Katrina Spade's house the night of the Kickstarter party for her Urban Death Project in Seattle. My colleague
Jan and I were representing A Sacred Moment Funeral Services, but,
really, we were there because we couldn't stay away. Who in their right
minds would miss out on the launch of such a wild and wonderful
idea—to compost human bodies into fertile soil in urban areas? And
to do so in ways that brought back participation and ritual and meaning to after-death care? Jan and I loved the concepts, and the minute
we stepped inside the door, we loved the crowd. The house was overflowing with fascinating people, most of them young, like Katrina,
full of energy, interest, and enthusiasm. As I wandered from room
to room, I felt as if I had entered the future—one where death was
a household word again, and people could laugh and joke and make
merry while musing over the temperatures needed to cook a corpse. It
was surreal and very real at the same time. I felt immediately at home.

Excitement was high because the Kickstarter was flying off the
charts and exceeding everyone's expectations. The project had fans
all over the world, and now it was garnering the needed foundational
money. Best of all, the project had Katrina.

I knew the minute Katrina began talking that the Urban Death Project had every chance of succeeding. There she was, standing in her own house, amid a sea of people waiting to hear from her—eager to understand her vision, drawn to her presence and passion. Katrina was calm and steady, showing us a video of her ideas, with graphs and illustrations, because she is an architect and designer. She's also a strong voice for nature and the earth. It's part of the beauty of what she sees, who she is—part of why Recompose has so much going for it. There is a brightness of being in Katrina, a clarity that feels refreshing and true. Because she is so much herself, she asks you to be yourself as well—and so you are. And, like any fine midwife who is focused on birthing something into the world, she has no need or time to be the center of attention herself. It's the vision that needs our tending and care. So we are invited to jump on board, roll up our sleeves, and get to work. With such a warm welcome, it's impossible to say no. And that's why I'm sure Katrina is going to open the first Recompose facility in Seattle someday.

I use the word "recompose" because, as of 2018, the non-profit organization Urban Death Project has metamorphosed into a Public Benefit Corporation called Recompose, in order to move forward in its mission to make recomposition a viable alternative for the future. ("Recomposition" is the term that will be used for this kind of after-death care.) The two major goals on the horizon are to complete a program with Washington State University to pilot the recomposition process, and to raise funds for the actual facility to be established in Seattle by 2023.

So what will recomposition be like, should we choose such an end-of-life plan? Let's imagine for a moment that our Aunt Tilda has died in Seattle, and she has expressly asked for her body to give back in some way to the city she loved. On the day of her ceremony/committal, family and friends arrive downtown at the Recompose facility, where our aunt's body will soon become compost, something that as a gardener she found delightful.

It is a cold February day, but inside the building we are greeted not only by the warmth of the Recompose staff, but by the heat softly generated by the Hive of units where the actual process of decomposition and recomposition of bodies is taking place. That warmth, along with the beauty of a building full of spaciousness and light and green, growing plants—intermingling with death as one—brings us comfort and a strong sense of the cyclical nature of things. The whole environment feels sacred, its deep stillness holding us in our grief. Outside, the center offers a public park and memorial site, available to all. This is no standard funeral home. This is the way we will be greening death for the future.

We are not arriving with Aunt Tilda, although many home funeral families will transport a loved one's body in their own vehicles, which is perfectly legal to do, provided they have a burial transit permit. Aunt Tilda lived in a tiny apartment and chose not to have a vigil, knowing we would be able to bathe and adorn her body at the facility anyway. Susan, a staff member trained in home funeral body care, and gifted with ceremony and ritual, is the perfect person to greet us at the door. She directs us to a smaller room, where Aunt Tilda's body lies in state waiting for us.

We spend the next hour brushing Tilda's hair and anointing her with essential oils she loved—lavender and rosemary. We are given a simple shroud, part of the Recompose offering, and we tenderly place our aunt inside, tying the straps while singing "I'll Fly Away," her favorite song. Tilda loved fiddle music and harmonica, so two friends play old Southern tunes as we process slowly toward the Hive, where our aunt will be placed in her own hexagonal cylinder to begin her composting journey. As we carry Aunt Tilda—singing, crying, and laughing together—we do so in the silent presence of all the other people whose bodies are already in the Hive. Our ceremony feels like an offering to them as well—an honoring of the power of collective vision and action to co-create with nature and give back to the earth when we die. That embracing gesture captures the heart of Recompose for all of us.

When we reach the Hive, someone remarks that Aunt Tilda always sang to her bees, so how perfect that her chosen way to decompose mirrors those wise and wonderful creatures. After we recite a poem by Wendell Berry and offer prayers, the door of Tilda's resting place opens. Some of us place her body inside on a bed of wood chips. Others take shovels and blanket her with additional ones. We say goodbye and seal our dear aunt inside.

At the end of her journey, Aunt Tilda's body—bones and all—will not be recognizable as human. With the aid of special staff who will screen out metal and mercury fillings, the coarse loam left will be cured and made into compostable soil. So in roughly six weeks' time, the form of the aunt we loved so well—with her gnarled hands, tiny feet, and blue-blue eyes—will have transformed into living compost, ready to be mixed with other soil and earth. She will metamorphose into a maple tree, lending her grace to a busy street corner in a crowded part of the city, a place where harried people rushing by might suddenly stop and look up, hearing the leaves rustling in the wind as a fiddle tune, seeing the branches dance in scarlet hues against a blue-blue sky.

Katrina's original vision was to place human bodies in a Core unit that would be at the center of the Recompose building, where families could process up a spiraling walkway to the top and place their loved one inside. The body would join others already in the process of decomposition, and make its way down to become collective compost at the bottom. The most startling part of this vision was that the remains a family received back would not be individual, just a sampling of "soil" jointly composed of all the bodies that were in the Core with their loved one.

This vision is a radical shift in ethical and philosophical views of how to care for our dead, and it has been controversial. Family members would have to be okay with not holding onto any tangible part of their loved one. And we ourselves would have to release any attachment we might have to "continuing on" as individual substance after we die. Instead, all of us would be embracing another

way of seeing entirely—one that recognizes our interdependence
with each other, and our essential oneness with all living beings.
Personally, I find this exhilarating—this invitation to let our individual "stories" go, and simply be human beings together—with a
common goal of giving back to life.

Interestingly, however, it turns out that this part of Katrina's vision
is not practical at the present time. Perhaps we are not quite ready for
such a unified way to care for our dead. Katrina, ever a pragmatist, has
had the courage to move forward now with technology that already
exists: the cylinders to compost bodies individually. She has stayed
true to her dream of being collective by designing those units as hexagonal, and stacking them in ways that invoke the collective beauty of
a hive. And she has placed her vision of the Core lovingly away, as a
potent imagination of what is possible for us all in the future.

For the present, Recompose has a host of team members from
all walks of life who are eager to work together: soil scientists from
universities, biologists, social and cultural pioneers, lawyers eager
to tackle the pioneering aspects of this work, and funeral directors
like me who are committed to bringing more ecological and sacred
practices into the industry. There is no doubt that urban areas are
already running out of land for cemeteries. Recomposition offers an
elegant and practical way to address this problem. It also provides
an excellent way to sequester carbon and improve soil health, just
as Promession does. Recomposition can save more than a metric
ton of carbon per person. This is a tangible and sustainable way to
address climate change issues for the future.

One of the elements of Katrina's vision that I love most is that
it innately builds and nurtures the idea of community—from the
smallest microorganisms that are helping a human body decompose,
to the creation of vibrant urban centers where death can become a
natural part of life again. Katrina's design plan will be a structural
blueprint that any city can use in building its own facility. Beyond
that, each Recompose center can be custom designed to meet the
creative and practical needs of the community it serves. A universal

plan, designed to also be unique and local, will reflect the spirit of the place and the people who will come. What's more, existing buildings can be used—like empty strip malls, warehouses, and old apartment buildings in downtown areas—bringing recycling to a whole new level.

We need ways to build true and sustainable community in cities, where it is so easy to feel disconnected and alone. I can imagine Recompose centers becoming places where people hang out in Death Cafés to talk about mortality openly with one another; to create marvelous art, music, and theater to help people get more comfortable with dying; or simply providing a nurturing place to be together in daily life.

Who knows, some day municipalities and our tax dollars might fund Recompose centers, radically transforming the existing funeral industry as we know it. City folk will simply have a card, like a library card, that is handed over at the time of death. This can aid people from all walks of life to become nourishment for the parks and other green spaces of the city where one has lived and loved. Whatever happens, it is clear that looking to nature for the best ways to care for our dead opens up exciting and unknown vistas we are only beginning to imagine. Recompose is a leading voice and model for this regenerative and healing change.

Promession

I am honored to include Promession in this chapter on more ecological ways to care for our dead in the future. Susanne Wiigh-Mäsak—a visionary biologist, composter/gardener, and engineer—embodies all that I am trying to convey in this book about reimagining death and what is possible in end-of-life care. She is part of the collective field of human beings who know that the way we are handling our dead must change, and she is passionate about modeling a different way. One that works co-creatively and in partnership with nature itself, and that comes from a nonprofit perspective that believes in the potential of "seeding" ideas that can take root and flourish

around the world naturally and organically. Susanne has worked tire-
lessly since 1998 to bring the idea of Promession to the world, as
an environmental and ethical alternative to existing funeral industry
practices. Her husband Peter joined her efforts in 2005.

Promession (a name derived from the Italian word for "promise") is a method that turns human bodies into nutrient-rich com-
posted soil, allowing our deaths to nurture and contribute back to
the cycles of life. Susanne's devotion to composting, and to rebuild-
ing and sustaining healthy soil, lies at the heart of Promession's
contribution to after-death care. Such a system also "grounds" the
carbon of our bodies back into the soil, rather than releasing carbon
into the atmosphere, as flame creation does—effectively addressing
and minimizing climate change, rather than adding to the problem.

Here's how Promession works:

1. The body is frozen and placed in a casket, to support the
   traditional funeral practices a family might choose. This
   casket is made of wood, biodegradable to minimize the environmentally harmful process of manufacturing caskets from
   metal or endangered wood.

2. Inside the Promator, the frozen body is removed from the
   casket and exposed to liquid nitrogen, a by-product of the
   liquid oxygen production already needed for medical procedures. Through a process of cryogenic freezing at temperatures
   of $-196°C$, the body becomes crystallized and very brittle.

3. Applied vibration breaks down this brittle body into a powder
   within minutes.

4. The powder is then freeze dried in a drying chamber, to
   remove all moisture left from the process. This leaves about
   30 percent of the original weight.

5. Metals left (amalgams, medical implants, etc.) are removed by
   a well-proven metal-separation technology.

6. The remaining material is placed in a biodegradable coffin, which is then buried at a shallow depth of 20–40 centimeters, thus supporting a rapid and effective decomposition that turns the body into nutrient-rich humus in as little as six to twelve months.

7. Families are encouraged to plant a tree or shrub in connection to the burial ground to commemorate their loved one, and as a symbol of death becoming life once again.

Promession ensures that a body will produce rich, nourishing soil within a year's time. This offers a solution to countries where cemetery land is increasingly scarce, as Promession's ecological burial system will transform the way we have traditionally buried our dead and provide sustainable land resources for the future. It addresses the environmental problems we already have with traditional burial—rampant use of resources, toxic manufacturing of caskets, use of pesticides and embalming fluid, creation of methane gas, and pollution of groundwater. Promession also offers a far more ecological alternative to traditional flame cremation: there is a guaranteed zero emission of mercury, dioxins, and other harmful pollutants from Promession's technology, and fewer resources will be used to operate the systems.

Because approximately 80 percent of Swedes are cremated today, the Swedish funeral industry does not yet feel threatened by Promession's "promise." And yet, more than 70 percent of Swedes interviewed about Susanne's system claim that they will choose Promession over cremation if and when it becomes available to them. Those numbers are certain to increase over time, as Sweden is known for its environmental awareness and concern for climate change. It seems from everything I've read that the country of Sweden is very proud of its visionary gardener/composter turned entrepreneur, Susanne Wiigh-Mäsak, and looks forward to having this more ecological and ethical way to care for the dead. Promession's ethical stance is clear: Susanne prefers to follow the principles of nature, which for her means continuing to bury human bodies, but to do so in ways that follow nature's way of decomposition, and that rebuild carbon-rich soil for the future. The dead body can then become a gift back to nature rather than a pollutant to the environment. I support Susanne and Peter in their admirable mission, and I uphold that Promession will become a viable after-death alternative for the future. In Susanne's words, "It will be a gift to the soil and to us all when it does."

Practical Wisdom: The Environmental Cost of Cremation

In the United States, close to 60 percent of families today are choosing cremation, because it is simpler, easier, and more economical. In addition, people think cremation is a more environmentally friendly alternative to conventional burial. Both my mother and father opted for cremation, even in Alabama, where burial is still the most traditional and accepted choice, thinking it would be easier and more economical for us as a family. (And it was.) In some states this cremation percentage is even higher, closer to 75 percent. These numbers are only going to increase over time, so I am including a discussion of flame cremation (to distinguish this method from water cremation, discussed below) here, in acknowledgment that many readers will choose cremation for their after-death plans. I offer, also, ways to minimize the environmental impact of such a decision.

Most people do not realize that flame cremation is unsustainable for our future and cannot be considered a green, eco-friendly choice of disposition, because it is dependent on fossil fuels and contributes in large measure to global warming and climate change. Each cremation lasts three to four hours, burning at 1,700–1,900°F. That is a huge amount of fossil fuel, at a time when we wish to reduce our dependency on oil. Each cremation emits 250–350 pounds of carbon dioxide into the atmosphere. Some estimates say more. Multiply that by the countless number of cremations that occur each day all over the world, and the result is sobering.

In addition, each cremation releases toxic mercury from dental amalgams, dioxins, nitrogen oxide, furans, and other harmful emissions and particulates into the air. Though newer, more fuel-efficient and filtered cremation retorts are reducing these statistics, the impact cremation has on our planet is far too high and must be taken into consideration when choosing more ecological after-death care.

Another unknown fact about cremation is that the ashes (which are not really ashes, but ground-up bone, more like fossils) are not beneficial to the natural world. In fact, they can be harmful. The idea of scattering cremains and giving them back to nature is one that many people carry today. Yet cremains do not decompose, and decomposition is the process by which nutrients are returned to the soil in beneficial ways. Anything that does not decompose efficiently is problematic, in fact can be toxic to the surrounding ecosystems. The high levels of sodium and alkaline pH (11.8, whereas soil is between 5 and 8) make cremains a source of pollution rather than nourishment for the environment.[1]

Because many people reading this will or must choose flame cremation for their families and themselves, it is important to know that there are ways to help minimize the impact of this choice on the environment. One is the work Bob and Annette Jenkins are doing with Verde Products, Inc. Their product, called Let Your Love Grow, is enriched with bacteria that, when added to cremated remains, will "break down the bone fragments and neutralize their detrimental effects" to the environment.[2] Verde Products is also studying a product and a system that will optimize the natural decomposition of bodies, similar to Recompose (discussed at the beginning of this chapter).

---

[1] Bob Jenkins, "ZPG—A Product to Attain Zero Pollution Growth after Cremation," in *Changing Landscapes*, ed. Lee Webster (2017). See the Resources section for more information on Verde Products, Inc.

[2] Ibid.

Some funeral homes are now offering "carbon neutral" cremation services. This means that the amount of CO_2 that your cremation will emit into the air will be "neutralized" by some kind of carbon-offset program that promotes energy efficiency efforts, reforestation, renewable energy development, and CO_2 sequestration projects, to name a few. Do some research and find out if there is a funeral service near you that offers such a carbon-offset program. If people begin choosing this option, more funeral services will provide it. These endeavors are at least a start in the right direction.

Available Eco-Friendly Alternatives

Aquamation

Alkaline hydrolysis, aquamation, resomation, or water cremation (it would be nice if the companies offering this would settle on a name!) is fast becoming the number one eco-friendly alternative to burial or cremation. At the time of this writing (2018), eighteen U.S. states have passed laws to allow families to choose alkaline hydrolysis, and it is legal in every state for pet disposition. And many other states have legislation on the table to approve AH in coming years. In Canada, three provinces, constituting more than 66 percent of the population, have legalized the technology. Australia is not far behind, led by a company called Aquamation Inc., whose intention is to have a working system by the end of 2018, and where it is legal for anyone to choose this option.

So what will happen to your body if you choose AH? You will be placed on a wire tray inside a stainless-steel cylinder, which is then filled with water and an alkaline agent, which is potassium hydroxide or sodium hydroxide—essentially lye. The water, in constant motion, is heated to temperatures ranging from 200° to 300°F, depending on the unit used. Everything but the bones becomes liquid, essentially returning the body to its natural state of 73 percent water. It takes as little as four to eight hours, or as long as eighteen to twenty, again depending on the type of unit being used and the amount of heat and pressure applied. The liquid eventually finds its way to the local water-treatment facility. The bones, very white and scoured clean, are ground into a fine powder and returned to the family of the loved one in a container, just as cremains are.

Alkaline hydrolysis is not a new concept, as it has been used for decades to dispose of contaminated animal carcasses safely. The first alkaline hydrolysis systems were created in Great Britain in the late 1990s to handle the disposition of cattle thought to be carrying prions, which cause mad cow disease. The original idea of safely breaking down animal carcasses to nourish plant life came from a Scotsman, Amos Herbert Hobson, who patented the method in 1888. For more than a decade now, alkaline hydrolysis has also been the disposition of choice for many medical facilities to dispose of cadavers donated for scientific research. These facilities maintain that AH is the safest and most reliable technology for body disposal.

I have not had a direct experience with this water method of disposition yet, but I have had wonderful conversations with Joe Wilson and his daughter Sam Sieber, whose family-run business, Bio-Response Solutions, Inc., in Danville, Indiana, is leading the way in providing alkaline hydrolysis technology to funeral homes and families today. Steeped in years of working with AH technology for animals and toxic-waste management, Wilson has developed low-temperature and high-temperature AH units, which gives funeral homes wanting to offer AH far more options and opportunities to tailor systems to their budget, and also to meet the needs of the families they serve. In creating a low-temperature unit, which does not require pressurized components and is simpler to operate, Bio-Response offers one of the most economical and environmentally sound alternatives to cremation and conventional burial practices today. Bio-Response has also patented a very successful system for disposition of pets, which is fast taking off as the most gentle and eco-friendly way to care for our animals' bodies after death. (See the Resources section for more information.)

Any "newfangled" idea about caring for our dead is going to be fraught with controversy, and alkaline hydrolysis is no exception. Think how long it has taken normal cremation to enter the mainstream and be accepted. And there are still areas of the country where cremation is regarded with suspicion, and where burial is still the only "respectable" choice to make. Much of this resistance has been cultural and religious in nature, as well as a refusal on the funeral industry's part to embrace change, especially when such change involves a loss in profit and the bottom line. Aquamation is meeting this same kind of resistance, though the general public seems very interested, even enthusiastic, about this option when they understand what AH actually entails.

There are always going to be sensationalists playing up the gory details of anything to do with disposal of dead bodies. When I start explaining AH, I often hear, "Oh, that's what mobsters have done forever—boiling bodies in lye and flushing them down the drain." It is important to understand that AH does not use boiling methods, nor is the entire body sent down the drain, as the bones are left intact, and the family receives 20–30 percent more remains back than they would with ashes from flame cremation. Let's take a closer look at some of the concerns and celebrations of aquamation, or water cremation, so that you will have a greater understanding of what this disposition choice really means.

Here are some of the concerns:

- The idea of having most of your body "flushed down a drain" and sent to a wastewater treatment plant does not appeal to some people, even if it is not remotely like the "mobster method." Many members of the Catholic Church have been fighting water cremation on the grounds that it is not a "respectful" way to treat a human body. Others agree, though they may not do so on the grounds of religion, just a felt sense that human bodies should not end up as wastewater. Interestingly, arguments against this stance are convincing.

Much of our bodies are sent "down the drain" when we are embalmed (a practice the Catholic Church has never forbidden), and one could argue that seepage into water happens even when we are buried. This realization has caused some in the Church to reassess their stance and call alkaline hydrolysis for humans "morally neutral" now, although the topic remains controversial.[3]

- Some people are concerned that human remains entering public wastewater systems is not a safe practice, arguing that not enough research has been done to prove otherwise. This is a valid concern. In my research on AH, however, I found that extensive studies made in Florida, where alkaline hydrolysis has been used for years to dispose of medical cadavers, found no tangible evidence that water is being contaminated. On the contrary, the AH effluent is considered beneficial to the wastewater systems, and even potentially nutritional for gardens, though not all regulatory bodies agree on this. My strongest affirmation that AH is safe for the environment and wastewater systems comes from speaking extensively with Joe Wilson and Sam Sieber, who are experts in implementing units that can deal effectively with contaminated water and waste products. Bio-Response guarantees that everything in a human body is cleansed and neutralized during the alkaline hydrolysis process—including disease pathogens, all chemotherapy and other pharmaceutical drugs, and even the chemicals used in embalming, making AH one of the safest ways to care for our dead.

- Some people cannot bear the thought of a disposition where they are "cooked" until the bones are bare, leaving a "coffee

---

[3] Renée Mirkes, "The Mortuary Science of Alkaline Hydrolysis: Is It Ethical?" *National Catholic Bioethics Quarterly* 8, no. 4 (2008): 683–696.

colored" soup behind. Hopefully, over time this reaction will change. It's interesting to tune into one's felt sense about this. I admit I have a slightly visceral aversion to the thought, though I believe I could get used to the idea, especially because AH is so much more ecological than flame cremation. (See below for the contributions of AH.) It's important to note that not everyone feels such an aversion. On the contrary, more and more families say they will choose AH, given the chance, because it "feels" like such a gentler and more nurturing way to handle a loved one's body—far less harsh than being burned in a retort in an industrial crematorium.

- Some people say that aquamation will be too much of a drain on water resources, at a time when water supplies for the future are in question. In reality, the amount of water used in each disposition is only 285 gallons (this is the number used in the Bio-Response machines). This may sound like a lot, but remember that the average household uses 400 gallons and an individual up to 150 gallons of water *each day*. Seen from this perspective, using 285 gallons at the end of life doesn't seem so bad—especially compared with the carbon footprint of flame cremation or conventional burial.

Here are the contributions and celebrations of alkaline hydrolysis:

- Families who want the convenience of cremation over burial—which includes simplicity, less financial cost, and flexibility in timing for memorials—receive the same benefits as flame cremation, without the concern that their disposition of choice is harmful to the environment and to our future health and well-being.

- The carbon footprint of a water cremation is as little as one-tenth of the carbon footprint of flame cremation. (This is a conservative estimate. Bio-Response states that their low-temperature unit is probably closer to one-fifteenth.)

- Alkaline hydrolysis leaves all medical devices—titanium hips, implants, gold in teeth, etc.—intact, sterilized, and looking almost brand new. Terry Regnier, director of anatomical services at the Mayo Clinic in Minnesota, and a passionate proponent of AH, believes that recycling some of these devices, in a time of rising health costs to the public, and in the name of decreasing environmental waste in landfills, could be a win-win solution for all concerned.

- The bones left after an alkaline hydrolysis disposition are in a completely scoured and purified condition, not carbonized and broken up as they are in flame cremation. Some traditional cultures utilize the bones of their dead in ritual and ceremony. I have worked with Tibetan Buddhist families who asked for the bones back after cremation. Provided facilities are open to working with families in this way, AH makes whole bones available (albeit very fragile, with a need to handle them carefully). This is also a very useful contribution for medical and forensic examiners, who need to study the bones of severely decomposed bodies as the only means of determining the cause of death.

- There is a growing desire to have more aesthetically pleasing environments, even sacred spaces that feel more reverent and nurturing for the dead and for their families. Though some funeral homes still have a crematorium as part of their facility, many retorts today are in industrial areas due to economics, zoning, and residential restrictions. Alkaline hydrolysis systems can be installed in ways that support a softer and less industrial atmosphere.

When I expressed my wish to Sam Sieber that AH would come full circle and make pet and human remains a generative gift to the environment, rather than simply wastewater, her response was telling. An avid environmentalist herself, Sam agreed. But she said such

innovation requires time. Even the liquid left over from pet aquamation is not being utilized in the way it could. Such remains could
easily become garden fertilizer, which would complete the cycle of
the AH process, making it an alternative that actually gives back to
the ecologies of life. Sam and I did not speak of the possibility of
human liquid remains also becoming fertilizer for gardens and green
spaces. But this question is already on the table with the process of
recomposition, which proposes to compost human bodies for intentional fertilizer uses. Such exploration will ask all of us to be open
to the rich complexities of what it means to be human, and to enter
the controversial realms of religious belief, ethics, respect, and values
together as a society while pondering this question. Perhaps it is too
early for such partnering with nature to be a reality, but the promise
of such co-creation is on the horizon.

Coeio: The Infinity Burial Suit

Jae Rhim Lee, founder of Coeio, made history with her TEDx
Talk in 2011, when she wore a "mushroom burial suit" on stage
and spoke about how fungi, embedded as biomaterial in the suit a
person wears when buried, can aid and enhance the decomposition
process after death. Her talk has had millions of views, and her
vision has certainly sparked the imagination of people all over the
world. She has gone on to create newer renditions of the suit—now
called the Infinity Burial Suit—and other products such as shrouds
and casket liners, all of which contain the biomaterial that can accel-
erate decomposition and also remediate toxins in the body and soil.

It is this latter purpose that makes Jae Rhim Lee's vision stand
out for some people, as few green burial methods specifically focus
on the issue of our bodies and soil being so overloaded with toxins
today. I quote from an article by Jae Rhim Lee, which is included in
Lee Webster's book *Changing Landscapes*. (See the Resources section.)

Mushrooms remove or eliminate toxins from the environment through a process called mycoremediation. They break down molecular bonds in many toxic,

organic compounds such as arsenic and Polycyclic Aromatic Hydrocarbons, thus neutralizing them. In the case of inorganic toxins, such as heavy metals, the mushrooms bind the toxins through a process called chelation and in turn make the toxins innocuous. These processes save energy and resources, improve the soil, and enrich surrounding plant life ... and the biomaterial prevents the toxins from re-entering the environment and causing further harm.[1]

Some natural and conservation burial advocates are not convinced we need such remediation, believing that nature's powerful decomposition process is enough. This stance is a move toward greater simplicity, rather than ever more complicated technologies and more costly "burial products." A simple shroud in a hole dug in the ground will do, in many people's eyes. The verdict is still out, and the discussions and arguments continue. (*Changing Landscapes* presents these different views, so it is well worth reading.) These differences of opinion are good, for it means we are looking at all the complexities of our efforts and are staying open to the questions. This is a wise stance, as we reimagine, both individually, with our own dreams and visions, and collectively, as human beings partnering with nature and the earth at the threshold of death once again.

Elemental Musings

I have come to see, over my years guiding others with end-of-life plans, that most of us have a natural affinity for one element over another, when it comes to choosing how our body will be handled after death. Some of us feel drawn to the purifying nature of flames and cremation; others feel an actual fear and aversion to fire. Some are certain they want their whole bodies to return to the earth and become soil when they die; others feel claustrophobic about being buried. There are those drawn to water burial, wanting to disappear beneath the waves of the sea; perhaps these people will now be drawn to aquamation. Others have a fear of drowning and will never choose these ways. Some feel an affinity with air and want to be shot

---

[1] Webster 2017, 184.

off into space or have their cremains scattered from an airplane. Or they long for a sky burial, where vultures come and feed upon their corpse, or plead at least to be placed high in a tree, as some Native tribes practiced, so that all the elements can work upon the body simultaneously. (These last two are not legal practices in today's world, though there are those who claim such ways should be reinstated, in the name of partnering with nature again.)

When I share my elemental musings with people, they often have an "aha" moment, and enjoy tuning in, as a kind of bodily felt sense, to what kind of disposition they might choose, based on the element they love. Such a game can be fun and even useful, but it is important now to include all the elements, all of the natural world, in our after-death choices and to come from a more informed place of planetary consideration and care.

10

BE PREPARED:
Creating a Plan with Family and Friends

When you start preparing for death you soon realize that you must look into your life now and come to face the truth of your self.

Death is like a mirror in which the true meaning of life is reflected.

—SOGYAL RINPOCHE

A friend and I were discussing my education and consulting business: doing presentations and trainings about home funerals and green burials, and companioning/consulting with others about the gifts of adding an Advance After-Death Care Directive to end-of-life paperwork. She looked at me wryly and said, "Leave it to you, Lucinda, to start a business based on a subject everyone actively avoids." The next question hung in the air between us, unspoken: How then, will I ever have enough clients?

How, indeed? I laughed in the moment with my friend, as if agreeing with her dire forecast of my future. I do share her concerns, but I keep going on my mission anyway. It's something I've done all these years working in the home funeral/green burial movement—stubbornly forging ahead despite all the odds. And I'm still here, still working away. That's because the more clients I have, and the more presentations I do, the stronger my conviction grows that this kind of education and consulting support is an invaluable part of transforming the very fears and avoidance that prevent a person from contacting me in the first place.

Take my friends Betsy and Andy (not their real names). They were one of my first couple consultations, but I ended up working individually with each of them, as they discovered they had different needs and wishes when it came to after-death care. Betsy wanted a three-day home funeral based on her spiritual practice, which was Celtic Christian in origin. If she ended up dying in a hospital, she wanted her body brought home. Andy didn't care about a home vigil, but Betsy did care about having time with his body, so we worked on ways to make that happen in different kinds of scenarios. Andy also began imagining a special memorial service, and I encouraged him to work on those plans as an engaging project, so it would all be in place if he died suddenly, which could happen, since he had a heart condition.

Sitting down together and opening to the idea of being dead is not for the faint of heart. I know this to be true. That's why I call my work "companioning" as well as consulting. I never simply consult with someone when it comes to contemplating death. I actually create, to the best of my ability, a safe and supportive space for that person to turn toward dying as best he can, and to actively imagine what his ideal death and after-death care could look like. Such attentive work is bound to bring up our fears and resistances. So this is not an easy task, for me or the client. Far from it. It's bone-deep work; it stirs the soul.

I remember Andy leaping up from his chair during our consultation and saying, "This is what I feel like trying to do this planning." He walked over to a closed door and began banging his head against it over and over. "I just can't bring myself to open the door. I have so much resistance, but I know I must, so I'm here knocking at the door as best I can." That image of Andy has stayed with me all these years, for it so captures what most of us feel when we decide to complete our end-of-life and after-death care wishes.

Betsy felt similar resistance, but her wish to work out all the details of her plans for a three-day vigil was stronger than her struggle. Betsy had a group with whom she practiced, and so she had a built-in spiritual care team, which was a comfort. Of course, nothing is guaranteed, since life is uncertain, people move away, people die before we do. But it was helpful for Betsy to go to her group and ask if they would be part of her spiritual care, and to then make a list of close friends who could help with the physical care of her body during the vigil. She contacted them as well. I am on that second list, as a consultant and guide, and will do my best to be available, at least by phone. There are backups for me if for some reason I cannot help. All these plans were reassuring to Betsy, and she was grateful we were giving everything so much thought and attention.

For example, we walked through her house and assessed where the best place for her to lie in state would be. We decided on her bedroom upstairs, because the stairwell is easily accessible and straight, not curved, and leads directly to the outside door. We decided which window would be opened, as, in her tradition, this is a way to aid the soul in leaving. We spoke about which chants and songs would be sung; whether she wants her body touched and bathed and dressed, or whether she prefers to be left alone; what she wants to wear after death, what kind of container she wants her body to be cradled in, what sacred objects she wants with her when she is cremated—all these considerations and imaginings.

Metaphorically, I feel we walked up to Betsy's doorway and even opened it a wee bit to peer over to the other side. It was hard but rewarding work, and Betsy told me afterward she was deeply relieved to have it behind her now, and especially to have it written down and shared with the right people. Together, we created a tangible field of support she could rest in, and this helped her turn back to life with a greater sense of well-being and ease.

Many people, when asked to approach end-of-life planning in a more imaginative and creative way, do so with greater openness and enthusiasm. So far, that has been my experience. This approach does not really eradicate someone's fear or resistance. It just helps balance those feelings with a greater sense of possibility and engagement. So the task is not so daunting, because one is less contracted and defended, and is, instead, coming from a place of interest and curiosity, perhaps even wonder and mystery. This is an excellent way to turn and face one's own demise. I like to think Death would approve of such ponderings.

Granted, these kinds of plans happen best if a death is not imminent. It's far easier to approach such work in a more lighthearted way when time stretches indefinitely before you. And yet, I have found the intense pressure of death's nearness also to be a great catalyst to get plans in order. It's much harder then, however, to be more buoyant and spacious about everything. That's why I encourage people to think about all this in the midst of life. It works out better for everyone.

The heart of an Advance After-Death Care Directive is really your own heart, what matters most to you. But it takes courage to ask the questions. We are so cut off from death, we may not even know how to begin. A Directive can help you open the doorway and get started, with questions like: What is your ideal place to die? Where would you feel safest—at home or in the hospital? Or this: Spend some time imagining the moment of your death. Do you wish to be alone, so you can concentrate on your spiritual practice; or do you want your family and friends around you, singing four-part harmonies to carry you across the great divide? Perhaps great parties were your love, and your ideal death would be to slip away in the midst of laughing and drinking and reveling among good friends. If so, write that down. The likelihood of your having such a death is already greater by doing so. I like to think that the act of strongly imagining what we want when we die could set up an energetic field of intention that actually makes our ideal death more possible. Wouldn't that be wonderful?

More contemplations: Do you like the idea of a home funeral vigil? If so, would you like your body to lie in state in the alcove, on the window seat where you have spent so many early mornings greeting the day? Or downstairs in your meditation room, where the field of presence generated by your own daily practice can sustain you in your transition? Or right in the midst of everything, with the TV in the background, because it always has been, and people sitting around drinking beer and coming over to toast you and make jokes about your present sorry state of affairs? The possibilities are endless—because each of us is a unique human being, and our send-offs can reflect in death who we were in life. Especially if we plan.

How could you invite the natural world to participate in your send-off? That's a question I find many people don't think to ask, and yet, when they start imagining nature's presence, they have all kinds of ideas: Cracking the window at your vigil so visitors can hear your favorite birdsong at twilight. Or letting the patio doors remain open so all the plants on the balcony can feel included in your passage. Or asking for your cat to have a special pillow next to your body during your days at home. Or making sure the smell of your favorite iris greets people when they walk in the door.

Then there's the choice of your disposition, as we have seen, which will either add to the toxicity of the earth and environment or help heal it. Spend some time looking into more innovative, eco-friendly options. Find out if aquamation, Promession, or recomposition will at some point be available in your area. Remember that the legacy you leave with a natural or conservation burial can reverberate for generations to come. Choose wisely where you want your body to rest, and be proactive in connecting with, even supporting, that burial ground long before you need their services. Contemplating this final choice is an essential way of including the earth and all webs of life in your Advance After-Death Care plans.

Who will be your team? This is an essential question, and a vital part of your Directive. Think of the people who you know will be at your death, short of dying themselves. Think of the ones you would trust with your life (and your death) and who will be physically, emotionally, and mentally able to make your plans happen, however wacky your wishes. Talk about what you want, early, way before you need to. It could be a great way to start the dreaded "death talk" with everyone concerned. It's a favor to your team. Believe that, and get started now.

These kinds of imaginings do serve as levity for habitual dread. Suddenly, an element of creativity, even joy, can make its presence known, like a fresh breeze blowing the tightly shut doorway of death open for a time. Yes, you will be there, dead—and sadness, even trauma and tragedy, might also be in the room. But the richness of your life will be there as well, your intricate and fascinating Incarnational Field. The people showing up will feel and take part in that larger tapestry of who you were and are. Having the time and space to feel and celebrate you in such a way, with your body still there, still present in the room, can do so much to help people grieve and come to terms with losing you. It can be an experience of wholeness. And that's the greatest send-off any of us could hope to have.

As satisfying as such planning can be, it's still extremely hard to actually sit down and complete the onerous task. I have lists of people who have said they are going to call me for a consultation, and they never do. So of late, I have been reimagining ways to consult and be of service. Group work is one answer, preferably an ongoing group that can explore all aspects of death and dying together, hold each other accountable for getting their paperwork accomplished, and share deeply to create lasting bonds of support for one another.

The bonus of such groups is that one has a built-in team of people who will probably be there to help when a member of the group dies. This care team is often a natural, organic outcome of opening the doorway of death together. This can be very helpful for single people who have no family or close friends to call upon, or people who are aging in places far away from family. The other advantage is that such a group can ask a knowledgeable person to educate and hold the first few sessions, and then the group can continue to meet afterward on its own. This is preferable if the group is going to meet over a long period of time.

Education is essential. The more we get together and explore death and dying issues, the easier it will be for folks to actually engage in completing their wishes and plans. We've come a long way in being able to speak about the process of dying itself. It's important now to reimagine and talk about all the possible choices we have in after-death care as well.

Practical Wisdom: Advance After-Death Care Directives

We are all encouraged to create a Living Will and/or an Advance Health Care Directive, and establish for ourselves a Medical Power of Attorney, as well as a Durable Power of Attorney. This is all pre-death paperwork—the essential documents we need in case we can no longer speak or advocate for ourselves regarding medical intervention treatments. Most people are aware of the importance of completing such paperwork, and it is the focus of standard end-of-life planning and preparation.

I see an Advance After-Death Care Directive as the next vital step beyond the Advance Health Care Directive, as it addresses the other side of death's threshold. Many people do not realize the importance of, or simply put off or avoid, preplanning for what happens after death. It is incredibly helpful for everyone to think way ahead about how you wish your body (and soul) to be cared for after you die, and to get those wishes in writing, witnessed, and shared with the person who will be handling your funeral arrangements, and with anyone else who would benefit from knowing your plans. It is also a great gift to survivors if you can set aside enough funds to cover the cost of such choices.

Working in a funeral home for six years helped me see how difficult and stressful it can be for families (especially your children or dependents) to have to make these important after-death care decisions on your behalf, at a time when they are least prepared and able to do so. Families who came in knowing what their loved one wanted, and having funds already set aside for funeral arrangements, often exhibited a greater sense of calm and well-being, and there were fewer family disputes, because the signed and witnessed wishes of the deceased always take precedence over any other person's opinions or needs. When someone takes care of everything beforehand, survivors often have more opportunity to focus on grieving and simply being together, rather than madly running around in chaos, trying to make last-minute, uncertain decisions.

This is true for any death, but it is especially important if you are interested in anything alternative, such as a home funeral vigil or natural burial, or specific spiritual care and practices that depend on the body being present. For example, green burial is increasingly popular, but many local cemeteries are now owned by corporate funeral homes whose policies require vault burial, embalming for viewing, and lawn maintenance with toxic herbicides. And there are often local regulatory laws that make establishing natural burial grounds more difficult. At the time of this writing, there actually is a shortage of places where one can be buried naturally in the United States. Hopefully, this will change, but for now it is vital to think ahead and discern whether you can actually have a green burial in your local area. If you can, then purchase a plot long before you need it, and state your intentions clearly in some kind of after-death care document.

For those of you who want a home funeral vigil after death, I recommend getting a copy of the NHFA's publication *Planning Guide and Workbook for Home Funeral Families* (see the Resources section), filling it out, and putting it with your other Directives and important legal paperwork. Revisit the workbook every few years, as our lives and circumstances change over time. (Perhaps fill it out in pencil, or purchase several to use over the passing years.) This booklet can be invaluable to your family and care team at the time of your death.

As in Betsy's story, whenever you desire specific spiritual practices, it is very important to have these wishes clearly written down and shared with those who are likely to be there to carry out such care at the time of your death. For example, people in my Buddhist sangha actually have Dharma Wills, and Death Kits with all the necessary sacred texts, mandalas, a shroud, and other relics inside, kept in a special place that others know about. Those who are caring for a dying or dead practitioner will turn to this Dharma Will (which is, itself, a Directive) and Death Kit and follow all the instructions outlined within. I have an Episcopalian friend who knows her family will want to have a priest offer holy communion around her body, and she feels this will be healing for everyone, so she has written these instructions down in her Directive, and has shared her wishes with her priest and family.

Planning your funeral or memorial service beforehand can also be part of your Directive. I know people who have created their entire service—choosing the music, readings, prayers, and practices they love most, and actually enjoying this process, as the next best thing to being there! This is a wonderful gift to family and friends, who are then not left with planning a service in the midst of everything else they are handling.

It is important to understand that an Advance After-Death Care Directive is an ethical document, not a legal one. It will not stand up in a court of law, but it should take precedence over anyone else's wishes, as the good and right thing for families and friends to try to do. If a person has taken the trouble to plan and put her preferences in writing, and to have these papers witnessed, dated, and signed, then it is ethically correct to help make those wishes happen if at all possible.

After-death care choices can be part of a legal will, as well, where you choose a method of disposition—burial or cremation—and designate either your next-of-kin or a chosen designated agent to handle your affairs. But if you are interested in all that we have been exploring in this book, I highly recommend spending additional time and energy to complete some kind of Advance After-Death Care Directive that describes in detail what your wishes are, both practically and spiritually. This can be an attachment to your legal will.

The Importance of Planning Ahead and Being Proactive

I heard recently of a situation where a woman kept her husband at home after death for several days without notifying anyone. She finally called the funeral home to come get the body, but because the man had not been on hospice, and the death had not been reported, the funeral home notified the police. Within an hour, the woman's home was inundated with police officers with suspicious stares and probing questions about the nature of her husband's death. What had, up until that point, been a peaceful and healing experience for her became instead a nightmare. She was shocked that such a thing could happen when she had such good intentions, and thought all was well.

All was not well, however, because this couple had no idea that, in order to keep someone at home legally after death, there need to be certain parameters in place, and protocols followed, to avoid the situation in which they found themselves. None of the aftermath this woman experienced would have happened if she had been better informed, and more properly prepared, and if she had notified the right people beforehand. Though the idea of home funerals is becoming more widely known, thanks to the NHFA and all those working in the field, it is surprising how many people in public positions—doctors, nurses, hospital staff, and law enforcement, even hospice staff—still do not know it is legally possible to care for one's own dead at home.

This is why planning ahead for a home funeral, and making sure that everyone has all the necessary information and practical details in place before the death, can be so important and helpful. "Be Prepared" is an apt and appropriate motto for all of us to follow in contemplating our deaths. But it is especially important for those who wish to have anything alternative, like home funerals and green burials, since these practices are still not widely accepted in mainstream life. It is also important to understand that putting such plans in place at the last minute, amid the upheaval of death itself, is a much harder task and can create a situation where many of your wishes cannot be fulfilled or, worse, things go awry, as they did in the story above.

The woman who experienced so much trouble keeping her husband at home was unaware that she needed to work within the system in order to avoid misunderstandings and confusion for everyone. If she had proactively consulted a home funeral consultant, or a funeral director aware of families' rights to care for their own, they could have helped her in these ways:

- **Engaging Hospice.** A home funeral consultant or cooperative funeral director might have suggested the woman engage hospice, to avoid having law enforcement arrive at the house. Remember, some hospice staff will notify the doctor and coroner of the death right away, leaving the family free to simply be present with the person who has died.

- Families who decide not to use hospice must report the death of a loved one to the police or medical examiner themselves—preferably right away, but at least within a few hours of the death. The woman in our story did not know she had to report the death in a timely manner to avoid suspicion.

Perhaps if she had been proactive with the funeral service and shared her plans to keep her husband at home for a few days, they could have assisted her, rather than reacting as they did.

- **Families Reporting a Death.** The timing to report a death depends on the nature and circumstances of a person's passage. *If the death is from old age or known natural causes, and it was expected,* then it is usually okay to take a few hours before reporting the death, especially if it is in the middle of the night. *If the death was unexpected, and the cause of death unknown,* it is important to report the death as soon as possible.

- It is more complicated to have a home vigil if a person's death is unexpected, as the medical examiner must examine the body and perform an autopsy. This means the body will be taken away from the home. The family can request that no autopsy happen (especially if this is a wish based on spiritual conviction that the deceased had intentionally expressed in writing). The final say will always be the coroner's, however. The family can also ask for the body to be brought home to the house after going to the medical examiner. I recommend that the family work with a home funeral guide or sympathetic licensed funeral director under these circumstances.

- **Attempting a Home Vigil Alone.** I do not know all the details of our couple's story, but it sounds as if the woman was attempting to care for her husband alone. This is always more challenging. Home funeral vigils are most successful when a team of people are present to help with all the necessary details and tasks, including, if possible, working with an experienced home vigil guide.

This Practical Wisdom section is by no means a complete legal or practical guide for someone creating an Advance After-Death Care Directive. It can be helpful to find a home funeral consultant or a sympathetic licensed funeral director near you to assist you in your plans. This is part of being prepared—to know who to call, and to have that person's name in your Advance After-Death Care Directive. It is also important to understand what is legally necessary where you live, and to incorporate this information into your Directive. That way, if your death should happen unexpectedly, the wheels of medical, law enforcement, and funeral industry services can turn more smoothly and without mishaps or added stress and confusion.

The last and most important step of completing an Advance After-Death Care Directive is to share your documents with your family; and make sure they are on board with your wishes, and are willing to either carry out your plans or have your chosen team do so for them. Sometimes having a family meeting can be hard, especially if your children do not wish to talk about your death, but it is a vital and necessary component of being prepared.

In that meeting, you may discover that your children and extended family are not supportive of your wishes to have a home funeral, and are resistant and unwilling to help. It is important to know this upfront, as you may have to reassess your plans, or figure out a way for friends and community to make a vigil happen. Even with this plan B, it might be problematic if the family truly does not wish to have a home funeral. On the other hand, for family who are supportive of your wishes, they will have a heads-up long beforehand and will be able to fulfill your wishes for alternative care with far less stress and confusion, whether your death is expected or unexpected in the end.

In my experience, creating a team of willing friends or turning to a community care group to help with a home funeral can be a good way to go, no matter how supportive your family is. Your closest people will be in grief and might need others to help them cope with all the details anyway. Having a home funeral guide, a case manager, and a team of people who can carry out your wishes, as well as a fully thought-out and completed Directive everyone can follow—these elements can help make your wishes more possible, even within the uncertain and mysterious territory always present at death's threshold. Since any of us could die at any minute, preparing ahead and getting everything in order is a very wise and compassionate thing to do—for yourself and for everyone you love.

EPILOGUE

$\mathcal{I}$ remember sitting at the foot of my friend Judy's bed, gazing at her dead face, spellbound by the light pouring from her open eyes. It was the second day of her vigil. Right after death, her eyes had been closed, her mouth open. It was hard to look at her then, so skeletal and emaciated from her cancer. But as the hours progressed, Judy's eyes gradually opened. Like portals into another vast and beautiful realm, they shone with a luminosity so large it spilled out into the room, affecting everyone. So many who came to be with Judy's body experienced this. They felt bathed in an energy of peace and well-being, just by sitting next to her and looking into her eyes.

My daughter Eliza, then barely thirteen, sat on my lap, and we shared this wonder together. It was Eliza's first up-close encounter with death, and it would become a supportive experience for her to draw upon years later when she helped me bathe her grandmother's body in Alabama. We would never have experienced Judy in this way if a funeral director had come and taken her body away right after death. It was Judy's gift to us, the Buddhist sangha friends who showed up to care for her body and soul. She had begged us to do this for her, rather than engage a funeral service. So we did, and we were forever changed by the experience.

I will never forget the vibrant colors and creativity showered upon Judy in her death. The wooden casket that friends built outside in the August heat; the painting of the lid, bright with symbols and messages of farewell; the multihued coverlet of a thousand paper cranes made by the students in Judy's elementary school class, laid upon her body in final blessing. Judy's death allowed her entire community to grieve and to celebrate. (Photos of Judy's vigil are in the color insert.)

In the years I have been working as a home funeral and green burial guide, I hear these kinds of stories over and over: someone we love dies, and we are called to imagine a different way to care for them—one that allows us to be ourselves, to have a direct and visceral experience of death again, and to create life-giving and healing ways to ease the shock and pain of saying goodbye. Such experiences help transform our relationship to death, and we naturally want to explore more deeply, and to share with others, the gifts we have been given.

These individual stories are like seeds, germinating in the soil of our collective consciousness, and emerging in many different places simultaneously all over the Western world. They are both unique and universal, and together they have helped weave, one family at a time, a loving fabric of reclamation and renewal. I have been tracking the larger story of this generative movement to reclaim home funerals and natural burial since its nascent stages. It has been a remarkable experience to see how tiny the seeds were in the beginning, and how this awareness is springing up in so many hearts and minds, in so many varied ways today.

The power of our creative imaginings burns at the core of this shift in awareness. Death itself has captured our imaginations again; thank goodness, since we have been wandering in the wasteland of fear and denial of our mortality for so long. I am thinking of the Reimagine End of Life expo being held in San Francisco and New York this year (2018), where seven thousand people are expected to attend; the Death Café movement springing up all around the world, in which people gather to discuss with others their fears and hopes around dying; and countless other collaborative gatherings happening each year everywhere. We can now discuss death in the news and on social media without flinching. We are waking up slowly, together, responding to Death's call in ways as different as we are as human beings.

It is the artistic, inventive engagements with death and dying that I find most fascinating and inspiring of late. Do a bit of exploring online, and you will find stunning examples of the human spirit's capacity to create art and beauty in the face of our mortality. Perhaps because the home funeral and green burial movement is so fundamentally woven with the natural world, the creations of artists inspired to work with biodegradable materials from nature seem especially alive and beautiful to me. The task of figuring out how to care for our own again, in ecological ways, demands that we all be more original and inventive, and this is part of the gifts and richness of the movement.

Creative and pioneering endeavors also build and strengthen community. We have seen how crafting a home funeral vigil together for someone, or sharing the job of filling in a grave, can forge lasting bonds of connection and intimacy among people. Shared artistic and living responses at the time of death (casket building, rituals, prayers, poetry, singing or keening, or whatever feels right to those gathered) can be the very means by which we are able to handle or bear what is happening to us. It is this sense of community, where we are not alone, but are being carried by the love and support of others, that can make all the difference in our journey of loss and mourning.

Often, being part of a community helps us talk about and prepare for our deaths more easily as well. The very popular Coffin Clubs in New Zealand, which are taking off in other countries as well, are a fine example of turning toward death together. These clubs were initially started by Katie Williams, a former palliative-care nurse who saw the great need for lonely elders to come together to share and talk about death and dying over tea. Out of that impulse arose the idea for members to actually build and decorate their own coffins together (with plenty of tea and biscuits to sustain them!). I imagine one's fear and trepidation of dying cannot stick around long if one is pounding nails for one's own coffin, in the midst of fun and hilarity and camaraderie with others doing the same. The idea is brilliant, and it captures all that I am speaking of here—facing death in the midst of life, in more lighthearted and creative ways; so that, when the time comes to "shed our mortal coils," we have a greater capacity to find acceptance, peace, even joy in the midst of loss and sorrow.

Such endeavors are reweaving the circles of life, and healing the profound sense of disconnection and brokenness we can so often feel living in the madness of modern times. Part of this reweaving is remembering the communities of the dead, our ancestors, and finding living ways to connect with them again. Most importantly, by choosing more natural ways to be at the threshold of death, we are consciously and reverently reweaving our lives with the larger circles of life, the communities and ecologies of the natural world, both physical and subtle, and with the planet itself, as a living and loving organism.

In all my explorations and conversations with people working in the home funeral/natural burial movement, one phrase often arises like a song, a litany—catching my heart and imagination each time. My fellow colleagues say, in many different ways, that they have done what they have done "for love of the land," for the preservation of a certain place or ecology, or because they are so concerned about the disappearance of nature's way in human lives.

This is especially true for those working with natural and conservation burial efforts, but it is increasingly true for those who start out as home funeral advocates and guides. The two movements go hand in hand, and it has been that way from the beginning. Many home funeral guides also become green burial guides, as I have done. It is as if our longing to care more naturally for loved ones after death takes us organically to a deeper longing to care for all living beings in sacred and honoring ways. Or vice versa: many conservationists, whose sole intention is to protect and preserve land, have found themselves gatekeepers at death's threshold, charged with the sacred care of families and their dead as well. This was certainly true for me; my love of the land and the natural world was the wellspring from which my ministry and home funeral work arose.

All along, in writing this book, I have felt in touch with a larger story, a more expansive dream, one that seems to come from the earth itself. Each time I meet someone new who is saying "yes" to caring for the dead and the environment in healing ways, I sense the earth's dream fulfilling itself in the unique story and manifested passion of that particular individual or group. Like a great weaving that depends upon each of our threads, each of our ideas and stories, this dream is incarnating now, through the love and dedication of all those who are daring to "do death differently" today.

―――――――――――――

I returned to my Alabama land recently. It was a joyous occasion, for my daughter Eliza and I were bringing Gwenna—her baby daughter and my first granddaughter—home for the holidays. Ten months old, Gwenna was to be with the entire family on our land for the first time in her brand new life.

In the early morning, I bundled Gwenna up in her red corduroy coat and took her out to greet the forest, the blustery wind in the trees, and our spring, overflowing its banks after a night of heavy rain. She immediately opened her tiny arms wide, as if to embrace every living creature great and small. A chortle of glee let me know how happy she was, her little voice singing out into the quiet morning air, her body dancing in my arms with delight. When Gwenna turned and looked at me, her eyes were bright with a sense of knowing and belonging. I felt the shifting tides of time and space—my mother walking out the screen door to stand beside us in joy; my father whistling over by the woodpile, stacking logs to stoke the winter fires. Later that evening, our family gathered round the old oak table in the kitchen for feasting and fun, toasting Mama and Papa with lifted glasses and grateful hearts. We were there together, celebrating the sacred continuum of life and death and life again, ever emerging, ever flowing, ever returning home to love and wholeness.

RESOURCES

Prologue: The Calling

National Home Funeral Alliance (www.homefuneralalliance.org). This all-volunteer 501(c)(3) nonprofit organization is the best resource available to families and communities wishing to care for their own dead, providing the most up-to-date information on all aspects of the home funeral movement. It also serves as a network of support for all who are working as home funeral guides, and for those wishing to become more involved in this work. The NHFA's extensive and informative website provides everything you need, including finding local home funeral guides/consultants and supportive funeral directors in your area. See the Practical Wisdom section of chapter 2, "Greening the Gateway of Death," for more information about the NHFA.

Green Burial Council (www.greenburialcouncil.org). The Green Burial Council (GBC) is an independent nonprofit 501(c)(6) organization that supports environmentally sustainable death care and burial as a means to protect and restore natural ecosystems and land. The GBC was established in 2005 by Joe and Juliette Sehee, who understood that a creditable organization was needed to oversee the evolution of natural burial grounds in North America, and who gave much time, energy, and financial support to make this vision a reality. See the Practical Wisdom section of chapter 4 for more information on the GBC.

Funeral Consumers Alliance (www.funerals.org). The FCA is "a nonprofit organization dedicated to protecting a consumer's right to choose a meaningful, dignified, affordable funeral." The FCA, under the strong and capable leadership of Josh Slocum, executive director, has been a stalwart ally of the home funeral and green burial movements, and serves as a sounding board and monitor for all the evolving trends in the industry, as well as an advocate for legal and regulatory reform—all of which strongly supports the efforts of the NHFA and the GBC. Josh Slocum and Lisa Carlson (author of *Caring for Your Own Dead* and one of the first strong voices in the home funeral movement) collaborated on a very useful book for families and consumers, *Final Rights: Reclaiming the American Way of Death* in 2011. This is an important resource for families wishing to care for their own dead, as it outlines, state by state, the legal parameters within which individuals, families, and communities can work, and also how to interface with the funeral industry in effective ways. The book recapitulates Jessica Mitford's pivotal book *The American Way of Death*, published in 1963, which exposed the foibles and flaws of the modern funeral industry, and led to funeral reform laws and guidelines that keep a tighter watch on the practices of funeral homes and funeral directors today.

Lisa Carlson, *Caring for Your Own Dead* (Hinesburg, VT: Upper Access, 1987).

Jessica Mitford, *The American Way of Death* (New York: Simon and Schuster, 1963).

Joshua Slocum and Lisa Carlson, *Final Rights: Reclaiming the American Way of Death* (Hinesburg, VT: Upper Access, 2011).

A Sacred Moment Funeral Services (www.asacredmoment.com). Founder: Char Barrett. Char Barrett began her alternative funeral home in 2007, creating one of the first licensed funeral services in the country to offer home funeral vigils and green burials to families who wished to be more actively engaged in caring for their dead. Char has been a key leader in the green funeral movement from its beginnings. I am grateful for the years I spent at A Sacred Moment, and for the chance to obtain my funeral director's license in a place where home funerals and green burials are an integral part of after-death care.

Chapter 1: Return to the Mother

Crossings: Caring for Our Own at Death. A Home Funeral and Green Burial Resource Center (www.crossings.net). Founder: Beth Knox. New Director: Jane Ellen Johnson. I called Beth Knox when my mother was dying, and her gentle and loving guidance was of great support to me at that time. She is one of the pioneering women of the home funeral movement, and I wish to honor her here.

Crossings' Resource Guide: A Step-by-Step How To Guide for Home Funeral Care (2009). This was my main aid in caring for Mama's body after her death. It can be downloaded at www.crossings.net/store.html.

Chapter 2: Greening the Gateway of Death

Madeleine L'Engle, *A Wind in the Door* (A Wrinkle in Time Quintet) (New York: Square Fish, 2007).

Louis M. Savary and Patricia H. Berne, *Kything: The Art of Spiritual Presence* (Mahwah, NJ: Paulist Press, 1989).

John O'Donohue, *Beauty: The Invisible Embrace* (New York: HarperCollins, 2005).

National Home Funeral Alliance (www.homefuneralalliance.org) has published several books that are invaluable:

Lee Webster, *Planning Guide and Workbook for Home Funeral Families* (2015).

Lee Webster, *Essentials for Practicing Home Funeral Guides* (2015).

Lee Webster, Lucy Basler, and Su Jin Kim, *Building Bridges along the Death Care Continuum: Advocating for Home Funerals in Hospices, Hospitals, and Care Facilities* (2016).

Holly Stevens, *Undertaken with Love: A Home Funeral Guide for Families and Community Care Groups* (2016).

Joshua Slocum and Lee Webster, *Restoring Families' Right to Choose: The Call for Funeral Legislation Change in America* (2015).
There are lists of other helpful books and resources on the NHFA website.

Joshua Slocum and Lisa Carlson, *Final Rights: Reclaiming the American Way of Death* (Hinesburg, VT: Upper Access, 2011).

Josh Slocum and Lee Webster, "Quick Guide to Home Funerals by State," www.homefuneralalliance.org/state-requirements.html.

Lee Webster, "The Advantages of Alternative Cooling Techniques," www.homefuneralalliance.org/cooling-techniques.html. All you need to know about the use of dry ice, Techni-ice®, and other techniques to cool the body of a deceased person at home.
Techni-ice® can be ordered through Amazon or Walmart online. Make sure you order the HDR four-ply for best results.

Final Passages (http://finalpassages.org). Founder: Jerrigrace Lyons. I am grateful to have received my home funeral training with Jerrigrace, in the early years of the movement. Jerrigrace and her husband Mark Hill, of Final Passages and the Institute of Conscious Dying, are leading pioneers in the home funeral movement and continue to offer trainings for home funeral guides and practitioners today. Final Passages has a three-part workbook in binder form that can be purchased:

Guidebook for Creating Home Funerals: http://finalpassages.org/product/guidebook-for-creating-home-funerals

Only with Love (www.onlywithlove.co.uk). Founder: Claire Turnham. I am including Claire's work with home funerals and green burials in Great Britain here as a resource, as she is one of the leading voices in the United Kingdom, and her work exemplifies everything I have been trying to convey in this book.

Chapter 3: Partnering with Nature When We Die

David Spangler and **Incarnational Spirituality** (www.lorian.org). To become more embodied, more incarnated, is an evolutionary task humans collectively must embark upon if we are to find right relationship with the earth and with all sentient life again. The Lorian Association educates and supports us to be unique and sovereign individuals as well as planetary Gaian citizens, working in partnership with the earth and the natural and subtle realms of life, to bring hope and resiliency and wholeness to our present time.

David Spangler has written many remarkable books over his more than fifty years of teaching. Most are available on the Lorian website (http://lorianpress.com/dspangler.html). Here are some good introductory ones:

An Introduction to Incarnational Spirituality (Traverse City, MI: Lorian Press, 2011).

Journey into Fire (Traverse City, MI: Lorian Press, 2015).

Subtle Worlds: An Explorer's Field Notes (Traverse City, MI: Lorian Press, 2010).

Findhorn Foundation (www.findhorn.org). Findhorn is an international community of spiritual seekers and ecological innovators, started in humble ways by Peter and Eileen Caddy and Dorothy Maclean more than fifty years ago. Findhorn is now a thriving eco-village that weaves the intangible with the tangible, modeling both spiritual and practical ways to co-create with nature to build a new and sustainable way to live as human beings.

The Findhorn Community, *The Findhorn Garden: Pioneering a New Vision of Man and Nature in Cooperation* (New York: HarperCollins, 1976).

Reginald A. Ray, *Touching Enlightenment: Finding Realization in the Body* (Louisville, CO: Sounds True, 2008). Reggie Ray, one of my Tibetan Buddhist Vajrayana teachers, says that we of the Western world are all disembodied, that the frantic machinations of our minds and the stressful ways we live "achieving" our to-do lists each day mean we are never "home," never aligned with the wisdom of our bodies and our felt senses, with the somatic wholeness of who we really are. Ray's Somatic Meditation practices focus on relaxing the extraordinary tensions of our bodies, and relaxing also the thoughts and emotions that are, in his teaching, also energetic tensions we can consciously release into the earth in order to begin to heal—and in order to recognize that our soma is not ever separate from the body of the earth, and that such a body is already awake and interdependent with all. We can practice and wake up to this understanding. And in doing so, we realize that our very lives are a co-creation with the earth in each and every moment, all the time. This same realization can help us relax and let go into the larger dimensions of who we are, with greater ease and awareness when we die.

David Abram, *The Spell of the Sensuous: Perception and Language in a More-Than-Human World* (New York: Vintage Books, 1996). This is a masterpiece by an ecologist and philosopher who writes from such an embodied and alive perspective that one receives a different way of perceiving simply by reading his words. This is remarkable, since Abram argues that written language was the beginning of our conceptual minds and of our separation from nature. A landmark, revolutionary book, this has become a handbook for how to be fully human, and how to participate with "convivial curiosity" and communion with the "more than human" world.

David Abram, *Becoming Animal: An Earthly Cosmology* (New York: Vintage Books, 2011). In Joanna Macy's words, "This book brings us home to ourselves as living organs of this wild planet. Its teachings leap off the page and translate immediately into lived experience." An essential read.

Thomas Berry, *The Dream of the Earth* (Berkeley, CA: Counterpoint Press, 2015). Thomas Berry was a cultural historian and remarkable human being whose seminal book, first published in 1988, has become an inspirational foundation and wellspring within the canon of ecological books written for our troubled times. Berry argues that planetary well-being must be the measure of all our human activity now and in the future.

Chapter 4: "Bury Me Naturally": Stories and Guidance for Green Burials

Where to Find a Natural Burial Ground

As of 2018, there are at least 160 known cemeteries and burial grounds in the United States where vaults are not required, and where "green burial" is either allowed or intentionally supported. There could be hundreds more not discovered yet. Former GBC International (the education wing of the GBC) education writer and board member Lee Webster keeps a list of known green burial cemeteries on the New Hampshire Funeral Resources, Education and Advocacy website (www.nhfuneral.org/green-burial-cemeteries-in-the-us-and-canada.html). Cynthia Beal, green cemetery owner and operator and the owner of the Natural Burial Company, offers the Natural End Map (www.naturalend.com), where providers of truly environmentally responsible natural burial products and services sign a pledge to provide products and services with integrity and natural options.

Environmental journalist Ann Hoffner's book *The Natural Burial Cemetery Guide* (South Orange, NJ: Green Burial Naturally, 2017) is also an excellent and valuable resource for readers, for she has traveled all over the United States, researching, visiting, and connecting personally with operators of many natural and conservation burial grounds, as well as rural and hybrid cemeteries that offer green burial services today. Ann updates her book yearly, which is invaluable, for as the green burial movement catches on, more and more burial grounds will be available in the future.

One of the things that stood out for me in perusing Ann's guidebook is how different each cemetery or burial ground is, and how the spirit or flavor of each place is shaped so much by the land itself, by the culture of the region of the United States where one lives, and by the visions of the people who helped make those places a reality. Because the guide covers a wide range of options, from old, established cemeteries to the more recent conservation burial grounds whose main purpose is to protect land and wilderness, readers can get a sense of both the past and the future of burial disposition options in America. Ann's website is: Green Burial Naturally (www .greenburialnaturally.org).

Natural Death Centre in Great Britain (www.naturaldeathcentre.org).

Memorial Ecosystems. Ramsey Creek Preserve in Westminster, South Carolina (www.memorialecosystems.com). Founders: Billy and Kimberley Campbell.

Green Burial Council (www.greenburialcouncil.org).

Green Burial Product Resources

Note: A list of green burial products would be pages long. I have included only those products that appear in this book and/or are creations for which I have a personal connection and love.

Kinkaraco (www.kinkaraco.com). My friend Esmerelda Kent, founder of Kinkaraco, is a shroudmaker extraordinaire. She is one of the pioneering creators of shrouds in this country and is a foremost and tireless advocate of green burial and natural death care practices today. You can see one of her creations in the last episode of the well-loved television series *Six Feet Under*. The shroud on the cover of this book is Esmerelda's PureLight linen one, with attached lowering straps and a backboard to support the body.

Mourning Dove Studio (https://mourningdovestudio.com). My chapter's title "Bury Me Naturally" is borrowed from Carol Motley, a natural burial advocate in Asheville, North Carolina, whose first company carried this name. Carol provides ecologically sound funeral merchandise for burial and cremation.

Natural Burial Company (www.naturalburialcompany.com). Founder Cynthia Beal has pioneered bringing natural burial products to the public since the beginning of the green funeral movement. See her Shrouding Board as an option for transporting shrouded bodies.

Final Footprint (www.finalfootprint.com). Jane Hillhouse is a good resource for families who want biodegradable wicker, bamboo, or banana leaf woven caskets. Her Casket Tray can also be used to support and transport shrouded bodies.

Pia Interlandi (www.piainterlandi.com). Pia Interlandi is a fashion designer and artist from Australia who is a passionate advocate of natural burial and caring for our own at death. Her Garments for the Grave and other offerings are stunning examples of the creativity possible when we work in co-creation with the natural world at death.

Chapter 5: "You're Dead. Now What?" Humor and Laughter at the Threshold

Green Burial Council (www.greenburialcouncil.org).

Chapter 6: Sacred Care of the Dead

David Spangler, *Partnering with Earth: The Incarnation of a Soul* (Traverse City, MI: Lorian Press, 2013).

Rudolf Steiner, *Staying Connected: How to Continue Your Relationships with Those Who Have Died* (New York: Anthroposophic Press, 1999). Selected talks and meditations by Rudolf Steiner, 1905–1924.

Nicholas Wijnberg and Philip Martyn, *Crossing the Threshold: Practical and Spiritual Guidance on Death and Dying* (Forest Row, UK: Temple Lodge, 2003). Based on the work of Rudolf Steiner. Vigils and after-death care are included.

Sogyal Rinpoche, *The Tibetan Book of Living and Dying* (San Francisco: HarperSanFrancisco, 1993). This is a classic guide, very accessible to Western readers, with practices that can be translated to one's own way of life and traditions. It includes chapters on "The Bardo of Becoming" and "Helping After Death."

Andrew Holecek, *Preparing to Die: Practical Advice and Spiritual Wisdom from the Tibetan Buddhist Tradition* (Boulder, CO: Snow Lion, 2013). This book includes very informative sections for practical and spiritual care of the dead.

His Holiness the Dalai Lama, *Mind of Clear Light: Advice on Living Well and Dying Consciously* (New York: Atria Books, 2003).

Joanna Macy and the Great Turning. Film. www.joannamacyfilm.org.

Chapter 7: When We Die in the Hospital: Field Notes for Finding Our Way Home

Lee Webster, Lucy Basler, and Su Jin Kim, *Building Bridges along the Death Care Continuum: Advocating for Home Funerals in Hospices, Hospitals, and Care Facilities* (NHFA, 2016). Lee Webster, president emerita of the NHFA, and writer of most of the NHFA's incredibly useful material, has written a workbook with Lucy

Basler and Su Jin Kim that addresses these needs. I highly recommend that anyone thinking of having a home funeral purchase this book, and have it with your paperwork and Advance After-Death Care Directives. That way, families can refer to the book if someone dies in an institutional setting. The excerpt in the chapter is from this book.

Chapter 8: Conscious Dying: A Death with Dignity

Death with Dignity National Center (www.deathwithdignity.org) is a "501(c)(3) nonprofit organization that expands the freedom of all qualified terminally ill Americans to make their own end-of-life decisions, including how to die; promotes Death with Dignity laws around the United States based on the groundbreaking Oregon model; and provides information, education, and support about Death with Dignity as an end-of-life option to patients, family members, legislators, advocates, healthcare and end-of-life care professionals, media, and the interested public." This is the main website for all information one might need when exploring Death with Dignity options.

End of Life Washington (formerly Compassion and Choices) (https://endoflifewa.org). This is the main website for Washington State Death with Dignity support.

List of hospitals in Washington State that support Death with Dignity: https://endoflifewa.org/hospitals

Example of application process in Washington State: https://endoflifewa.org/wp-content/uploads/2012/09/WA.DWDA_.An_.Overview.for_.Patients.and_.Families.10.2015.pdf

Laurie Riepe, psychotherapy focused on conscious dying: www.laurieriepetherapy.com

Chapter 9: Reimagining the Future in Ecological After-Death Care

Recompose (https://recompose.life). Katrina Spade.

Promessa (www.promessa.se). Susanne Wiigh-Mäsak.

Lee Webster, *Changing Landscapes: Exploring the Growth of Ethical, Compassionate, and Environmentally Sustainable Green Funeral Service* (Ojai, CA: Green Burial Council International, 2017).

Verde Products, Inc. and Let Your Love Grow (www.letyourlovegrow .com). Bob and Annette Jenkins. This company advocates adding nutrients to cremains to make them more environmentally friendly.

Bio-Response Solutions, Inc. (www.bioresponsesolutions.com). Joe Wilson, Samantha Sieber, and family. Alkaline hydrolysis/aquamation.

Coeio (www.coeio.com). Jae Rhim Lee. Mushroom/Infinity Burial Suit.

Chapter 10: Be Prepared: Creating a Plan with Family and Friends

Lee Webster, *Planning Guide and Workbook for Home Funeral Families* (NHFA, 2015).

Sacred Crossings, *Advance Death Care Directive* (Los Angeles, Sacred Crossings, 2015). You can purchase this Directive at www .deathcaredirective.com or www.sacredcrossings.com. It was created by Olivia Bareham, reverend and home funeral educator and guide. Olivia does wonderful death midwifery and home funeral trainings.

National Home Funeral Alliance Advance Directive list: www .homefuneralalliance.org/advance-directives.html

Limina LLC—Thresholds Consulting and Ministry (www
.lucindaherring.com). I have created an Advance After-Death Care
Directive, which one receives in hard copy and electronic form as
part of my consultation and companioning work.

Epilogue

Death Café (http://deathcafe.com). The Death Café movement
was started by the late Jon Underwood. This nonprofit endeavor
creates opportunities for people to meet over tea, coffee, and cake to
explore and discuss death together.

New Zealand Coffin Clubs:

A wonderful video about the movement: www.youtube.com/watch
?v=KsmWV3vzni4

"Kiwi Coffin Club Throws Glitter on the Idea of Dying": https://
news.nationalgeographic.com/2017/10/new-zealand-coffin
-club-death-music-spd/

Appendix A

THE THREE STAGES OF DEATH'S THRESHOLD

*T*here are always three stages of a threshold: the beginning or opening, which includes the time of preparation and movement toward a specific event or time; the actual event or happening; and the time afterward, which offers integration, completion, and closure. Understanding the three stages of death's threshold can serve as a map to help us navigate all that we encounter at the end of life. I define these three stages as follows:

I. **Stage One: Turning toward death.** When a person knows there is no way back from the inevitability of death, he or she enters what Buddhists call the "bardo of active dying." ("Bardo" means "thrown in between, a liminal state.") This stage is as varied and individual as the persons themselves, in terms of timing and circumstances and how someone's final journey unfolds. Someone dying of cancer, and their caregivers, could have a very long experience in this first stage. This was true for my mother and family. Our first stage lasted a full lunar month before Mama was able to let go. When Papa learned he had terminal cancer, he declared "transition time," refusing to get treatment, having gone through that nightmare with Mama. He vowed he would see Alabama football season and die before the New Year, when estate tax laws would change and make it harder for all of us who would inherit the land. He did just that, dying the night before Halloween, his favorite festival.

Someone who dies suddenly in a car accident will go through the first stage, but it is barely noticeable. For such a death, the threshold appears, but the gap between the opening and the moment of death is very brief, perhaps only a few seconds or minutes in physical time. For such a person, there is no time to prepare inwardly or outwardly for dying; and, according to teachings that believe consciousness continues after death, this can be problematic on the other side. A prolonged stage of dying can be difficult but also potentially helpful to all concerned, especially if the person can accept that he or she is dying, and can make use of the time left to be with loved ones, prepare, tie up loose ends, and appreciate the gift of those final days.

2. **Stage Two: The event or actual moment(s) of death.** The time when a person ceases to breathe, and the life forces of the physical body begin to dissipate. For those who feel consciousness continues after death, this is the time when a person's awareness actively begins its journey out of the body. There is a vast difference in opinion between Western and Eastern thought about when the moment of actual death occurs. Western medicine pronounces a person dead when they take their last breath and the pulse ceases. Eastern medicine and teachings say that a person's consciousness can take much longer to actually depart the body, and that a person is not dead until an inner dissolution, actually a "second death,"

is complete. For those who die suddenly, the process of leaving the body behind may be greatly accelerated. According to spiritual teachings that have made the moment of death an exploration and a focus, a person experiencing a rapid death may need help to realize what has happened.

There is a story in Sogyal Rinpoche's book *The Tibetan Book of Living and Dying* about an American couple who witnessed a man's sudden death along a road, when he was hit by a passing vehicle. A monk who happened to be nearby knelt down by the man, who had by that time been pronounced dead at the scene of the accident. The monk bent over the still form and did prayers and practice to bring the man's consciousness back into his body. The monk then helped him die again, but this time in a much more calm and peaceful way. Such understanding helps us see that the *way* a person dies, and *how* they die, what their state of mind is at the moment of death, what the environment around them is like—all these elements are important to consider.

3. **Stage Three: The time after death, between the moment of the last breath and the final disposition of the body.** This book explores Stage Three in depth, as this is the time when home funeral vigils and caring for our own dead are possible. A deceased person will normally be in a morgue until the necessary paperwork is completed for burial or cremation—still the most acceptable disposition choices today. Keeping a person at home, whether for a few hours or a few days, or bringing the deceased home from the hospital for a time, opens up many opportunities to understand this final stage of death's threshold again, and to come to terms with "being dead." We collectively lost such awareness when we handed over the care of our loved ones to the funeral industry. This is the time-out-of-time stage we are rediscovering.

Appendix B

BEING A HOME FUNERAL VIGIL CASE MANAGER

*O*ften, it is difficult for the people closest to the dying person to oversee a home funeral. Primary caregivers are taken up with helping a loved one die, and may find it challenging to also plan and track the after-death care. It is helpful to enlist a family member or friend who is good at managing a project, or someone who wants to "hold" the overall intention and picture of the unfolding event. This person will help keep things on track and be the go-to person for questions, concerns, and guidance if needed. This person can be designated the home funeral case manager.

Here are some considerations and tips for performing this role:

1. There are no hard-and-fast rules or "shoulds" when it comes to managing home funeral vigils. The most sacred and meaningful experience will emerge from who you are, and how you and your family and community best work together.

That being said, any team can benefit from basic elements like organization, delegation, and management. This holds true in creating home funeral vigils, especially for families choosing the direct-it-yourself option or who are doing most of the tasks themselves.

2. A person holding the larger picture may have an easier time if he or she is able to focus on the task at hand, and not have other major distractions during the vigil days. This is a tall order for anyone in today's busy world, but often someone can come forward who is retired or not working full time or caring for young children.

3. When strong emotions are present, clear communication can often break down. Therefore, it is helpful if a case manager has good communication skills and knows how to listen.

4. Death is a mysterious and uncertain time. It is helpful to be flexible, and unattached to outcome, while still holding the larger picture as a helpful structure or map. Knowing how to be present to "what is" rather than what one might want or expect, and to be able to let go or change plans midstream, are often what enable a home funeral vigil to emerge in the best way possible for everyone.

5. Being able to stay calm is also a gift. None of us can manage this all the time, especially if we, too, are grieving. However, being someone in whom others can "rest" is invaluable.

6. Knowing the importance of delegating responsibilities helps create an experience that is meaningful for all. Family and friends who can creatively participate and be of help report feeling greater closure and support in their grieving process. A person who can be sensitive to the needs of others, and knows how to empower people to contribute in their own ways, while holding the larger picture throughout, makes the most successful case manager for home funerals.

INDEX

ACKNOWLEDGMENTS

Reimagining Death would not exist without Tim McKee, publisher of North Atlantic Books, who trusted his intuition and the power of synchronicity enough to reach out to me and ask if I would be interested in a possible book project on natural burial and home funeral vigils. Thank you, Tim, for believing in this book and in me from the beginning.

It has been a privilege to work with the North Atlantic team. My appreciation goes out especially to Susan Bumps for patient help with the contract, and to Hisae Matsuda for being a positive and supportive editor through the months of completing the writing. Thanks too to the production and publicity staff for your help in shepherding the book into the world.

I could never have attempted this goal without the financial and prayerful support from everyone who contributed to my GoFundMe book project. Your gifts literally made this book a reality. Communities are at the heart of true change; your generosity and love have proven this so beautifully. All of you have my heartfelt gratitude and blessing.

To Claire and Ed Blatchford, whose initial seed money enabled me to reclaim my writer's self, and have the courage to take time off and say "yes" to this journey. I will be forever grateful to you, my kindred friends. Thank you, Claire, for your own books, which were a source of comfort and delight for both my mother and father, in life and in death.

I count David and Julia Spangler and my Lorian colleagues and friends as one of the great blessings of my life. Their support and love are woven throughout this book, and have helped make it what it is. Thank you all, and my deep gratitude, David, for writing the book's foreword, and for the gift of your life and teachings in this time.

I honor the contributions of my friends and fellow writers Laurie Riepe, Judith Adams, Donna James, Shelley Sherriff, and Lee Webster. Your stories, poetry, and wisdom make my book a richer and more creative offering.

To Lindsay Soyer, for the cover photograph, and for our shared adventures in the green funeral work. Thank you for your love and support and for who you are.

To Lee Webster, leader extraordinaire in the home funeral and green burial movement, and my colleague and friend. I could not have navigated this journey without your input and encouragement. Your practical wisdom permeates every page of this book, and I am so grateful.

To all my colleagues and friends in the home funeral and green burial networks: May your passion and tireless dedication and love continue to transform the way we "do death" in our society today. Thank you for all you do.

A special thank you to all those in the conservation burial movement who contributed photographs and helped me articulate your history and vision. May your work flourish for future generations of all beings on the earth.

I honor and give thanks to all the families who were willing and courageous enough to share their intimate death experiences and photographs in this book. Thank you for trusting me and allowing me to tell your stories. What an uplifting and humbling task it has been. Your offerings are the heart and soul of this book, and are a sacred gift to us all.

I am so grateful to my family, who have graciously allowed me to tell the stories of our mother's and father's deaths (from my perspective!). To my sisters Shay, Margaret, and Nancy (for your skilled editing!) and to my brother Hal. Thank you for being my kin; for living creative lives, dedicated to the well-being of earth and nature, animals, land and ecologies.

To my cherished daughter Eliza, who inspires me every day. Thanks for being my staunch advocate always, and for your editing skills and love, in a time when you had few resources yourself. May your gifts find their authentic way into the world, and may you know joy and fulfillment in everything you do.

To dear Gwenna, my granddaughter. Thank you for arriving in the world at the beginning of this book's life, and for bringing so much joie de vivre to so many people in your one tiny, very precious year of being alive.

Thank you, Stu Ryman, for your courage, determination, and positive spirit. Your life is a beacon for me, and you have inspired me throughout my writing this year. May you find your way forward to healing and renewal, wherever that journey takes you.

I am grateful for the hidden web of connections behind the book's inception. To Jake Seniuk across the veil, to Donna James, his partner, and to his sons Markus and Tristan, whose beautiful photographs in a Grist.org article about Jake's death helped Tim McKee find me. To Erica Rayner-Horn, thanks for your part in this story, and for our friendship over the years. Without these connections, this book may never have come to fruition.

To the spirit and land of Hedgebrook; to Nancy Nordhoff, the founder, and all those who, over the years, have made it possible for "women authoring change" to have time and space away from busy lives to dream, create, and bring their voices into the world. Thank you. What a tremendous honor to be part of your community.

To my dear friend Autumn Preble. Thank you for your ongoing support, and for knowing a retreat at Hedgebrook would inspire and strengthen me to complete this project. Your part in getting me there is a gift I will treasure always.

My heartfelt appreciation to Deborah Koff-Chapin, and Ross and Aleah Chapin, for your lifelong love, friendship, and support.

Thank you so much, Deb and Ross, for helping me create the video for the GoFundMe project, and for being such loyal allies in my life.

To Dana MacInnis, for your past and future comradeship in all things death (and life!) related. Thank you for your bright spirit and your willingness to be part of the evolution of this work.

To Mara Grey, who generously gives me nourishing gardening work, and whose sage advice as a fellow writer and friend is invaluable.

To all my beloved friends and community: I am enriched by your presence, by the beauty of your lives. If I begin to list you here, my book will grow beyond its allotted pages! You know who you are. How happy I am that we are a communion of souls together this lifetime.

Last, but not least, I honor the Dead—all those whose lives and deaths are interwoven with mine. I have felt your inspiration and celebration of this book from the beginning. May this book bless the Borderlands and bring peace and well-being to us all.

ABOUT THE AUTHOR

Lucinda Herring has worked at the cutting edge of the green funeral movement for more than twenty years, beginning with others in the 1990s to quietly care for loved ones after death. Today she is one of the leading voices for more healing and ecological ways to care for our dead. Herring is a home funeral/green disposition consultant and guide, an interfaith minister, and a licensed funeral director in the state of Washington. She speaks regularly about her work, and through her company Limina LLC—Thresholds Consulting and Ministry, she offers Advance After-Death Care planning, home funeral/green disposition education and trainings, and celebrant/ministerial services for families and communities who are reclaiming their innate right to care for each other and the earth at the end of life.

Contributors

Judith Adams is an English-born poet living on Whidbey Island in Washington State, where she is lovingly honored as the Poet Laureate of Langley. She has published four books of poetry and recorded several CDs of her work, she reads and teaches poetry, and she conducts grief workshops in many arenas of life. Her husband Robin died in 2014, and his home vigil and green burial are the inspiration for the poem Judith wrote for this book.

Donna James, PhD, has practiced psychotherapy for thirty-five years. As a poet, she wrote her way through her husband's illness, his dying, and her first year of grieving. She now incorporates her experiences of caring for the dying and grieving the dead into her twin disciplines of clinical work and writing.

Laurie Riepe, MA, LMHC, is a psychotherapist in Seattle. She works with couples, families, individuals, and groups at all stages of life. Following her husband's use of Death with Dignity, Laurie deepened her study of conscious dying. Through public speaking, Laurie shares the rich, nuanced, and vital conversation about choice and responsibility that lies at the center of our right to a death with dignity. Laurie has written an excerpt about her experience in the chapter on Death with Dignity.

Shelley Sherriff is a home funeral guide and educator living in Victoria, British Columbia, Canada. Combining her passion for end-of-life work with her experience as a writer, researcher, and web developer, Shelley is the founder and director of Walking You Home, a comprehensive online directory of holistic end-of-life support, information, and resources.

Lee Webster is a career writer, editor, and researcher, longtime hospice volunteer, trained home funeral guide, ardent conservationist, and frequent speaker and published author on funeral reform, including end-of-life support, home funerals, and natural burials. She is the director of New Hampshire Funeral Resources, Education and Advocacy, former president of the National Home Funeral Alliance, and former board member and educational consultant for the Green Burial Council International. She currently serves as a founding member on the board of the National End-of-Life Doula Alliance, the National Hospice and Palliative Care Organization, the End-of-Life Doula Council, and the Conservation Burial Alliance.

About North Atlantic Books

North Atlantic Books (NAB) is an independent, nonprofit publisher committed to a bold exploration of the relationships between mind, body, spirit, and nature. Founded in 1974, NAB aims to nurture a holistic view of the arts, sciences, humanities, and healing. To make a donation or to learn more about our books, authors, events, and newsletter, please visit www.northatlanticbooks.com.

North Atlantic Books is the publishing arm of the Society for the Study of Native Arts and Sciences, a 501(c)(3) nonprofit educational organization that promotes cross-cultural perspectives linking scientific, social, and artistic fields. To learn how you can support us, please visit our website.